THE MAN THAT PETER KNEW
The Historical Jesus According to Mark

Cover image: **This design is taken, by kind permission of the Quaker sculptor Gill Ledsham, from a photograph of her 'Crucifixion/ Resurrection', now installed at All Saints Church, Dedworth, Windsor. It vividly expresses the warmth and eagerness of the out-going love of God, as seen in the resurrected Jesus.**

The Man that Peter Knew

The Historical Jesus According to Mark

by

Philip Oakeshott

Sessions Books

York, England

First Published 2011

British Library Cataloguing

ISBN 978-1-85072-411-7

Printed in Times New Roman
from Author's Disc
by Sessions Books
York, England

Table of Contents

TO MY MOTHER
FOR HER LOVE OF TRUTH
AND MY FATHER
FOR HIS
INTELLIGENT APPROACH TO THE BIBLE

Preface

Recent reading has convinced me that modern New Testament scholars have too often failed to see the essential differences between the four canonical gospels, with the result that both Mark and John are misjudged, the high factual content of one and the extreme lack of fact in the other being alike ignored. Hence most modern scholars deny that any gospel can be eye-witness, which easily becomes an excuse for unsound or fanciful theoretical interpretations of Jesus; equally erudite opponents reassert eye-witness in *all* the canonical gospels; and the disillusioned take refuge in The Gospel of Thomas, so avoiding the historical Jesus altogether. This study re-examines the evidence about gospel origins, and then, without overstating the case, affirms the Gospel of Mark as the Roman interpreter's recollection of sayings, parables and anecdotes which he had heard from the Galilean apostle; an honest but by no means flawless record.

While I hope that scholars may find this study clear, logical and soundly based on evidence, it is intended rather for general readers who would like to meet the credible historical Jesus as he steps off the page in Mark's account. He does not accord entirely with ancient tradition nor with modern studies, but is recognisably the same person, seen more objectively; a Jesus of his own time, but vitally relevant to ours.

Teenage reading introduced me to A. J. Cronin's young doctor, saying that his maxim for research is 'Take nothing for granted'; and to H. C. Bailey's Mr. Fortune, explaining that the reason he so often sees what police and lawyers overlook is because 'I *believe* evidence' – which others ignore or put aside if they cannot see at once what it means or how to use it. This study has tried to follow those two precepts, and they have led at times to unanticipated conclusions.

Acknowledgements

All Old Testament citations are, unless otherwise stated, made from the Greek of the Septuagint, using Benson (1851) and Rahlf (1924) for the text; for the few citations from the Hebrew I have mostly used the New English Bible. For the Greek New Testament I have used Aland (4th rev. ed.), classical citations are from the texts of Harvard University's Loeb Classical Library editions, and the Ancient Fathers from J. P. Migne's *Patrologiae Graecae* and *Patrologiae Latinae*, but *all translations from Greek and Latin texts in this book are mine*. I am greatly indebted to previous translators, but often standard translations, especially of Mark, and even occasionally the Loeb translations, conceal or underplay some point I wish to make. Biblical and other ancient quotations are printed in bold type without quotation marks; the words of modern authors are in plain type.

I would acknowledge as having been particularly helpful: *Jesus by an Eye-witness*, by H. D. A. Major, *Jesus the Jew*, by Geza Vermes, and A. E. Harvey's *Jesus and the Constraints of History*. Although I dissent from all three on various points, much of what I have written derives from them.

I gratefully acknowledge permission from Keith Gilley, who edits the Unitarian *Faith and Freedom*, and from Stephen Plant, editor of the SPCK's *Theology*, for permission to use in this book material which was first published in their journals.

I wish to express my warmest thanks to my friend Keith Treacher, to Professor Paul Anderson of George Fox University, Washington, and to Professor Howard Jacobson of Illinois University, all of whom gave me good advice and encouragement during the earliest stages of my research; to Professor David Catchpole for more recent criticism; and most especially to Canon John Davies, formerly of Southampton University, who has generously expended much time and effort as my friend, mentor and sharp-eyed critic over the last ten years. Finally, my heartfelt thanks to my ever-patient computer instructor, adviser and trouble-shooter, who prefers anonymity, but without whose unfailing help and support this book would literally never have been written. None of these persons, however, are to be held responsible for any of the opinions or inferences expressed in this book.

INTRODUCTION

Il faux reculer pour mieux sauter. We must go back a little and re-examine that twentieth century criticism which claimed to rule out the possibility that any gospel could be close to eyewitness, before we can take the big leap forward towards a detailed account of the ministry of Jesus which shall depend, not on church tradition nor modern speculation, but on sound history, logic, modern knowledge and common sense. The aim is not to restore the *status quo ante Bultmann*, as some conservatives are trying to do, but, taking fully into account the considerable truths of modern criticism, to establish firm ground from which to begin our study of the life of Christ.

The Validity of Mark

The primary importance of Mark, once commonly accepted, fell victim to the Form Criticism which, led by Martin Dibelius and Rudolf Bultmann, dominated the 1920-1950s, classifying all gospel material into various 'forms' such as 'Examples' and 'Tales', making the common mistake of assuming that the four canonical gospels are all of one *genre,* and arguing from these 'forms' that all the gospels were far removed from eyewitness. That inference remains generally accepted today, even though the Form Critics' more extreme conclusions have been rejected; with the result that most modern criticism, taking for granted that Mark edited and invented material to suit his purpose, concerns itself largely with his supposed theological, partisan or literary intentions. Alternatively, conservative scholars try to make a case for Controlled Tradition, arguing that the Christian communities would themselves have ensured the reliability of the oral traditions which lie behind the gospels. Recently R. Bauckham and later still C. S. Keener have pointed to the weaknesses and fallacies of most modern readings of the Gospels, but both, in my opinion, try to prove too much: I cannot agree that even Mark's gospel can be taken as almost infallible eye-witness, the direct testimony of the apostle Peter, recorded by the John Mark of Acts; nor that every canonical gospel has historical value.

Here it will be argued, contrary to all the above schools of thought, that Mark, although certainly not a perfect record, is almost our only source of authentic history, although Matthew and Luke offer the best of Jesus' teaching and John has its own spiritual and dramatic qualities.

Mark: Historical Evidence

The historical evidence about our evangelist is remarkably strong, and says that Mark was Peter's *hermēneutēs*, his guide-interpreter, who wrote this gospel in Italy, after Peter's death. (Although scholars have generally translated both Greek *hermēneutēs* and Latin *interpres* as 'interpreter', the prime meaning of each is courier or dragoman, one who guides a traveller in foreign parts, interpreting as needed.) The gospel itself is usually dated around 65 AD at the earliest, and less than a century later comes what is almost certainly a reference to it: Justin Martyr, writing his *Dialogue with Trypho* c.150 AD, mentions '*the reminiscences of Peter'*, which, since he quotes from them words found elsewhere only in Mark 3.7, can hardly refer to anything but the gospel of Mark,[1] with which Justin elsewhere seems to be familiar.

Next, a fragment of a Latin preface to Mark, the Anti-Marcionite Prologue, probably c.160-180 AD, is more specific:

> **[...] stated Mark, who is nicknamed 'Stubby-fingers' because he had small fingers in relation to the size of the rest of his body. He was Peter's guide-interpreter (*interpres*); after the death of Peter himself he wrote out this very gospel in the land of Italy.**

Then Irenaeus, writing c.180, after mentioning Peter and Paul at Rome, continues:

> **And after the departure of these men, Mark, Peter's guide-interpreter (hermēneutēs), also handed down to us in writing the things preached by Peter** (*Adversus Haereses*, 3.1.2)

'Departure' here almost certainly means 'death', but to take it literally would make no difference to the validity of Mark: for the important point, we shall see, is that when Mark wrote his gospel Peter was not there to correct him.

Fourthly, c.190 AD, Tertullian comments: **And the [*gospel*] which Mark published may fairly be called Peter's, Mark [*having been*] his *interpres*** *(Adversus Marcionem 4.5).*[2]

So the earliest evidence is solid, different from each source but always consistent: in sum, Mark, Peter's guide at Rome, wrote down, after Peter's death, what he had heard Peter teach. But this tradition was 'improved' early in the next century, Clement of Alexandria advancing unlikely claims that Mark wrote while Peter was still teaching at Rome: which would have strengthened the gospel's authority. One of these passages survives in Latin translation, alleging that when

Peter was preaching to men of wealth and position in Rome, they asked Mark to write down for them what Peter said, and Mark responded with the gospel 'known as' his;[3] the other passages – quoted more, or less, accurately, a hundred years or so later, by Eusebius – have Peter knowing but not hindering Mark's writing, or even authorising it 'to be read in the congregations'.

It was also, it seems, found unacceptable that the writer of the gospel should be this unknown and undistinguished Mark; so Eusebius, writing his *Ecclesiastical History* c.315 AD, claims the evangelist as the Mark who was the first bishop of Alexandria – an identification which Eusebius' own dates contradict. But Eusebius, although as liable as Clement to 'improve' the record, includes much material cited from earlier writers, of whom one was Papias, bishop of Hierapolis, who from his youth had zealously collected all the stories and sayings of Jesus' disciples that he could, and finally wrote out five books of '*The Lord's Sayings*' (estimated dates vary between 130 and 160 AD).

Papias quotes at length from John the Elder, a disciple of Jesus but not one of the Twelve:

> **This also the Elder used to say: Mark, having become Peter's *hermēneutēs*, wrote down accurately, though not in order, everything he** (Mark) **remembered of the things said and done by the Lord. For he** (Mark) **did not hear the Lord, nor did he accompany him, but later, as I have said, [heard and accompanied] Peter, who organised his teaching as the occasion demanded, but not as though making an orderly arrangement of the Lord's sayings, so that Mark was not wrong, writing down individual items like this, as he** (Mark) **recalled them.[4] For he made it his one concern not to omit anything which he had heard nor to misrepresent anything in them** (Eusebius, *EH*, 3.39.15)**.**

Since Mark's mistakes in the order *would* have been blameworthy if Peter had still been there to consult, this critique of Mark's gospel, from a well informed contemporary, agrees perfectly with the testimony of the second century witnesses.

(This is a difficulty for scholars who prefer Mark *not* to be Peter's follower. They usually claim that only the first sentence is from the Elder, the rest by Papias; and cite Eusebius' comment that Papias was a man 'of very little intellect'. But Eusebius' contempt meant that he would probably *not* have quoted anything he thought was Papias' own; he seems to use him only as a source for the words of earlier Christians.)

The passage also confirms the *primary* insight of Form Criticism, that the gospels are basically some writer's arrangement of material received as separate sayings and episodes. The Form Critics' further inference, still the basis for most modern gospel studies, that all the gospels were far removed from eyewitness, will be shown here not to be true of Mark's, which is eyewitness at one remove; although even that does not guarantee its total accuracy. Mark had to put his material into the best order that he could, Peter was no longer available to check the detail in individual stories, and even an eyewitness can himself be mistaken. A few detectable errors still leave Mark's gospel likely to be as near the truth as most historical biography.

Not John Mark

During the first half of the twentieth century, the evangelist was commonly identified with John Mark of Acts – a view supported by later traditionalists like V. Taylor (1953), R. Gundry (1993) and R. Bauckham (2006). – which would allow the evangelist to have known at first hand some events and much of the background. Yet apart from the folly of identifying John Mark from Jerusalem, on the strength of half his name, with one out of thousands of 'Marks' in Rome, no Jerusalem disciple could have guided Peter around that sprawling city, whose sheer size, and one million inhabitants, made it a marvel of the ancient world: 'See Rome and die!' What Peter needed, and must have had, was a denizen of Rome, someone who knew his way around, fluent in Latin as well as Greek. The oldest tradition stands firm: Mark was simply Peter's guide and interpreter in Rome, who after Peter's death wrote down all he could remember of what he had heard from Peter about Jesus, being as exact as possible and trying to omit nothing and distort nothing.

The latest gambit by the traditional school comes with Bauckham (2006, pp.210-7) claiming that Mark would have been putting down Peter's Aramaic reminiscences in Greek, almost while Peter was telling them. His evidence is a questionable translation of Papias (note 4, below), and his theory depends on the evangelist's identification with John Mark, which seems implausible. It is unlikely that an ordinary Roman would know Aramaic; or that an ordinary Galilean like Peter would have travelled so far without himself having a working knowledge of Greek; and even if this Mark had the knowledge, and the leisure, to have written down the teaching while Peter was alive, he had no motive. As long as Peter was there, perhaps a vigorous man of about sixty, to tell and expound the stories, what need to write them? But at Peter's death the Roman church suddenly lost its highly prized witness, whose testimony was the guarantee of the gospel message; and when he was suddenly gone, the need was obvious.

We may imagine the elders of the Roman church, as soon as Nero's persecution had eased sufficiently, deciding that Mark, now without his previous occupation, should be set to write down the teaching of the martyred Peter, of which he would surely have the most comprehensive knowledge. Yet, however it came about, this was, with no previous 'gospel' as a guide, a formidable undertaking. How would one set about it?

Compiling a Gospel

Common sense suggests first writing down every story, parable or saying one remembered, word for word; the Elder says Mark wrote them down accurately, and that he tried not to alter or omit anything. Then, from the general picture that he had gleaned from Peter, he might compose a brief outline, into which to insert his material; and such a 'framework' of connecting passages in Mark, written in a plainer style than the stories themselves, was identified by the German scholar K. L. Schmidt in 1919. Later, the scattered link-passages identified by Schmidt at different points throughout the first part of this gospel were assembled by C. H. Dodd (see McArthur 1970, p.115) to show how, when put together, they make a simple summary of Jesus' Galilean ministry. Slightly adapting from Dodd's version, this would run:

> **But after John's arrest, Jesus came into Galilee preaching the great news of God and saying that 'The time is fulfilled, and the Kingdom of God is at hand; change your ways and trust in the great news'.[5] And straightaway, on Sabbath days, going to the synagogue he would teach. And they were astonished at his teaching. For he used to teach them as someone with authority, and not like the scribes. And he went preaching in their synagogues all over Galilee, and casting out demons.**
>
> **And he went out again beside the sea and the whole crowd would come to him and he used to teach them. And from Judaea and Jerusalem, from Idumea and Peraea, and from around Tyre and Sidon, a huge crowd, hearing of the things he was doing, came to him. And he told his disciples to keep a boat handy for him because of the crowd, so that they should not crush him. For he healed many, so that all who had diseases kept pressing on him to touch him. And the unclean spirits, whenever they saw him, used to fall in front of him**

and cry out, saying, 'You are the son of God'. And he strictly commanded them that they should not make him known.

And he goes up into the hill-country, and summons those he himself wanted, and they came to him. And he appointed twelve so that they might be with him and that he might send them out to preach and to have power to cast out demons. (And he was leading [*them*] round the villages in a circle,[6] teaching.) And he calls the twelve together and began to send them out two by two, and he would give them power over the unclean spirits, and going out they preached a change of heart. They were exorcising many demons and they used to anoint with oil many sick people and heal them. And the apostles gather round Jesus and reported to him all the things that they did and taught (Mark 1.14, 15; (Dodd adds 1.21a here); 1.21b, 22, 39; 2.13; 3.8-15; (Dodd adds 3.17-19, omits 6.6b); 6.6b, 7,12, 13, 30).

This outline is perhaps as much as Mark might be expected to have gathered from Peter, and probably reasonably reliable, as far as it goes. Into the outline Mark had then to fit stories, parables and sayings to make a coherent narrative.

In Mark's gospel we find all the Form Critics' types of material: Sayings and Parables, with some context or none; 'Examples', which are stories in which details have been lost, eroded by their use as examples in preaching; and 'Tales', stories which are rich in detail and colour; even, perhaps, in the account of the Baptist's death at Herod's court, a 'Legend', a good story which has grown from little or misunderstood fact. But these 'Forms' do not, in Mark, tell against eye-witness. The Tales (accurately, but cumbersomely, named 'Miracle-Stories' by Taylor, 1949), are really much better explained as the reminiscences of Peter, told off duty, perhaps over a drink or a meal, than as the later deliberate expansion of previously eroded stories, as suggested by Dibelius;[7] and the obvious erosion of the Examples through preaching does not mean that they must also have been handed on from person to person, time and again; only that, as I know from experience, someone has *used* them time and again; while the only partly eroded stories, noted by Dibelius in Mark, fit perfectly here as stories which Peter had used, but not often.

Where Form Criticism was right was that all this material reached Mark as separate items, and their sequence now is not historical, but contrived by Mark as best he might. The outline, Dodd showed, gives three stages: the obvious first approach is preaching in the synagogues, but the anecdotes show how often he meets with hostility from the well off and highly religious. He responds to popular demand by preaching instead to large crowds, using a boat on the lake to let them hear him but not crush him, for many come wishing to receive, or perhaps only to witness, healing; thirdly, he withdraws to the hill-country (ie. Upland Galilee, the northern part)[8] and there trains the chosen Twelve, and sends them out to spread his message. Many episodes clearly fit best into one particular stage; controversy in the synagogue, for example, plainly belonging to the first. That is as much as we can know, or need to know, about the progression of Jesus' ministry in Galilee. The various episodes must usually be taken separately; but Mark has done his best to arrange them.

Parables and sayings are largely in groups linked by phrases, such as In My Name (9.33-41); by words, like Stumble (9.42-48); or by topics, like Salt (9.49,50). In Mark 4.3-32, the main theme of Seed, in three parables (4.3-20, 26-32), is present also with the Corn Measure (4.21), which leads onto Measuring Out to Others (4.24, 25); but here there is also the subsidiary theme of Hearing (4.9, 14-20, 23, 24). With equal ingenuity, Mark appears to dispose of three items, which might have happened anywhere but for which he had found no obvious link or context (Divorce, the Little Children, and the Rich Man), by setting them in Jesus' time of teaching in Perea (10.2-31), the last point in the narrative before the Passion Story, where they would have seemed less appropriate.

Some stories are placed to satisfy their own details.[9] For instance, a leper can only be met outside the towns, so Mark places that healing to follow a reference to Jesus *touring* Galilee (1.39); but since the episode ends with Jesus unable to enter towns himself (1.45), Mark places next a story starting (2.1) **And coming back to Capernaum *after a while*** (2.1). Occasionally this method leads to misplacement: Mark has set the healing of the epileptic boy (9.14-29) after the Transfiguration, because it begins with Jesus rejoining his disciples; but in that setting its details make little sense, whereas, if we put it at 6.30, with Jesus at last returning, as we may infer, from the hill-country, to meet his returning disciples at Capernaum,[10] all the details, from the crowd's great surprise at seeing Jesus to the final retreat into 'the house', make perfect sense, and explain also why the house next became so continuously thronged (6.31b) with, as we may assume, sensation-seekers. Other episodes are linked by theme, like the string of controversies with scribes and Pharisees (7.1-23), or the insertion of the scribes from Jerusalem, who say Jesus is demon-possessed, into the story of Jesus' family, who think he is out of his wits (3.20-35).

The Passion Narrative

For the very last days of Jesus' life, however, there was already a written summary. Taylor (1953, pp.653-64) has shown that Chapters 14 and 15 are in two distinct styles: a narrative in better Greek, such as a well educated Diaspora Jew might have used, into which are inserted stories and details, probably told by Peter, in the usual heavily Semitic Greek of this gospel. A probable reason for an early written summary of the Passion at Rome is that Claudius had, c.49/50 AD, ordered all Jews to leave Rome,[11] thereby depriving the Roman church of all its Jewish Christians, some of whom might well have been visiting Jerusalem for Passover when Jesus died. It would have been sensible for one of these to write down the known facts about trial and crucifixion before they had to leave the Gentile members of the church to manage alone.[12] Not until the reign of Nero could any of the expelled Jews have returned; Simon of Cyrene was possibly one who did, since his sons are known there later, when the gospel is written.

There is plentiful corroboration in the text itself that most of this gospel comes from Peter; it may often be in his exact words and phrases, for an interpreter who must translate a speaker's words promptly, paragraph by paragraph or story by story, requires an excellent memory; again, I speak from experience. The Semitic flavour of most of the Greek is probably all from Peter, conscientiously recorded by Mark; of the latter there is no reason to suppose that he even came from a Jewish family.[13]

Irrelevant Detail

That there is much, often vivid, detail in the 'Tales' does not prove them true; comparison will show just as much in the stories in John, which, we shall argue, are mostly pure fiction. But in John the details are purposeful and usually clear, typical of a constructed story; in Mark they are often unnecessary, like the hired hands in Zebedee's boat or the pillow for Jesus' head when he slept in the boat; or meaningless, like **other boats were with them** (4.36), since these are never heard of again. They are the words of a vigorous but unliterary raconteur; and sometimes the narrative is obscure, or even misleading, because the teller has not thought to explain to *us* what seemed obvious to *him*.

A clear example of this unexplained detail is **And going along beside the sea of Galilee, he saw Simon and Andrew the brother of Simon round-casting in the sea** (Mark 1.16). *Amphiballontas*, 'round-casting', means, as Matt.5.18 elucidates, using an *amphiblestron*, the circular, weighted net thrown spinning to trap fish as it settles. This activity, still to be seen in early twentieth century

Galilee (Major 1925, p.26), is done standing in the shallows; so Peter and Andrew, standing literally 'in' the sea, were so close that Jesus spoke (*eipen*) to them, but called (*ekalesen*) to James and John, who, in their father's boat, would have been out in deeper water. Right to the end we find unimportant, irrelevant or inexplicit details, like the unimpressive brushwood cut to strew before the donkey, Jesus not permitting anyone to carry a load through the temple premises, the hymn sung to close the Last Supper, the youth who fled naked from Gethsemane, and the identification of Simon of Cyrene as **the father of Alexander and Rufus**.

Appropriate Vocabulary

Many words accurately reflect conditions in Galilee. The use of **Pilate**, with no rank, or **the high priest**, with no name, suggest a speaker who takes for granted that everyone knows who these people are. A. N. Sherwin-White (1963, pp.129-137) cites, as appropriate for a minor local ruler, the terms used of Herod's entourage: *megistanes* for local bosses, *chiliarchoi* for his army commanders, the Latin *spekulator* for his executioner (Mark 6.21, 27); and also approves the usually correct distinctions made in Mark between *polis*, a city or borough, and *kōmē*, a village or town with no self-government, with *kōmopolis* coined for those very large villages in fertile Galilee noted by Josephus.

There are also in Mark a large number of Aramaic words, like *Korban, Rabboni, Abba*, and expressions like *Ephaphtha* or *Talitha Koum*, always instantly translated; more than in any other gospel. Yet there are also Latinisms like *kodrantēs (*farthing*), krabbatos (*bed*), kenturiōn (*centurion*)*, again more numerous than in any other gospel, which suggest either the Roman milieu or the Roman interpreter.

Geographical Errors

However, the signs of a genuine Galilean background to this gospel are accompanied by a notable ignorance of Palestinian topography. There is much variation in the manuscripts between Gadara, Gerasa and Gergesa (5.1),[14] and between Dalmanutha (spelt four ways), or alternatively Magdala, Mageda, Melegada and Magada (8.10); it seems that whatever Mark first wrote here cried out for correction. The most notable lapse is the claim that Jesus, leaving **the territory of Tyre,** returned via Sidon, which is north of Tyre on the Mediterranean coast, to the Sea of Galilee to the south-east, through the midst of Decapolis, the string of Greek towns set, for defence, further to the east and south of that 'sea'. The proper sense that lies behind this absurd statement, which has been likened to 'going to Bannockburn by way of Beachy Head', is worked out in Chapter 7 below; here we are concerned only with the ignorance concerning the lands adjoining Galilee which it reveals. The evangelist is plainly capable of the grossest misunderstanding of geographical references which no doubt seemed clear enough to his source; which points firmly to a Roman interpreter and away from Palestinian John Mark.

Redundancy and Poor Syntax

Without looking further than Mark's first chapter, examples of redundant narration, very typical of oral, unliterate speech, are obvious: **everywhere, into all the region of Galilee** or **the leprosy left him and he was cleansed**; the speaker further amplifies the first statement with a second, which may or may not simply repeat the meaning of the first. On the day when Jesus first found himself healing people, **Evening having come, when the sun was set** sounds so tautological that Matthew only keeps one phrase and Luke the other; but this was a Sabbath day, so the sick could not be carried to the healer until it had formally ended at sunset. Then there are the triple adverbs in *proi ennycha lian*, **in the early morning, long before it was light**, or the double negatives of **See that you say nothing to nobody**. Later examples are the highly redundant, but graphic, **looking round at those around him sitting in a circle** (3.34), and the less explicit **when he was alone, those around him with the Twelve** (4.10): who are these others, not of the Twelve, who are also with Jesus when he is **alone**?

If these redundancies suggest an oral witness, the ways in which Mark treats his verbs tell against such theories as his knowledge of rhetoric,[15] and suggest that, although he could read, write, and translate from Greek to Latin, he was not sufficiently educated to feel obliged to amend the eccentricities of Peter's oral narration and rough Semitic Greek (glossed over by translators and amended by other evangelists), rather than to preserve them. For if the frequent use of Present tense for Past can be justified, as the Historic Present, the change of subject during the same sentence cannot: consider **And his mother *comes*, and his brothers, and standing outside *send* to him, summoning him** (3.31), or **And *Simon hunted* for him, and those with him, and *they found* him and say to him** (1.36); these are vivid oral communication, but not the speech or writing of an educated man. Nor are the changes of tense: **And the apostles *are coming together* to Jesus and *reported* to him ...** (6.30), or, **And *having left* that place he *comes* to the region of Judaea on the far side of Jordan, and again crowds *are gathering* round him and he *was teaching* them as *had been* his custom**

(10.1). The verdict that 'it is very ordinary, homely, untrained prose', the product of 'a rather ordinarily clumsy writer, probably working on materials that had come to him in ordinarily clumsy form' (Meagher 1979, 57f) seems fair.

Inexplicit Narrative

A great many points in Mark need explanation, but because we are all accustomed to the smoother narratives of the other gospels, and usually read or hear the gospels in short sections only, these are overlooked. Whose is the house or 'home' at Capernaum, so frequently mentioned? Why, when it creates such difficulties for many who wish to approach him, do we find Jesus teaching *indoors* (2.2; 3.31)? Is *to oros* (3.13) a mountain, as Matthew and Luke take it, or the north of Galilee, called, because of its higher, hilly nature, *Upland Galilee*.

In the episode of the epileptic boy, as it stands, the crowd are baffling. They are arguing with Jesus' disciples, yet are greatly surprised to see Jesus himself. They are already present, and rebuked, but just when Jesus seems about to heal, **a crowd comes running up**. At the end, Jesus retreats *eis oikon*, which, like the Spanish *en casa*, should mean 'into his home' or 'our home'; yet the story is not set in Galilee but, apparently, abroad, in Iturea (9.14-29). The whole story reads as the vivid narration of someone who was there; he has the whole scene before his eyes, but does not always realise that some details need to be explained. As suggested above, if the story is moved to 6.30, sense can be made of these puzzles, but that does not mean that the narrative is clear or explicit as told. It does not read as a story composed, or even edited, by an author; one has only to compare it with the short, smooth, much less colourful versions in Matt.17.14-21 and Luke 9.37-48a.

Again, the call of the fishermen (1.16-20) plainly requires that these men had met Jesus somewhere before; since Jesus, demanding great sacrifice from his disciples, did not recruit those who were so feckless and irresponsible as to leave abandon their work, property and families at a word from a passing stranger.[16] Matthew has Jesus already living in Capernaum, Luke offers a mighty miracle to persuade the fishermen to leave their trade, and John makes them disciples of the Baptist, who obligingly points out Jesus (as **the Lamb of God**) so that they can go and talk with him: the missing element in Mark's narrative is evident to them all. So it may have been to Mark, too; but he, being determined not to add invention to any of his material, could only record what he been told.

Explanation is also missing for what Jesus was doing between his time in the wilderness and the arrest of the Baptist; why he left Galilee to wander in foreign lands; and, most importantly, *why* Judas betrayed him. Comparison with the fourth gospel's smooth explanations for Jesus' movements, or its early presentation of Judas as evil, unkind and corrupt (John 6.71; 12.5f), shows how little artifice there is in Mark.

Artistry

Many scholars (eg. R. H. Lightfoot, 1950, p.39; Nineham 1992, p.112) have claimed to find evidence that Mark is artfully editing his story in the various instances of one episode sandwiched between the two halves of another; described as 'insertion', this is sometimes thought to have subtle theological significance. For example, the story of the withered Fig Tree is supposed to show that the Clearing of the Temple, coming as it does comes between the first and second parts of the Fig Tree story, foretells the uselessness and coming fate of the Temple, and so on; but the critics seem to be reading into Mark 11.12-23 whatever would support these assumptions about his method of composition. That the Fig Tree only withers overnight, so much more realistic than Matthew's version where it dies instantaneously at Jesus' word, is perfectly natural. That an auto-suggested healing might occur as Jesus was on his way to a sick child, the crowd about him giving the afflicted woman her opportunity to clutch his robe (5.22-43), is again the untidy way in which real happenings overlap in real life. In fact, Mark may well be historically correct in his placing of both incidents; but deep significance seems unlikely. We must allow Mark a good deal of ingenuity, as when he fills in the obvious time lag between the sending out of the Twelve to preach and their joyful return, by inserting there the highly coloured gossip about Herod's execution of the Baptist, which had happened earlier, introducing it with Herod's fear that Jesus was the executed Baptist, returned from the dead (6.7-30); but, fortunately for the historical value of his gospel, neither subtle artistry nor theological speculation seem to have been within Mark's scope.

Much has been made, too, of the subtle literary skills and theological thinking supposedly found in Mark 16, the ending of his story. The reasons for rejecting any such view of Mark, or of his ending, will be given in Part Four, when we reach that point in the narrative.

The Unvarnished Portrait

Mark presents a primitive picture of a warm and generous Jesus, more human but much less dignified than Matthew's wise rabbi or Luke's *theios aner*, the superior, god-like man. In Mark only a foreigner begging a favour calls Jesus *Kyrie* (Lord), the disciples address him as Rabbi or *Didaskale* (Teacher), and remonstrate with him quite naturally (Mark 4.38, 53.1, 6.27, 8.32). He cannot heal everybody (1.32ff; 3.10): nor does he raise the dead, for it is Matthew and Luke who stress that Jairus' daughter was really dead, Jesus himself says that she is not (Mark 5.39). He is a willing and welcome guest, with a lively sense of humour. His strong emotions, often smoothed away in Matthew and Luke, are unconcealed in Mark; anger and indignation (1.41, 43; 3.5; 10.14), or warmth and affection: he first embraces the leper and then is very short with him (1.41), he picks up and hugs little children (9.36; 10.14), and shows affection for the rich (young) man (10.21)[17]. He is distressed and bewildered at Gethsemane (14.33). Peter knows the man too well for the picture to be blurred by his reverence for the earthly Messiah who will soon return to judge the world (an early, basic theological reading of Jesus) and he remains frank about his own shortcomings and those of the other disciples.

Incredible Stories

What greatly assisted the general acceptance of the Form Critic's claim that all gospel material was far from eye-witness was the fact that, even in Mark, there are stories which most people would judge incredible; and many twentieth century Christians were happy to be freed from such embarrassments. Yet in fact there is nothing in Mark which is inconsistent with believable facts, sometimes slightly misunderstood or misreported.

The healings in Mark usually lie within the range of non-medical healings such as occur today, and which even today are sometimes claimed as miraculous (See Ch.3 below). We need not perplex ourselves by asking whether these are really miracles, breaking the laws of nature, or cures according to natural forces not yet fully understood, or short lived self-delusions; the point, as regards Mark's historicity, is that such things, still happening today, would then most certainly have been taken as miracles.

The same applies to prophecies, which Bultmann confidently claimed to be always stories invented after the happening. Invented stories of prophecy undoubtedly exist, but prophecies which come true, and others which do not, are also facts, and there need be nothing unhistorical in Jesus' prophecies that Jerusalem and the temple would be destroyed – as indeed they were – and that the apocalyptic Day of the Lord would follow – which it did not (See Ch.2, below).

Where credibility breaks down, however, is when Jesus destroys a herd of pigs by allowing the many demons, which he has just exorcised from a demented man, to possess the animals and drive them over a cliff; or when he blasts a fig-tree with a curse because it could not supply him, out of season, with some fruit;

acts as malicious as they are unlikely. In both cases, these seem to be Peter's misinterpretations of events for which we can easily find better explanations.

We must sympathise with Peter; for, having seen Jesus perform cures which seemed miraculous, he had no way of knowing how far such powers might reach; and his Jewish culture strongly endorsed the miraculous. Mark too, having heard from Peter of those cures and 'miracles', was in the same case; and so when Peter told him of the time when Jesus came walking out towards the boat, looking as though he were walking on the water, and they all mistook him for a ghost, Mark could also leap to a mistaken conclusion, which Peter was not later available to correct. Such mistakes, by eyewitnesses, and such misunderstandings by those who hear their stories, are the stuff of everyday life and reporting.[18]

In sum, all the internal evidence in Mark bears out the historical testimony: that, after Peter's death, Mark, Peter's *hermēneutēs*, wrote down accurately, though not in order, everything he (Mark) remembered of the things said and done by the Lord. Peter organised his teaching as occasion demanded, but not as an orderly arrangement of the Lord's sayings, so that Mark could only write down individual items like this, as he (Mark) recalled them; and he made it his main concern not to omit anything which he had heard nor to misrepresent anything. He may therefore have included a second version of the same story, if this seemed sufficiently different; he may have misunderstood; and at best he heard eyewitness from a single person, who may not have seen everything that took place. Yet, even with these caveats, Mark stands as reliable recording of a truthful account of the ministry of Jesus.

Matthew and Luke

These two, probably the earliest gospels to follow Mark, and datable to perhaps 80-90 AD, seem to be much as previous scholarship has said. Both use not only Mark, but also the hypothetical but usually accepted Q, a collection of sayings (such, for instance, as the one which Papias says the apostle Matthew compiled in Aramaic, or the so-called *Gospel of Thomas*); Q, like Matthew's collection, is now lost, but may fairly be inferred from many sayings of Jesus, not found in Mark, which appear in both Matthew and Luke in identical or closely parallel wording. Both Matthew and Luke have each a source of his own, too, from which come episodes almost always more marvellous or more dramatic than those of Mark.

For his narrative, Matthew seems, after his Birth legends, always to rely on, or to adapt from, Mark's; but Luke's story-line is often distinctly different, and suggests that his own particular sources included some alternative narrative scheme as well as certain parables and legends. Both have edited and arranged their material, as ancient biographers did, to suit their own concepts of Jesus, polishing up not only Mark's grammar but also his homely peasant hero; Jesus in Matthew is clearly a successor to Moses, reforming the Jewish law, while in Luke he resembles a Greek philosopher who also works miracles (like that Apollonius of Tyana who was more or less Luke's contemporary, and whose life was unreliably written up by Philostratus in the early third century). Apart and together these two gospels are much the best sources for the teaching of Jesus, for it seems that both had a version of an early written collection of Jesus' sayings and parables; but for the facts of his life and death they must be considered secondary at best. In this study a likely extra detail may occasionally be drawn from either but, wherever there are differing versions, Mark, who is not a biographer but a painstaking recorder, is always to be preferred.

Thus Matthew and Luke seem enough by themselves, without even considering the more bizarre excluded gospels, to refute the historical value of a 'Controlled Tradition'. The Christian communities of that time may well have preserved some concise statement of essential facts, such as Paul gives in 1 Cor.15.3-7; even, perhaps, one as long as the so-called Apostle's Creed: but even these two accepted gospels reveal an alarming growth of exaggeration, and of pure legend narrated as fact, within those communities. Even Luke, who wisely excludes, for example, the Walking on Water and the Withered Fig Tree, produces a great many other miracles, and more dramatic but less likely versions of such episodes as the Rejection at Nazareth and the Call of the Fishermen; his story of Zacchaeus could easily be a much developed version of 'the Call of Levi', but if so, Luke is unaware of it. Matthew, as well as many unlikely stories of his own, has Peter walking on the water as well as Jesus; and his Fig Tree withers, not overnight, but instantly, at a word. Thus the acceptance as tradition of invention and exaggeration, whether by the evangelists, by their sources, or by both, was rife no more than fifty or sixty years after the Crucifixion.

John:
A Realistic Early Critique

John's Gospel, however, is something quite different. Published perhaps between 100 and 110 AD, it was slow to gain acceptance as an authoritative gospel: as late as c.180, Irenaeus knew that not all Christians accepted it. However, c.210 AD the scholar Clement of Alexandria approved it; but on his own terms, saying that,

> **John, last of all, aware that the physical facts** (*ta somatika*) **had been set down in the [synoptic] gospels […], divinely urged by the Spirit, created** (*poiēsai*)[19] **a spiritual** (*pneumatikon*) **gospel.**

We should pay attention to this judgement; for Clement is saying that the last of our four canonical gospels is not concerned to set down historical fact, but rather to create a work presenting spiritual and theological truth, as understood by the author. John is a treasure house of riches, but history is not one of them: as Clement says, the history had already been written.

In John, Jesus is shown as a confrontational Sabbath-breaker, which in real life would have allowed his opponents to dispose of him quickly and legally;[20] as an egocentric controversialist, constantly preaching his own importance; as showing supernatural power by 'signs', ie., by cures and miracles unprecedented then and highly incredible now; as moving incessantly between Judaea and Galilee, and as the hero of hairbreadth escapes and secret journeys: Stibbe neatly likens him to the Scarlet Pimpernel. All these unlikely aspects come from reading as biography what was intended as drama or historical novel.

Drama

My own opinion is that the author originally drafted a Greek tragedy. That was an obvious medium for the striking presentation of an interpretation of Jesus, for in classical tragedy,

> Most important of all, the affairs of the characters which move us are given a moral setting which is argued and explored within the play. They act and suffer within *situations of moral conflict, of social, intellectual and theological conflict* (Taplin, 1989, p.169; my italics).

The play would have covered only the final week of Jesus' earthly life, at Jerusalem, thus meeting drama's basic need for Unity of Time, and of Place:[21] hence the fact that, even though now expanded, so much of this gospel is set in and around Jerusalem, unlike the Synoptics. Hence too the Prologue (John 1.1-18), a normal opening for a play, which sets out the cosmological, theological significance of the plot; and later the proliferation of speeches starting 'I am', which in fact sound natural enough from an actor on a stage, but nowhere else.

In John, Jesus is cast as a tragic hero defying and dominating all opposition, in a sequence of Jerusalem scenes which, running from the Clearing of the Temple, through three increasingly marvellous cures (the lame, the blind and the dead), bring him to a triumphant climax of popular acclaim as he rides through the city.

Then, after a short Last Supper (perhaps only the Washing of Feet and the promise that the Counsellor will come after Jesus has gone) comes the *peripateia*, the sudden reversal of fortune which brings down the hero to his doom: his Arrest at Gethsemane, followed by Trial and Crucifixion. Yet tragedy to the Greeks meant simply a serious play, it did not preclude a happy ending; the Resurrection scenes follow, featuring Mary Magdalen and Thomas, to end the play with the great avowal, 'My Lord and my God!

This outline plot may perhaps be dismissed as arbitrary selection; but there can be no doubt that the author deliberately creates dramatic scenes, with many echoes and even plagiarisms from classical Athenian tragedy. Many scenes borrow from Sophocles: Jesus with his whip, driving cattle from the temple, recalls the popular role of 'Whip-Wielding Ajax', who flogged sheep and cattle in a fit of frenzy; Lazarus, hobbled by his grave-clothes, coming out of his cave tomb when called by Jesus, visually reproduces Philoctetes, hobbling out on a poisoned foot, from the cave into which he had gone to die, when called forth by Neoptolemus. What Jesus tells Pilate, Antigone had told king Creon, that there was a higher authority than earthly power, which she would obey to the death. The mockery of Jesus, led out in scarlet robe and crown of thorns to be displayed by Pilate to the crowd, recalls not Sophocles but Euripides, with the righteous king Pentheus in *The Bacchae* led out by Dionysus to be made ridiculous on the stage before being led away to death.[22]

The author creates dramatic scenes of his own, perplexing to scholars who suppose them to be intended as history. Only Pilate had soldiers at Jerusalem, yet the soldiers who come to arrest Jesus, falling back in terror at the words 'I AM', seem unlike any troops in the Roman army; it is, however, a powerful scene, which shows Jesus as the willing sacrifice, *consenting* to his own arrest, with 'soldiers' in place of servants to exploit the visual menace of men in helmets. Later Pilate, setting Jesus on the raised 'judgement-seat' to present him to the crowd as 'your king', is acting as no Roman governor ever would; but it makes a striking, theatrical, tableau.[23]

Dramatic factors control the Crucifixion in John. Jesus carries the cross himself, for the theatrical effect of the victim toiling under his burden to the place of his death. Four soldiers, dicing for Jesus' clothes, make a wholly inadequate squad to guard the execution of yesterday's national hero, but are an effective stage-army – they *imply* a military presence. The attendance of Jesus' mother and disciple at the foot of the cross could never have been allowed really, but makes a fine scene.[24]

For the Resurrection, Mary Magdalen plays the non-recognition scene so popular in Greek drama. However, to be mistaken for a gardener, Jesus must wear ordinary clothing; but heavenly persons should wear shining robes, so he is given a line saying 'Do not cling to me, for *I have not yet gone to the Father*'.[25] Then, for his final appearance to close the play, he will be splendidly and brilliantly clad, to show him in his glory and leave no room for doubt.

If much of John was first created for the stage, many problems noted by scholars are resolved. Greek drama had an imposed limit of three actors, covering between them all speaking roles; so that with these playing Jesus, Mary and Martha, then Lazarus, whose silence here (11.44) has been thought puzzling, can only be a mute extra.[26] The bafflingly variable identity of the Judaeans (*Hoi Iudaioi)* could derive from a chorus of *Men of Judaea,*[27] some of the singers costumed as priests and Pharisees, others as 'the people'; for a chorus often showed divided opinions. It might also show shifting attitudes; the same chorus could represent the outraged audiences who wish to stone Jesus (John 8.59; 10.31), the mourners for dead Lazarus (John 11.19), the enthusiastic Palm Sunday crowd, and the mob howling for crucifixion.

Historical Novel

Yet, either because the final stage of putting the play into Greek verse defeated the author, or because of the much greater scope available to a novelist, or for some other reason, the draft play was, I suggest, rewritten and expanded by the author to form a historical novel, a popular genre of the time used by both Greek and Jewish writers.[28]

For the one point of general agreement amongst Johannine scholars is that *some* original version has been worked over and extended; what, why, how or by whom are argued various ways. The clearest example amongst the abundant evidence of reworking is John 20.30f, clearly written as an ending, yet immediately followed by another chapter, with a second ending at 21.24f. The suggested expansion of play into novel could explain this – for a novel requires a more leisurely and detailed closure than the climax of a play – *and every other* problem posed by this 'gospel'.

However that may be, many indications show that this gospel is written in a fictional style, like the ancient Greek 'romances'. It is frequently told from the 'God's eye view'; the author knows everything that happens, in all places and at all times; telling us, for example, what the Samaritan woman says to her neighbours in the village, and they to her, or everything said by the man born blind and his parents when interrogated by the Pharisees. He knows what Pilate says to Jesus in private, as well as in public. He knows everyone's motives, and also knows the will of God, which otherwise only Jesus understands. He drops hints about Judas' shortcomings to prepare us for his treachery; and he invents, as historical novelists so often do, a fictitious witness to the 'truth' of his story, in this case the Beloved Disciple. He heightens the tension with repeated escapes, journeys, danger and subterfuge. He plunders the early gospels, particularly Mark and Luke, for suitable names and unusual vocabulary. He creates new scenes by taking themes, mostly from Mark, and using them with a freedom that has induced scholars to imagine a 'Signs Gospel', and one or two early, possibly Aramaic, sources supposedly used by both Mark and John, to account for similarity of themes but discrepancy of detail.[29] His time-schemes are arbitrary, and sometimes muddled[30], but he writes memorable episodes, like the Wedding at Cana or the meeting with the Samaritan Woman, well and clearly written, with delightful touches of humour.

This brief outline does not attempt to convince readers of the exact truth of these particular theories, but only of the fact that this gospel makes no attempt to be history. The three Jerusalem miracles may illustrate the writer's technique. The basis for each is a theme from Mark, but instead of a paralysed youth (in Mark, Jesus calls him *Teknon*, Child), John has a man paralysed for thirty-five years; Mark's blind man at Bethsaida has now been blind from birth; and rather than Jairus' unconscious young daughter (Mark 5.35-42) we have Lazarus, an adult, dead four days in a hot climate (John 11.38-44). All three events have been made marvellous beyond normal possibility, and all are suited to stage production; whereas an attempt to stage, say, walking on water would simply look ridiculous. The stories are distorted beyond recognition, were it not that unusual details (carrying away the bed, applying spittle to the eye-lids) and particularly Marcan vocabulary (*krabbaton* for bed; *embrimaomai*, to be overcome by emotion) reveal the source. It is these, with closer correspondence in miracles not intended for the stage (Mark 6.35-52: John 6.5-21), which have suggested the hypothetical sources mentioned above, but can more simply be explained as the normal techniques of a historical novelist.

John and History

It must not be thought that the fourth Gospel is devalued by this interpretation; rather, it allows the work to be properly appreciated, without nagging doubts about physical or historical improbability. It sets out, as Clement recognized, not only an advanced theological view of Jesus, but a doctrine of the Spirit working in the early church which Clement certainly approved (and which George Fox, for one, has built upon). But as well as the theology, there are some incomparable vignettes in John of a very human Jesus, in which fiction may bring us nearer to the truth than mere fact: Jesus washing the disciples' feet, for example, makes vividly concrete and memorable the attitude recorded in Mark's dictum that the greatest must be the servant of all; Mary Magdalen's sudden and overwhelming recognition of Jesus, alive and present there beside her, perhaps conveys best what the Resurrection experiences, whatever their objective nature, really felt like, and how overwhelmingly convincing they were, to those who experienced them.

The dating of the Crucifixion in this gospel to the *eve* of the Passover is, however, not only inherently more likely than Mark's trial and crucifixion on the day of Passover itself, but authoritatively affirmed by Polycrates, bishop of Ephesus, and corroborated by a story in the Talmud.[31] It makes the sole point on which John may be preferred to the Synoptics. Without similar independent corroboration, however, nothing from John should be accepted as historical fact, for fact, as Clement made clear, was not the evangelist's concern. We should not, therefore, accept as true that the first disciples of Jesus had been followers of the Baptist, that a crowd in Galilee wanted to make Jesus a king, that there were soldiers at Gethsemane, or that Pilate seriously wished to set Jesus free but was intimidated by the chief priests and the crowd; and we should, however regretfully, reject the beloved disciple as a historical character.

From Matthew and Luke we may occasionally cull items which amplify and explain Mark, and for the teaching of Jesus they must stand as our most reliable source; for Mark includes relatively little teaching, and while John may have much to teach us, it will not be not through Jesus' own words. The Gospel of Thomas, while containing some undoubtedly genuine sayings, is for the most part conformed to a later Gnostic viewpoint, in which individual salvation depends on the knowledge (*gnosis*) of spiritual mysteries. Where any gospel contradicts Mark's narrative, however, excepting only John's dating of the crucifixion, it must be considered inferior; the Gospel according to Mark stands as our prime witness, and the realistic picture of Jesus which it shows is its best recommendation.

This study will therefore attempt to present, perhaps for the first time since the first century, an account of Jesus nowhere adapted to those of the later evangelists. For John is historical fiction, and Matthew and Luke are aretalogy, retelling, 'with advantages', the life of a cult figure; only Mark attempts a plain account of the life and death of Jesus of Nazareth.

Mediterranean Custom

Yet even in the best historical sources, sometimes an incident can only be understood in terms of the culture of the society in which those people lived. Palestine, having been ruled successively by Assyria, Babylon, Egypt, Macedon and now Rome, was a society of many nations – one does not immediately think of a theatre at Jerusalem, but certainly there was one, and Jewish writers even composed plays. The 'hypocrisy' which Jesus denounced meant playing a part on the stage,[32] and 'hypocrite' was probably a Greek word adopted into Aramaic, as English words too are used in Urdu or Hindi, when no native equivalent existed.

One does not think of Jesus as taking a siesta (to use the best known word for the practice of every Mediterranean country) each afternoon, but in that hot climate it must have been so. Siesta time, which once allowed a *coup d'etat* in Rome while the Praetorian Guard were asleep, is not of major importance in the story of Jesus, but that habit often throws some light; on, for example, the afternoon of Good Friday.

Another custom which, in Spain at least, still held good in the twentieth century, was that no one ate in the presence of others without inviting them to share: such a custom would illuminate several occasions in Galilee. Mark is a good source; but can better be understood against the background of customs which he would have taken for granted.

Notes to Introduction

[1] *The Gospel of Peter* is late, far-fetched and patently not eyewitness.
[2] Tertullian excepted, all the ancient references to the authorship of Mark are set out in V. Taylor 1953 pp.1-8.
[3] Clement's *Adumbrationes in 1 Pet.5.13*; and Eusebius, *The Ecclesiastical History*, 6.14.6f, and 2.15.1f.
[4] Bauckham translates here 'as *Peter* recalled them', claiming that Mark wrote down the stories when Peter told them; but, since Mark is the subject both of the previous clause and of the following sentence, the 'he' in between would be Mark, not Peter.
[5] 'Great' news is my translation: '*euaggelion*' means *important* good news.
[6] By 'the villages' Peter probably meant *Tetracomia*, The Four Villages, the Greek term for Upland Galilee (like *Dekapolis*, The Ten Towns).
[7] This suggestion means that Miracles were rarely preached. Naturally so, since the *kerygma*, the basic message, concentrated on the great miracle of

---

Resurrection, claiming Jesus as unique; other miracles would only prove that he was, like others, **a man approved by God**.

[8] Josephus merely labels the two Galilees as 'the up' and 'the down' (*ē anō, ē katō*): Upland and Lowland Galilee seem a fair translation.

[9] These I take as details which Mark remembered Peter giving, and therefore kept, 'trying to omit nothing'.

[10] Capernaum is implied by the availability of the boat (6.32).

[11] Hence Aquila and Priscilla left Rome for Corinth (Acts 18.2).

[12] If this reason is correct, it offers no support for claims that a written summary of the Passion was the general practice of early churches.

[13] Kummel (1996, p.219) points out that the Epistle to the Romans (c.59 AD) seems to be written for a predominantly Gentile church; which agrees with the historical probability.

[14] Weatherhead (1959, p.63) identifies the place as Khersa (possibly Ger'sa in Peter's speech), a village near 'the only spot on the whole shore of the lake where steep ground falls into deep water.'

[15] Advocated by Tolbert 1996, pp.80-83. It is true, however, that where communication is largely oral, ordinary folk often tell stories artistically, although not in a literary style: I recall rural Western Ireland in the 1950's.

[16] Levi abandoned the day's takings at a word, but he was not being recruited as a disciple, and may have been back at work next day. Only in Matthew has the story of Levi been fathered onto the apostle whose name lends prestige to that gospel.

[17] It is Matthew who says the rich man was young, a reasonable inference from his 'running up' to speak to Jesus.

[18] In 1998, a bell-ringer's accident at Romsey Abbey was reported with a news-worthy spin and appeared in 8 daily papers next morning. Every account contained one or more of five or six different errors, mostly coming from eyewitness at either first or second hand.

[19] ***Poieō***, to a scholar like Clement, would probably have here its prime meaning in classical Greek, 'to create an original work', used particularly of sculptors, poets and playwrights. (This usage is not found in New Testament Greek, unless Luke is using it, as maybe he might, in Acts 1.1, about his own, somewhat creative, gospel.)

[20] In the Synoptics, arguments are only about the proper *interpretation* of the fourth commandment. Blatant defiance of that law (John 5.8-12) was tantamount to blasphemy.

---

[21] Aristotle recommends a single day; many plays require more, but do not emphasize the fact. A single location is usual, but that means various locations in the same general area, Athens, say, or Jerusalem.
[22] Stibbe (1992, pp.121-47) has listed many other similarities and echoes, but holds that they are unconscious plagiarising.
[23] Although the text is ambiguous, it must be Jesus who is seated on the *bēma*, or the whole clause in John 19.13 is pointless.
[24] Inspired by Sophocles again, in whose *Women of Trachis* the dying Heracles insistently commends his dear Iolē to the care of his son.
[25] This would solve theological difficulties which scholars have found in this cryptic remark.
[26] In Euripides' *Alcestis*, the actor who earlier played the dying Alcestis also plays Heracles, who rescues her from the underworld; so when he brings her back, she likewise is a mute extra.
[27] We might expect *The Men of* **Jerusalem**, but *Hierosolumitai* is very cumbersome.
[28] One of the earliest was *Joseph and Aseneth*, a romance spun from a mere two verses of Genesis.
[29] Hypothetical sources: Fortna 1970; Morton Smith 1974; Wills 1997.
[30] **About the middle of the feast** of Tabernacles, Jesus is teaching in the temple, and the chief priests send officers to arrest him; not until the last day of the feast do the officers report back, empty-handed (John 8.32-46).
[31] Polycrates, bishop of Ephesus c.190 AD, tells how the correct date had always been kept, in unbroken succession, by the church of Asia; the Babylonian Talmud, *Sanhedrin 43* says, **Jesus was hanged on the eve of the Passover.**
[32] Another theatre was built at Sepphoris, a few miles from Nazareth, although probably after the time of Jesus.

PART ONE: MISSION TO GALILEE

CHAPTER 1

The Call

To accept Mark as almost our only source for the life and actions of Jesus loses us nothing; rather, we gain the chance of seeing Jesus as he was, before hero-worship and theological dogma overlaid the picture. On that basis we can begin to study his earthly ministry.

The Baptist

Mark's narrative of Jesus rightly begins with his baptism by John, for without that there would have been nothing to relate. This episode should be taken as being what Jesus told his first four disciples in order to explain the nature of his mission. That telling is nowhere recorded, but may safely be inferred: for sane, responsible adults do not abandon work and family to follow a complete stranger, however charismatic, at a moment's notice. The recorded summoning of the four fishermen from their nets (Mark.1.16.20) means that they must have met Jesus before, heard why he was changing the course of his life so drastically, and promised their support.

What happened to Jesus at his baptism can, like the calls of the Old Testament prophets, happen in any age to believing folk, as the records of 17th Century Quakers (who often committed their experiences to writing) can confirm. James Nayler briefly states the fact.

> I was at the plough, meditating on the things of God, and suddenly I heard a voice saying unto me, 'Get thee out from thy kindred, and from thy father's house' (*Quaker Faith & Practice,1955, 19.09*).

There seems to be a physical condition engendered by steady walking which can aid such a mental process; Marmaduke Stevenson also was ploughing:

> And as I walked after the plough, I was filled with the love and presence of the living God [...] which made me to stand still. And, as I stood a little still [...] the word of the Lord came to me in a still, small voice, which I did hear perfectly, saying to me in the secret of my heart and conscience, 'I have ordained thee a prophet to the nations' (QFP 19.17).

After such a call to service it is usual for the recipient to have to wait to learn what he or she is meant to do about it, and Jesus' time in the wilderness follows naturally, although forty days may be symbolic enhancement rather than exact reckoning. Ezekiel is said to have stayed 'astonished' for seven days; Paul retired to 'Arabia' for two or three years. Fox, like many others, had a continuing series of revelations, but maybe two years passed between his first revelation in 1646 and a clear call to 'go forth' and 'turn people to that inward light'.[1] Nayler, after his initial call, parted with personal property but did not at once leave home – not knowing, perhaps, where to go. He fell gravely ill, which he took to be because he had not fulfilled his first instructions; so when he recovered he got ready some clothes and other 'necessaries' for travel:

> But shortly afterwards going a gate-ward with a friend from my own house, having on an old suit, without any money, having neither taken leave of wife or children, nor thinking then of any journey, I was commanded to go into the west, not knowing whither I should go nor what I was to do there.

Stevenson's 'call' to be 'a prophet unto the nations' was not at first specific; but later, 'at the time appointed, Barbados was set before me'. From Barbados, receiving a hint that he should go to New England, he went as far as Rhode Island;

> and the word of the Lord came to me, saying, 'Go to Boston [...]' and at His command I was obedient and gave up to His will.[2]

We should expect that Jesus too would need time before he could discern even how to start his ministry, and that there might be stages in its development.

The Baptism story, then, seems likely to be substantially accurate; all the more so because, as Bultmann complained, it has *not* been conformed artistically to a literary type. Its setting provides a first historical correlation: Luke dates the Baptist's appearance to the fifteenth year of the reign of Tiberius, possibly 26-27, more probably 28/29 AD[3]. Josephus too records John, as a good man who called the men of Judea to live uprightly and, showing fairness to others and reverence to God, to gather together in baptism.[4] John's baptism – Josephus does not, perhaps, want his Roman patrons to confuse it with the inferior rites of Christians – required first the adoption of good ways, **fruits worthy of repentance** (Matt.3.9); it did not of itself remit sins, but merely sanctified the body once the soul was already cleansed by honest living. Since Mark 1.1 describes John's rite as *baptisma metanoias eis aphesin hamartiōn*, **a baptism of a change of heart**

for the remission of sins, and later says that Jesus, whom Mark never shows as baptising anyone,[5] also preached *metanoia* (1.15), it seems likely that Jesus taught the same.[6]

Josephus does not depict John as wearing clothing reminiscent of Elijah (2 Ki.1.8; cf. Zech.13.4), nor as prophesying the Coming Day of the Lord, as Mark does; but Peter would be the better witness. Not only may he have seen John himself, but the account of Josephus, not born until 37 AD, is inconsistent. Herod killed John, he alleges, when **others** joined the crowds, and the crowds **were excited to a high degree** by John's preaching, so that Herod opted for pre-emptive action, rather than waiting for riot (*stasis*) or revolution (*neōteron*) to start. Josephus says Herod feared the power of John's eloquence; but that implies that the preaching was not simply ethical, but urged or foreshadowed political change. For ethics, however eloquent, do not excite a crowd; and if the unidentified **others** who joined the crowds are, as seems implied, men seeking not spiritual cleansing but some nationalistic goal, their interest is best explained if John was preaching the end of the existing world order and the coming of God's kingdom.[7]

Elsewhere, Josephus has confirmed the prevalence of the Messianic theme amongst his people, blaming it as a principal reason for the disastrous Jewish War of 65-70 AD, and specifically for the destruction of the temple; which makes it probable that John too had preached, as Peter claims, that there would come one more important than himself (Mark 1.7), to bring in that kingdom. Nothing in Mark suggests that John knew Jesus, nor that he had any individual in mind for Messiah. Nor is there anything to suggest that Peter was himself present at Jesus' baptism; this story (1.9-12) must rather be Jesus' own account, for everything unusual takes place in his own mind, unknown to Baptist or crowd.

Burton Mack, who dismisses Mark's gospel as invention, holds that the Baptist was introduced into the Q material to help transform the image of Jesus from philosophical sage to apocalyptic prophet.[8] However, after Luke has merely repeated Mark's story, in all the other gospels we find early Christians using increasing exaggeration to diminish, rather than to invoke, the Baptist's authority. Clear in Matthew, this is clearer still in John, where the theology of the perfect sacrifice, hinted when the Baptist points Jesus out as **the Lamb of God**, may be the reason why there is no narrative of the actual baptism of the sinless one,[9] while the evangelist also contrives a meeting between the first disciples and Jesus such as Mark's narrative, I have argued, must imply. John may not be a historical author, but he is an accomplished artist.

A story needing constant revision to fit developing Christologies is not likely to be invention, but rather a report too early and authoritative to be censored completely. Yet the real case for the historicity of the Marcan story is that Jesus' subsequent career demands, at its human level, precisely some such overwhelming experience to account for his undertaking such a mission; just as Paul's career as an apostle confirms the basic truth of some shattering personal experience on the road to Damascus.[10] Had Joan of Arc never heard her 'voices', she would have remained an unknown peasant in an obscure village; had Jesus at his baptism not heard the *bath kol*, the heavenly voice, he might have done the same.

A Voice from Heaven

> **And just as he came up out of the water he saw the sky split open and the spirit like a dove coming down to him. And a voice came from the sky, 'You are my son, the one I love (*ho agapētos*), I have taken great pride in you (*en soi eudokēsa*).' And at once the spirit drives him out into the uninhabited land** (Mark 1.9ff).

There is not a hint that the experience could or did at the time concern anyone but Jesus; and it is in the nature of such experiences that they are entirely subjective. They must not, however, be therefore considered unreal; for they really happen, in the mind of that person, to whom they are the most real thing that ever happened; they have real effects on the lives of others, and sometimes they change the course of history. Whether the experience is 'really' the voice of God, or 'really' an illusion, may be debatable; that it really happens is not.

Its context, for Jesus, was that every Hebrew prophet was called directly by God; for it was in God's name that he must speak. Amos says, as briefly as Nayler, **the Lord took me from following the flock and the Lord said to me, 'Go, prophesy to my people Israel'. So now, listen to the word of the Lord** (Amos 7.15f, *RSV*).[11] Isaiah's very visual experience (Isa.6.1-13) is well known; Ezekiel's fills two and a half chapters with yet more complex imagery (Ezek.1.1-3.14). Jeremiah's, in contrast, is almost entirely verbal:

> **And the word of the Lord came to him. [...] 'before you came out of the womb I sanctified you, I appointed you a prophet to the nations.' And I said, 'Lord, Ruler of all, look, I do not know how to speak, for I am too young.' And the Lord said to me, 'Don't say, I am too young; for you shall go to all those to whom I send you, and you shall speak**

> **according to all the words that I command you. Don't be afraid when facing them; for I am with you to protect you, says the Lord'** (Lxx. Jer.1.4-8).

Fact or fiction, these accounts show that what was recognised as a prophet's call would be a summons in words quite clearly 'heard' by the recipient, possibly accompanied by some visual imagery.

The summons often presents itself in familiar phrases. Stevenson's is from Jeremiah, Nayler's from the call of Abram (Gen.12.1). The words which formed in Jesus' mind – **'You are my son, the one I love; I have taken great pride in you'** – came from the scriptures he knew. If he knew them in Hebrew, Isaiah 42.1 would offer **Behold my servant, whom I uphold, my chosen, in whom my soul delights. I have put my spirit upon him, he will bring forth justice to the nations** (*RSV*).[12] If, as may be more likely, Jesus knew the prophets best in the Greek of the Septuagint, the words in Jesus' mind may best be taken as a paraphrase of Isa.41.9 (cf. also 43.10, 44.21) **I have called you, and said to you, 'You are my servant (or, son), I have chosen you, and I have not deserted you';** crossed perhaps with Isa.49.3, **'You are my servant, Israel, and in you I shall be glorified.'**

Almost everywhere in this part of Isaiah the Greek word used is *pais:* primary meaning 'son' or 'child', but commonly used for 'servant' (like 'boy' or *garcon*). Mark 1.11 uses the unambiguous *huios*, 'son'; but the *bath kol,* the voice from heaven which alone, in Jewish stories, addresses anyone as God's son, always means someone who excellently performs God's will (Vermes 206-10). So whether *huios* was the word which came to Jesus then, or the sense in which he understood *pais* when later he told his disciples of his call; or whether, most probably, *huios* was Peter's word as he put back into Greek what he had been told in Aramaic, makes no real difference.

It should be noted that, given the very wide use of Greek throughout Galilee,[13] it is highly likely that Jesus, and Peter, could speak it. Aramaic was the mother tongue in which Jesus taught, but the scriptures were available only in Hebrew or Greek; and it is perhaps more likely that he read them in Greek; for archaeological evidence suggests a much wider use in Galilee and Judaea of written Greek than of written Hebrew;[14] and to any artisan living near Herod's new city of Sepphoris, and whose son was not destined to be priest, scholar nor lawyer, the greater commercial usefulness of Greek could have been important;[15] and if devout, then reading Greek might also give easier access to the scriptures. We do not know the usage of Galilean synagogues before the destruction of

Jerusalem led the rabbis to move north; but while Jesus no doubt heard some Hebrew in synagogue, and perhaps knew by heart familiar psalms or prayers in Hebrew, just as a mediaeval workman might know his *Ave* and his *Pater Noster* in Latin, Greek seems the most likely language which he might have been taught to read and to write. (Hence, unless otherwise stated, all further Old Testament citations are translations of the Greek text of the Septuagint;[16] only specified (*Lxx*) when necessary. Similarly, New Testament quotations are from Mark, if nothing is specified.)

To a devout Jew, the son and the servant of God would both mean the same thing, a man notably obedient to the will of God, his Father and Master.[17] To be chosen and approved as the servant of God, and now filled with his spirit – another recurring theme (Isa.42.1; 44.3; 50.4; 61.1) – could be nothing less than a summons to work as God's prophet. That he might be the Messiah, the one who would lead and rule the nation, probably did not enter his head at this time; he would have had enough to do in accepting the basic proposition that he, the builder from Nazareth, was being chosen for God's service.

Time to Consider

There is nothing to suggest that Jesus was seeking any new experience when he went to hear the Baptist. Since the Baptist operated in the south of Peraea, on the eastern side of the Jordan but not too far from Jerusalem, Jesus had walked some eighty or ninety miles from Nazareth and was most probably on his way to Jerusalem for one of the feasts, taking in the Baptist as he went. If so, his plans were overset. He was now driven (literally, **thrown out**) into the wilderness to come to terms with that experience, to learn what God's message might be and how his task should be performed. There is no suggestion in Mark of Jesus eating no food; nor indeed does Matthew's **having fasted forty days** necessarily imply that, either. Luke says that Jesus ate nothing, but Matthew may be rendering the version in Q more accurately here;[18] over a period of weeks, fasting probably means only eating simply and sparingly. Mark's **and the angels served him** suggests that his needs were supplied from time to time by kindly folk, for a 'wilderness' is not usually totally uninhabited, while the 'angels' might be Peter's naive explanation of the source.

Mark knows nothing of the nature of Jesus' temptation; but if we accord Jesus a full humanity, his first and strongest temptation may have been to go home and forget all about it, for such calls, however flattering, are seldom welcome. Jane Fenn, an 18th century Philadelphia Quaker, eventually a noted travelling preacher, records her dismay at being called to ministry by an inner voice:

> Yet I must confess, this awful word of Divine Command shocked me exceedingly, my soul and all within me trembled (...) yea, my outer tabernacle shook insomuch that many present observed the deep exercise I was under. I cried in spirit, 'Lord, I am weak and altogether incapable of such a task, I hope thou wilt spare me from such a mortification; besides I have spoken much against women appearing in that manner' *(QFP, 2.56)*

She struggled for six months against her call, before finally submitting and speaking a few words in meeting; from which she went on, by degrees, to travel farther and farther in her preaching.

A call is not usually immediately explicit, either. When, after a time of waiting for specific 'directions', these come, they come singly, one step at a time. Nayler says that he spent the rest of his life 'not knowing today what I was to do tomorrow'. Acts gives this account of step-by-step guidance:

> **So they went through the land of Phrygia and Galatia, having been forbidden by the holy spirit to speak the word in Asia. And when they came down to Mysia, they were trying to go into Bithynia, and the spirit of Jesus would not let them. So, going past Mysia they went down to Troas. And a vision appeared to Paul in the night, a Macedonian man standing there and begging him, saying, 'Come across to Macedonia and help us.' So when he saw the vision, we at once sought to go off to Macedonia, agreeing that God had called us to take them the great news.** (Acts 16.6-10).

It is this constant attitude of trustful obedience, which Brother Lawrence called 'the practice of the presence of God', that allows the prophet to hear the message. Note too that the source of guidance and power, which had come to the disciples at Pentecost and which was now regarded as the touchstone of a genuine disciple, is variously referred to as **the holy spirit, the spirit of Jesus,** and simply **God**. This confirms that those first disciples knew that Jesus had throughout his ministry been guided and empowered in the same way, by the spirit of God which had 'come' to him at his baptismal experience. And when perplexities arose, Jesus needed again to retreat into solitude, so as to hear more clearly (Mark 1.35; 6.46; 9.2; 14.35,39).

The Way Forward

This is not a Jesus who understands or knows God's plan in any detail. If there is such a thing as 'God's plan', it lies outside the range of human knowledge; and if Jesus was fully human, as the creeds insist, he would basically have *known* no more than that general understanding of the Kingdom to Come which he shared with the rest of his nation, although he *felt* deeply that he must proclaim it as imminent (1.15). What comes to humans who are serious about 'waiting on the Lord', who are ready to be of service, are specific 'commands', whether as individual flashes of illumination, or by a prompting from another person; or as insistent ideas, 'concerns' as Friends say, that take hold of one over a longer period, like the urge which drove the unqualified but indomitable Gladys Aylward (all her life a fine example of obeying the inner voice) to go to China as a missionary (Burgess 1959, pp.15-24); sometimes a request or suggestion from a friend, or something read in the scriptures, may become insistent. Whether these impulses come *from* the subconscious or merely *through* it, falls outside the scope of this book; the fact is that, in certain circumstances, they come, and to the subject they are the compelling, if often unwelcome, commands from their god.[19]

Such people retain their normal ability to plan and reason, and more often than not must rely on that; but with a continual readiness to have their own plans overturned by some new guidance. That Jesus too went forward one step at a time is confirmed by the fact that he taught his disciples to do the same: **Take no thought for tomorrow, tomorrow can take care of itself [...] Give us today enough food for today [...] Not what I want, but what You want.** So he lived and so he died.

But death would have been the last thing on his mind when he began his work. That 'the Synoptists are unanimous in presenting Jesus as exorcist, healer and teacher' (Vermes 1983, p.22) is true as far as it goes; but Mark puts first and foremost that, as soon as the Baptist was no longer at large to proclaim the coming kingdom,

> **Jesus came into Galilee preaching the great news from God, and saying, 'The time is up and the kingdom of God is at the door; change your hearts and trust in this great news'** (1.14f).

He came as a prophet, foretelling the urgent future, and calling folk to mend their ways while there was still time.

Notes to Chapter One

[1] George Fox, *The Journal*, 1646-1648; Penguin, 1998, pp.13-36.

[2] Steventon was executed in Boston in June 1659.

---

[3] The former is possible, dating from the time when Tiberius was appointed to share the imperium with Augustus, but it is unlikely that any foreigner would reckon Tiberius' reign other than from Augustus' death in 14 AD.

[4] Josephus, *Antiquitates Judaici,* 18.117. No date is given. Herod Antipas was tetrarch from BC 4-39 AD; his killing of the Baptist was still well remembered in 37 AD, when it was held to be the cause of the defeat of his army.

[5] It is only the fourth evangelist, writing when Christians were no longer accepted in synagogues, who wishes to show Jesus baptizing; and his hasty dilution of that claim suggests that he knew that the record stood otherwise (John 3.22; 4.2).

[6] The word 'repentance', which customarily translates *metanoia*, is now devalued to mean 'feeling remorse', rather than an active change of heart and life-style.

[7] Josephus has appropriated the **ambiguous oracle, also to be found in their sacred writings, that at that time some man from their country would rule the world** to flatter his patron Vespasian, who launched from Judaea a successful bid for empire.

[8] Mack 1993, pp.2f, 24, 177-180 (Mark); pp.149, 153-158 (Baptist). 'It was Mark who invented the story about Jesus being baptized by John', p.155.

[9] Cf. in the *The Gospel according to the Hebrews*: **The Lord's mother and brothers said to him, "John the Baptist baptises for the forgiveness of sins; let us go and be baptised by him." But he replied, "In what way have I sinned that I ought to go and be baptised by him? Unless perhaps what I have just said is a sin of ignorance."**

[10] For other examples, see William James, 1902, Lectures IX & X.

[11] Old Testament references are all given from the Septuagint, unless otherwise stated. Here I use the Revised Standard Version, which follows the phrasing of the Hebrew more closely than does the New English Bible.

[12] Any connection with Psalm 2.7, **You are my son, *today I have begotten you,*** depends on a minority of the texts of Luke 3.22.

[13] 'Greek was certainly widely used, even among the lower, uneducated classes' (Freyne 1980, p.144). Jewish *culture* was but slightly influenced (Reed 2000, *passim*, summarised p.217). Greek would have been, like Spanish in modern Bolivia, the main language of government, commerce and trade; used generally in large towns, by many in smaller communities, unknown in the most remote settlements.

[14] Eg., out of 194 inscriptions on ossuaries, 64% are in Greek alone, 26% in Hebrew or Aramaic, 9% in a Semitic language and in Greek also (Meyers & Strange 1981, p.65; full discussion of Greek, pp.78-88).

[15] During **the war of Titus (**the sages**) prohibited [...] that a man should teach his son Greek** (*Mishnah Sotah* 9.14); which implies that to do so had been common. A small building-and-carpentry firm at Nazareth might need to seek work in nearby Sepphoris, where Greek would be useful.
[16] *The Septuagint with Apocrypha: Greek and English*, Brenton 1851, reprinted Hendrickson 1986; and Rahlf, *Septuaginta*, 5th ed. Wurttembergische Bibel. Stuttgart 1952.
[17] See Harvey, 1982, pp.159-163; Vermes 1976, pp.190-210.
[18] Q, the hypothetical (Aramaic) early document which best accounts for the many sayings found with similar or identical phrasing in both Matthew and Luke, seems also to be the source for their Temptation stories.
[19] Socrates' 'daemon' was a similar inner compulsion.

CHAPTER 2

The Prophet

The Prophet's Role

If, however, Jesus knew himself called to be a prophet, how did he understand his mission? He must, with his own call having sprung from hearing the Baptist, have seen his own task in the context of the coming Kingdom, as Mark says. If this truly human Jesus ever speculated on his own role he might have wondered whether he was to be the 'prophet like Moses' (Deut.18.22) who would help to prepare the nation for the Coming Day of the Lord. The Pharisaic rabbis (Mark's **scribes of the Pharisees**) held that there would be no more prophets, except for Elijah, returning as prophesied by Malachi, and the prophet like Moses, promised in Deuteronomy (Vermes 1983, pp.91-4). The latter was now the obvious vacancy, since the Baptist himself was, if Mark's source is correct, picturesquely filling the role of the returned Elijah; as Jesus later confirms (Mark 9.13).

It is hardly meaningful to ask whether Jesus thought he might be *the* 'Anointed' (the Messiah)[1]; the title 'Anointed' was applied in many contexts, and often, therefore, further defined – the Anointed of Aaron, the Anointed of Israel; thus Caiaphas asks **'Are you the Anointed, the son of God'** (Harvey 1982, p.79). These various 'Anointed's do little to undermine the earlier view that to ordinary folk 'the Anointed' commonly meant the mighty man who, like David or Judas Maccabaeus, would by the power of God deliver the nation from all its enemies (T. W. Manson 1953, p.25). The ritually, publicly and literally 'anointed' were the kings, anointed by prophet or by priest,[2] and it was surely in the sense a kingly deliverer that the term was commonly understood in Palestine: certainly the disciples were thinking in royal terms when they piled their cloaks on the donkey to make Jesus a 'throne', spread cloaks and greenery to pave his way, and hailed **the coming kingdom of our father David**'; and Pilate always uses **King of the Jews** as his understanding of the term 'Christos'. Yet there is nothing in the account of Jesus' baptism, nor in his teaching, nor in his Galilean ministry, nor even in Caiaphas' question, to suggest that he ever felt called to lead Israel against her foes, nor to be her king. He knew himself to have been called, and in that sense 'anointed', but as one of **God's servants, the prophets**, to arouse and teach the people.

Jesus may not, so early, have looked beyond his immediate task. Yet, meditating in solitude on the words he had heard at his baptism, he might well have recalled the triple declaration in Isaiah 42.1-4 that the servant was to **bring forth justice to the Gentiles**, to **bring forth justice to truth**, and to **set justice on the earth**. Which might lead him to 42.6:

> **I the Lord God have called you in righteousness, and will take hold of your hand and make you strong, and I have given you as the covenant of a nation, for a light to the Gentiles, to open the eyes of the blind, to bring those in fetters and those who sit in darkness out of their bonds and out of the prison-house.**

What could be more truly to follow in the steps of Moses the Law-giver, who proclaimed the Lord's covenant with the nation, opened their eyes to the Law and led his people out of bondage?

The Pitfall

To believe oneself a prophet, however, was no light matter. If the age of prophecy was past, as Zechariah (13.3ff) had foretold, and there would be no more prophets except the two actual forerunners of the Day of the Lord, it would be dangerous to proclaim oneself a prophet, since Deuteronomy 18.20 imposed death as the penalty if such a claim were disallowed as false, as blasphemy. It was on that charge that Jesus was eventually condemned for blasphemy by the leaders of his nation; it was because he did preach the end of all earthly government that he was condemned for sedition by the Roman governor.

Prophets notoriously came to a violent end (Matt.23.23-37; Luke 11.47-51; 13.34); but if Jesus was to take forward the mission of John, he must live long enough to do so. So, no matter how sure he was that God meant him to play a role in preparing God's Chosen People for the great day, he never, according to Mark, throughout his ministry, admits to having been called as God's anointed servant, until finally he is questioned by the High Priest in terms admitting no evasion. He finds other grounds to justify his acts: 'Anyone can tell people that their sins have been forgiven' (which I take to be the original version of Mark 2.10)[3]; or, 'I cannot be healing by sorcery, since one evil cannot cure another' (Mark 3.24-27); or, 'I shall tell you the source of my authority when you have told me where the Baptist's authority came from' (Mark 11.28-33). The nearest Jesus ever comes to saying, 'Thus says the Lord' is when he commandeers a donkey on the grounds that **'The Lord has need of it'.**

Messiah?

J. D. G.Dunn, in his careful critique of Wrede's 'Messianic secret',[4] sees Jesus as asserting Messianic status by claiming to be able himself to forgive sins (2.10) or to overrule the sabbath (2.28); but these pronouncements might also be Jesus proclaiming *God's* readiness to forgive, expounding the true nature of *God's* sabbath and showing how the healings prove the growing power of *God* which will bind that strong man Satan (3.27), speaking as a prophet although without overtly claiming that role (3.27). He once applied to himself the proverb that a prophet was without honour in his own country, but proverbs are not taken literally; indeed, the question was asked, **'Why does this man speak like this?'**(2.7).

Nonetheless, as Geza Vermes (1983, p.87f) says, a prophet is how Jesus was commonly known and the designation he seems himself to have preferred, or at least, how he wished to be understood. In the speech ascribed in Acts 4.20-24 to Peter, Jesus' role in life is identified with the prophet promised by Moses, his role as the Anointed ruler yet to come at the Day of the Lord. As far as the disciples were concerned, the man they knew was Jesus, the prophet from Nazareth; and that role could not be at once discarded simply because of a post-resurrection conviction that he was also the Anointed One who would bring in the Kingdom of God. That conviction that Jesus was 'the Messiah', however, has left many Christians, including perhaps Peter, looking for evidence that Jesus thought so himself.

A. E. Harvey posed the question as to how Jesus, who had not in his life claimed to be Messiah – if indeed 'the option to represent oneself as "the Messiah" actually existed' – could so soon after his death have been claimed by the disciples, and notably by Paul in his letters, not even as *Jesus ho Christos* (Jesus *the* Anointed) but simply as *Jesus Christos*, as though *Christos* were a name and not a title; and he suggested that Jesus in his lifetime had been so nicknamed because his role as proclaimer of the coming kingdom qualified him to be seen as God's 'anointed'.[5] Given that, in Matthew's version of the trial, Pilate uses the phrase **Jesus who is called Christos** (in an episode which is marked as authentic because it refers also to **Jesus** the **Barabbas**)[6] it does seem probable that the nickname became current during the ministry. Nicknames, however, can go by opposites, as when the unusually big man is called Tiny; it is possible that as a nickname 'Christos' was meant to mock a pacifist as a most unlikely 'Messiah'.

However that designation may have arisen, Jesus the prophet, with his dependence on the direct revelation of the will of God, was undoubtedly, as Vermes has expounded, in the charismatic tradition of the Hasidim; with whose ways of healing and ethical attitudes he also had much in common. It may be a mistaken emphasis, however, to suggest that it was because of marvellous cures that he was known as a prophet; or that healing, exorcism and 'dispensing forgiveness to sinners' were the 'three fundamental aspects of his function' (Vermes 1983, p.58). Hasidic 'men of deed', like Honi and Hanina, who had some reputation for miracles, do not seem generally to have been called prophets.[7]

The Fact of Prophecy

Essentially, a prophet is one who foretells the future: a true prophet if all that he says comes true (1 Sam.9.6), or if he knows what he cannot know (Luke 7.6; 22.62). Such, Vermes agrees, was the meaning in which Jesus' tormentors and antagonists used the term. Jesus, I suggest, was known as a prophet not because of 'mighty works', although these greatly increased his prestige and drew the crowds, but because his basic message was the foretelling, albeit incorrectly, of the imminent coming on earth of the empire of God, and correctly of disaster soon to come upon the nation; and because he fulfilled the prophet's vital role by telling folk what they should therefore do.

Graphic though it is, the elaborate Temptation story from Q (Matt.4.1-11; Luke 4.1-13), which reads like the type of imaginative expansion of simple fact to which preachers are prone, does not add to our understanding of Jesus' work; for it appears to be based on a retrospective view of him as a miracle-worker and potential king. There seems no reason to believe that the human mind of Jesus foresaw at this point that he would be called upon to heal, nor to reveal himself as a national leader in Jerusalem, and the kingdom he preached was that of God, not of Jesus; 'king of the Jews' was Pilate's word, not his. It may be that Jesus did give his friends some inkling of the conclusions to which he had come by himself in the wilderness; but if so, Peter says nothing about them.

What can reasonably be inferred from Jesus' next actions and sayings is that he had now a strong presentiment of doom coming upon his nation; as indeed it did, some thirty or forty years later, when temple, holy city, priesthood and nation were simultaneously destroyed; within the life-span of **this generation**, as he had foretold (Mark 9.1; 13.30). Naturally, since his own life-changing experience arose directly from the Baptist's mission, he assumed that the troubles which he foresaw, perhaps not very clearly yet, would be those calamities which in Biblical prophecy precede the Day of the Lord. Before returning from the wilderness he was, we may suppose, convinced that that Day, which would usher in the Kingdom, was at hand. The matter was urgent.

Not everyone today finds the idea of premonition easy to accept; but it is well attested as a recurring feature of human life. A materialist may choose to see successful prophecy as the chance result of rational, or irrational, prediction, not of 'knowledge'; although in a relative universe it may also be regarded simply as telepathy working in Einstein's fourth dimension. The solid fact is that an inner compulsion to foretell disaster does seem to happen. It happened here, but in a context of apocalyptic in which the coming troubles would be the prelude to the establishment of God's kingdom on earth. When Jesus proclaimed that the Coming was at hand, he did so as one having authority, and not as the scribes; not quoting even the Baptist, but from his own deep conviction, nurtured in the wilderness.

Since so many New Testament critics have dismissed all prophecy as necessarily *ex eventu*, written later to fit what had in fact transpired, it is worth labouring the point that prophecy does at times occur beforehand, predicting, sometimes accurately, what later takes place. Josephus (*JW*.6.300-309) tells of Jesus son of Ananias who prophesied **'Woe to Jerusalem!'** daily, in spite of dire punishment, from four years before the outbreak of hostilities, until his death during the siege, in 69 AD; not a very precise forecast, but clear evidence of the compulsion to utter it. G. N. M. Tyrrell (1947, pp.73-90) offers a variety of modern instances of premonition. Fox's *Journal* for 1665 cites a Quaker who went up to London to foretell disaster in person shortly before the fire. Most cogently, F.Morison (1939 pp.260ff) pointed to the number of dated pamphlets prophesying disaster for London *by fire,* which appeared, in print, in the years immediately preceding 1666. He commented, caustically,

> Save for the practice of the Restoration typographers in putting dates upon their work, how many reams of valuable paper might not have been used by textual critics, seeking to prove that these indisputably historic documents were written after the event?

As it is, the evidence is inescapable that such foretelling happens, whatever its explanation; so too, be it admitted, do prophecies which fail of fulfilment.

To some, again, the thought that Jesus could ever be mistaken may be equally unacceptable; but the humanity of Jesus must, if it was truth and not appearance only, have been liable to error. However, a premonition of coming troubles would not by itself, however deeply felt, tell Jesus what to do. To him, as to most of his nation, a basic framework was clear: the world was, in this age, under the power of Satan, the Evil One, which would finally be broken at the Day of the Lord when, following the direst calamities, God's new age of peace and justice on the earth would be established. But, if the human side of Jesus is not to be undervalued, he must be seen as a man willing to listen and then to go forward, one step at a time; not as a privileged being whose path was, unlike ours, clearly lit by sure foreknowledge, but as our example in trustful obedience. The essence of a 'call' such as he had experienced is that it does not map out exactly what to do nor even who to be; it merely points in a certain direction and requires to be trusted and obeyed. To repeat Nayler's words, 'And ever since, I have remained not knowing today what I was to do tomorrow.' The prophet, like a subordinate officer, remains perfectly able to take a decision for himself, but prepared to have it overruled, at any time, by higher authority.

A Prophet's Method

Yet even a prophet has his own *modus operandi*. The outline discernible in Mark and set out in our introduction would read here:

> **and he came into Galilee, proclaiming the wonderful news [...]. And from the start (*euthus*) he would go to synagogue on the Sabbath and teach. And they were astonished at his teaching. For he taught them as one having authority, and not like the scribes.** (Mark 1.14, (15), 21b, 22).[8]

This is the first stage of Galilean ministry, as identified from the outline by C. H. Dodd.[9] Synagogue was the obvious place for a Jew with such a message to proclaim it, as Meeting would be to a Quaker; and Jesus attracted some notice, not necessarily approving, because he spoke from what was in him, citing no authorities. Yet he showed none of the outward signs of the holy man,[10] nor even of the highly religious, but ate and dressed normally, using neither fussy ritual nor ostentatious prayer. Plainly a man of the people, he confidently exhorted or rebuked his social superiors.

It is reasonable to suppose also that he was following then the same discipline as he later imposed on his disciples when he set them to the same work: travelling without weapons, money nor spare clothing, living on such hospitality as might be offered (Mark 6.8-11). To teach primarily on the Sabbaths suggests going on to a new place each week, some days being given to travel but others to staying on, after speaking in synagogue, to talk further with folk who showed interest; for the injunction to the disciples to stay in the same house until they leave the place

(Mark 6.10) must imply a sojourn of some few days wherever hospitality is found.

Some weeks, even a month or two, might therefore have passed before Jesus found himself walking along the shore near the north end of the Lake, and called his first disciples. Taking Mark 1.21a as properly the ending of that episode, it would appear that they all went back together to Capernaum;[11] and presumably stayed in the house of Peter and Andrew, where they are certainly found on the Sabbath (Mark 1.29).

Peace and Good Government

So far Jesus would have roused no more interest than any visiting preacher might expect, even if his style was unusual. Everyone knew that the Kingdom would come, some day, as the prophets had said; but why now? Where was the urgency? For they also knew that before that day there would be:

> **a time of affliction, such affliction as there has never been since there has been a nation on the earth** (Dan.12.2);
>
> **a powerful day of wrath [...], a day of anguish and distress, a day of untimely death and affliction [...] a day of trumpet and screaming against the strong cities and against the tall towers** (Zeph 1.15f);
>
> **and the city shall be captured and the houses looted and the women raped and half the city will go away as captives** (Zech.14.2);
>
> **the sun shall be turned to darkness and the moon to blood, before the great and glorious day of the Lord come** (Joel 2.39)

but here was this new preacher expecting them to take the Coming seriously when there was not a cloud in the sky.

This was Jesus' second great handicap as a prophet, that he was proclaiming impending catastrophe in a time of unparallelled peace and prosperity. Galilee was a particularly fertile and productive area, beginning to be even more widely cultivated in response to the market demands of Antipas' new cities of Sepphoris and Tiberias (Reed 2002, pp.77-96), which must also have employed much labour and generated new employment and commerce; only the peasantry, squeezed by the competition of larger estates and bulk trading, came off badly, and some of them probably found work in those cities.

Many scholars have written of over-taxation, the harshness of Roman rule, and rampant banditry; but that seems to ignore the realities of this early phase of the Roman Empire. Galilee was not directly under Roman rule, Tiberius was an emperor notably concerned that taxation should not be extortionate,[12] trade was booming and the years from 6 to 36 AD were a period of peace and good government, with hardly a bandit in sight.[13] Crossan (1991, pp.218-24) asserts that the country was in turmoil; but his economic evidence relates to a later period and primarily to Judaea; the sociological generalisations he deploys lack relevance; and the gospel record is against him. As colonial government goes, the rule of the Roman Empire under Augustus and then Tiberius was restrained, efficient and well-monitored, allowing few corrupt or cruel officials; Philo of Alexandria, denouncing the infamous Flaccus, says that he had ruled very well – until Tiberius died. Taxation was probably considered heavy, but then it always had been;[14] they were grumbling about their taxes in King Solomon's day (1 Kings 12.4). Herod Antipas was an able ruler, encouraging new economic growth (Jones 1967, pp.176-83).

Pilate

The Judaeans, who after the death of Herod the Great had invited the Romans to take over, were probably mostly pleased when they did so later, in 6 AD, after a period of notable misrule by Archelaus; and had as yet no great reason to regret it.[15] The Roman census had provoked a short lived revolt by religious fanatics, but there was no repetition of the Roman heavy handedness in administration which had sparked serious violence in Jerusalem in 4 BC, with great damage to the temple. Josephus, anxious to show Pilate (Prefect of Judaea, 26-36 AD) as a tyrant, yet found only three cases to cite. Philo, it is true, says additionally that Pilate provoked protest by decorating the outside of his palace in Jerusalem with shields, and was forced by the emperor to give way;[16] but this incident is implausible, since Josephus, born and bred in Jerusalem, does not mention it; Pilate, based at Caesarea, would scarcely have bothered to embellish his quarters in Jerusalem; and thirdly, shields were not controversial. Herod the Great *had* decorated the walls of his theatre with panoplies (breast-plates or shields with spears, etc.) but the protesters were confounded when Herod quite amiably showed them that there was not, as they had supposed, any human figure behind the armour.[17] Probably in Alexandria, some fifty years later, Herod's 'shields' had become confused with Pilate's eagle-headed, tutelary standards, to make a tale for Philo's diatribe.

Our best source, Josephus, says that there was outrage over Roman standards brought into the holy city; but in the end Pilate, unable to cow a huge delegation of senior Jews by threats of instant death, sensibly backed down.[18] Then there was a protest riot in Jerusalem when it was put about that Pilate's new aqueduct had been funded from the sacred Corbonas, money given for the sacrifices:[19] forewarned, probably by the competent and cooperative Caiaphas,[20] Pilate deployed soldiers with clubs rather than swords, as riot police; but his (probably Syrian) levies proved over-enthusiastic about clubbing Jews, and many of the crowd died in the panic rush to get away.[21]

The third case, probably later than Jesus' death, was when a potentially subversive Samaritan prophet led a fervent pilgrimage to their holy mountain, promising to produce there the sacred vessels of Moses. Pilate managed to block their path, swiftly deploying a screen or escort (*pompē*) of cavalry and infantry; but fighting broke out and, after the enthusiasts were dispersed, Pilate summarily executed the ring-leaders.[22] Each incident shows him as trying to minimise the use of force and the number of casualties, while maintaining law and order. To satisfy various lines of argument, Pilate has been depicted as harsh or weak; but in reality he seems hard, certainly, but competent and responsible. There was nothing in the way Pilate and Caiaphas administered Judaea and Samaria to cause anxieties in Galilee.

This does not mean, of course, that there was not the normal resentment of a colonial power by any strongly nationalistic subject people. A feast-time crowd would always be good for a riot, if urged to it by some political agitator – or charismatic prophet; and Mark 12.13-17 shows an attempt to turn that anti-Roman sentiment against Jesus. But at this time there were not the serious economic problems and political grievances needed to transmute sentiment into sustained violence.

The Coming Disaster

Real trouble for the Jewish people started under Caligula and Claudius, when the empire was less conscientiously run, when Antipas, Pilate and Caiaphas had all been replaced in office by less able, more extravagant or greedier men. Severe famine in the late 40s, with no Herod the Great now to take effective relief measures,[23] created widespread poverty; and brigands and terrorists began to flourish. The inevitable rebellion ended in 70 AD with the utter destruction of temple and city. Some inkling of those coming troubles must surely lie behind Jesus' conviction that the Day of the Lord was at hand; for, except that sun, moon and stars did not change or fall, the siege of Jerusalem fulfilled all the signs in the scriptures.

But in the lifetime of Jesus there was no sign of coming disaster. Like Edwardian England, it was a good time for any but the poorest, and even for them might have been worse;[24] there was peace and good order, and not even the down-and-out would starve in Jewish communities, who always looked after their own. So from first to last, when Jesus proclaimed the imminent Kingdom of God, people said to him, not unreasonably, 'Show us a sign. What trouble, what portent can you point out, to back up what you say?' And there was nothing he could show. As Tacitus wrote of Palestine, **under Tiberius [*there was*] quiet**;[25] and when a Roman said it was quiet, he meant primarily that law and order prevailed, without Crossan's 'turmoil'.

What made folk take Jesus seriously was, therefore, not that he could show any portent to back his prophecy, but that he suddenly began healing people, which proclaimed him a man of power. In the synagogue at Capernaum, he was challenged by a man mentally unbalanced, and he promptly exorcised the supposed 'demon':

> **And they were all astounded, so that they asked each other saying, "What is this? New teaching, with power! He even gives orders to the evil spirits, and they obey him!" And the fame of him spread at once everywhere throughout the whole surrounding land of Galilee.** (Mark 1.23-28)

Notes to Chapter Two

[1] Because 'the Messiah' now has such specific meanings (one for Jews, to whose national mythology the term belongs, and another for Christians) I prefer to use 'Anointed' instead wherever possible.

[2] 1 Sam.10.1, 16.13; 2.Sam.2.4; 1 Ki.1.32-40; 19.15f; 2.Ki.9.1-13; 11.12; 23.30; Ps.45 & 89.

[3] In Mark 3.28 Jesus asserts that all our sins will be forgiven – except that of calling the Light, Darkness. This implies that God forgives unconditionally; *c'est son metier*, as Catherine the Great said. Any one who understood this could tell people that they were forgiven.

[4] Dunn, 'The Messianic Secret in Mark', in Tuckett 1983, pp.116-131. Wrede had, in 1901, argued that Mark shows Jesus as the Messiah who deliberately conceals his identity.

[5] Harvey 1982, pp.139-151; he has a strong case.

[6] A minority reading, yet most unlikely to have been a Christian invention; accepted by *NEB*.

[7] Hanina specifically denies that he is a prophet; Vermes 1976, p.75.
[8] Into this Mark has inserted the Call of the Four Fishermen, which logically might end with v.21a, **and they went** (home) **to Capernaum**.
[9] Dodd, 'The Framework of the Gospel Narrative', 1st pub. *Expository Times*, 1932, repr. McArthur 1970, pp.109-118.
[10] Eg. Bannus, **living in the desert, wearing only what was provided by the trees, feeding on whatever grew wild and, for purity, washing himself with water frequently, day and night.** Josephus, *Vita* 11.
[11] Dodd includes this in his outline, using the variant 'he comes'; but it would be exceptional for the outline to specify a town.
[12] Tiberius famously told an over-zealous governor that he wanted his sheep shorn, not skinned alive.
[13] Horsley 1988, pp.66f, finds no bandits recorded between 6 AD and 44 AD, except for the two crucified with Jesus.
[14] Much has been said of the extra burden of Roman taxes (eg. Horsley 1988, pp.55-58; not, however, by Crossan). Egyptian and Greek empires also levied tax; the Hasmoneans too had lived like kings, built palaces, led armies – the peasants no doubt paid. The accusations made (by the upper class) against Herod the Great (Josephus, *Antiquitates Judaici* 17.304-308) amount to the fact that *he* levied heavily on the rich, too.
[15] Josephus, *Ant.* 17.300-314, 342ff, 355; *Bellum Judaicum* 2.80-92. Judas of Galilee and the Pharisee Sadok are named by Josephus as founders of the *'philosophy'* followed later by the Zealots of his own time (*B.J.* 2.118; *Ant.* 18.23; cf Acts 5.37); but there is no hint of an active Zealot *party* between Judas' short-lived revolt in 6 AD and the Jewish war, in which they first appear by name at the siege of Jerusalem (*B.J.* 4.160). Josephus is explicit that adherents of this 'philosophy' only became active after hostilities had started (*Ant.* 18.23-25).
[16] Philo, *Legatio ad Gaium*, 299-305.
[17] Josephus, *Ant.* 15.272-279.
[18] Josephus, *Ant.* 18.55-59; *B.J.* 2.169-174.
[19] Morison 1939, pp.132-147, shows that the funding must have been agreed by Caiaphas with the Sanhedrin, and would really have come from the temple building fund, the same from which Agrippa II later proposed repaving the streets (Josephus, *Ant.* 20.222).
[20] The Romans never hesitated to replace a high priest; Caiaphas' exceptionally long tenure speaks for itself.

---

[21] Josephus, *B.J.* 2.175-7; *Ant.* 18.60-62. Hostility of Samaritan and Caesarean troops, *Ant.* 19.364-6.

[22] Josephus, *Ant.* 18.85-87.

[23] As Herod had done in 25-24 BC.

[24] 'During the long and apparently peaceful reign of Antipas, the lot of the peasant must have improved somewhat': Freyne 1980, p.128. For those not squeezed by the competition of large-scale farming, this would be true; and even the destitute would then benefit.

[25] ***Sub Tiberio quies***: Tacitus, *Histories*, 5.9.

CHAPTER 3

The Healer

First Healings

Jesus was probably already staying with Andrew and Peter at Capernaum (1.29); and now that he was suddenly revealed as an exorcist, they told him that Peter's mother-in-law was ill: bad news with which otherwise they might not have burdened a guest. Jesus again was able to heal, and the word went swiftly round, for neighbour to neighbour is not even a 'sabbath day's journey', and no commandment bans tongues from working on the Sabbath. So that evening, as soon as the sun had set and Sabbath was over,

> **they carried to him all those who were sick or afflicted by demons. And the whole town was gathered round the door. And he healed many who suffered from different diseases and exorcised many demons, and he would not let the demons speak because they knew him.** (1.32ff).

Note that **the whole town gathered round the door**. This, from the very start, was the negative side of healing, a third handicap: it attracted sensation-seeking crowds, and the curious and inquisitive could make it hard for Jesus to reach or teach those who might truly be **looking for the kingdom of God**. This, it will be shown, may have been the factor which in the end drove him out of Galilee.

Healing Power

Conventional ideas of an omniscient Jesus whose mission runs according to plan, or who uses a controlled 'healing power' when he chooses, to draw attention to his message, to confound his critics, or even to foreshadow the kingdom of God on earth, should be put aside; for to be omniscient would be not truly human. The healings may be seen to result directly from listening to the promptings of God, which has been stressed above. Jesus might make his plans but, as the story above demonstrates, Jesus was repeatedly to find his intentions hindered or even thwarted by mass enthusiasm, and to experience the frustrations which commonly beset human planning.

It would seem that his healing role found Jesus unprepared. Even if his search for his own role had already led him to identify himself with the servant in Isaiah, it is unlikely that he would have expected to find himself literally **opening the eyes that are blind**, for he would surely have understood that phrase as metaphor, like the metaphor of deafness he used himself. But Isaiah 35.5f was probably thought to promise that God Himself would literally abolish all physical handicap as part of His new kingdom; therefore, when Jesus found himself impelled to heal, and felt the power flow through him, and shared the joy of the newly healed, this was not only uplifting but encouraging; a clear sign that the rule of Satan over 'this age', held to be the root of all disease, was now crumbling.[1] So, although it appears to have taken him by surprise, a deed of power (*dunamis*), and especially the exorcising of an ‘evil spirit’, would be to Jesus a useful corroboration of his message and his authority; the power, as he said, was not his but the power of God, but also a welcome assurance that he was following the true path, for God was showing his approval. But how should he now proceed?

Famed as a Healer

Should he stay at Capernaum, using his new fame to obtain a better hearing? In urgent need of guidance,

> **in the morning, having risen while it was still very dark, he went out and went off into the open country and he was praying there. And Simon hunted for him, and the others with him, and they found him and they say to him, 'Everybody's looking for you.' And he says to them, 'We must go away to the village-towns nearby, so that I may give my message there too. For that is what I have come out *(exēlthon)* to do’** (Mark 1.35-39).

To Jesus the fact that many people, fascinated by 'miraculous' healings, are looking for him is *not* good news: he and his four disciples must leave at once. Whether *exēlthon*, **came out**, means ‘left Nazareth’, or ‘left the peace of anonymity in Judaea’, or simply ‘left the house’, this is a clear statement of how Jesus saw his mission: it was to proclaim, as Mark's outline says at the start, the great news that the Kingdom of God was on its way, and to tell folk to change their hearts. And now, the outline continues, **he went proclaiming in their synagogues in the whole of Galilee and exorcising demons.**

By the Finger of God

Mark's healing stories should all be taken as the witness of Peter, given with more or less detail, and better or less well understood. For example, when Peter says that Jesus forbade 'unclean spirits' to speak *because they knew who he was* (1.34), this would be hindsight, reinterpreting the patients' outbursts and the exorcist's admonitions (1.24ff; 5.7ff; 9.25f), and remembering Jesus' usual injunction against publicising cures; all viewed in the light of Peter's later conviction that Jesus was the Messiah, the 'Son of God'. Similarly, the claim that Jesus destroyed a herd of pigs, by allowing demons, which he had just exorcised, to enter those unfortunate animals, must be Peter's inference about an accident whose probable cause was the distraction of the swineherds.[2]

However, claiming Peter as Mark's source forbids our selecting only the most plausible healings. There could be a 'doublet' healing, a different version which reached Mark through another source; but to assume this initially is to evade the issue. The entire record must be taken together and judged as basically possible or impossible, true or false. Readers who deny any possibility of non-medical healing may refer to the many examples given by, say, William James or Leslie Weatherhead.[3] Explain them as we will, healings *thought* by many to be 'miraculous' happen even today;[4] and the thirteen healings described in Mark, such as paralysis, fever, skin diseases, some kinds of blindness or deafness, for example, and the exorcisms, all lie within the range of credibly attested 'cures'. They may perhaps best be taken, not as 'miracles' overriding the laws of the universe, but as extensions of life's natural self-healing power through psychological or psychiatric means, sometimes beyond what science has yet found explicable. (Which is not to say that this is simply a form of 'alternative medicine': the prophet's healing power may be 'natural', but equally it is 'God-given', and cannot be produced to order.) Narrated without explanation, the healings in Mark are free of the exaggerations of Matthew and Luke, and lack the Johannine absurdities;[5] the Marcan record will stand examination, however we choose to interpret the actual events.[6]

If Jesus did not think healing was what he had primarily been called to do, and found his work handicapped by the resulting notoriety, why did he do it? The answer must be that here, as in all else, he was obedient to the spirit; for natural compassion would not explain in every case why he thought that he *could* help. He was, as Fox said of himself, 'moved' to do it. Jesus as prophet would seek to keep himself tuned to a sub-conscious wave-length – to put it in human terms – from which came those promptings which might tell him where to go and what to do. From the same source at times would come an overriding impulse to help some sufferer; words and actions might come without conscious thought, and healing may have been effected through a telepathic 'link' by which his loving concern and positive attitude reached the subconscious of the patient to cure the trouble at its source. The crux of what we may call 'spirit-led healing' (as opposed perhaps to 'faith-healing'), is that the healer obeys the healing power, but does not control it, and cannot foresee when it will come upon him.

Methods of Healing

Yet however spontaneous the words and actions, some patterns emerge from the individual healings described in Mark. In all cases thought of as demon-possession – the man in the Capernaum synagogue, the man amongst the tombs near 'Gergesa', and the epileptic boy (1.24-27; 5.1-20; 9.14-29) – suggestion is made through specific commands banishing the evil spirit. The patient's subconscious reaction may be imagined as, 'The prophet has driven out the demon! Now I am free!'

With the paralysed youngster, and the man with the paralysed hand, some rapport between patient and healer is developed in a preliminary interchange: in the one case, Jesus telling the young man his sins are forgiven; in the other, the placing of the man in the centre of the synagogue, with what words of encouragement we are not told. Only then is the command given to pick up the bed and take it home, or to stretch out the withered hand (2.1-12; 3.1-5). Sufferers lying unconscious or semi-conscious are taken by the hand and raised to sit up (1.31; 5.41; 9.27),[7] a bodily action which would reinforce any telepathic encouragement to be well again. The leper was taken by the hand by Jesus, who hugged him (*hēpsato*, **clung to him closely**) (1.41).[8] Spittle is used both with the blind man at Bethsaida and the deaf-mute, for actions possibly symbolic but which the sufferer would physically feel and mentally understand as 'He is healing me!' Blind Bartimaeus, who has already made clear at the top of his voice his complete confidence in Jesus' power, needs only the prophet's word; but in every case, the cure depends on powerful suggestion that the illness or disability has been removed: 'He hugged me! So I must be clean!' 'He says "Stretch out your crippled hand!" So I can!'

Very interesting is the auto-suggestion of the woman with the haemorrhage. **For she was saying to herself, 'If only I can even just touch his clothes I shall be cured'** (5.28); and she did, and she was. That Jesus on that occasion knew at once that someone had been healed demonstrates the telepathic factor which is probably always a main part of the process, and which is certainly required in the cases of Jairus' daughter (since Jesus believed, before even reaching the house, that a child reported dead was still alive), and the Syro-Phoenician woman's daughter, whom he never saw at all. To a person of Jesus' time this was not telepathy so much as keeping in touch with the omniscience of God; and it was through prayer, ie. listening to the spirit, that he could heal. **Cases like these can only be exorcised through prayer**, he once told his disciples (9.29).

It is plain that Jesus himself needed great faith, to trust that the inner voice which urged him to act would also deliver the healing power, and not leave him standing there looking silly. He also needed a response of trust, from friends or parents, or from the patient. Scepticism at Nazareth (6.5f), the scornful disbelief of the mourners at Jairus' house (5.40), the curiosity of inquisitive spectators in the Decapolis (7.33) and Bethsaida (8.23), any of these could obstruct the rapport between healer and spirit, patient and healer, which the process seems to have demanded.

Fox's *Journal* shows that although he too saw his real mission as preaching, he was also sometimes 'moved' to heal, just as he was 'moved' to speak or to go to a particular place; and his record of his own experiences may shed some light on the gospel healings, for which we do not have the healer's own account. No more than Jesus had Fox any special knowledge of healing, but he trusted the impulse that came to him and acted as he was prompted. Here is a simple cure of mental unbalance:

> Coming to Mansfield-Woodhouse, there was a distracted woman under a doctor's hand, with her hair loose all about her ears; and he was about to let her blood, she being first bound, and many people being about her, holding her with violence: but he could get no blood from her. And I desired them to unbind her, and let her alone; for they could not touch the spirit in her, by which she was tormented: so they did unbind her. And I was moved to speak to her, in the name of the Lord, to bid her be quiet and still: and she was so. And the Lord's power settled her mind, and she mended; and afterwards received the Truth and continued in it to her death. And the Lord's name was honoured, to whom the glory for all His works belongs (*Journal*, 1649).

The healer here explicitly responds to an inner prompting, and so releases a power which does not seem to him to be any power of his. The same inner prompting, I have suggested, was what led Jesus to heal; and whether it is a message from some extra-material source, or telepathic reception of the desperate concern of parents, friends or of the sick persons themselves, it would come to Jesus, as it came to Fox, as the voice of God. The same practised willingness to stay tuned to the 'holy spirit' would account for occasional healings by apostles and others in the early church.

We cannot know whether all such cures were permanent or not. In so far as the ailments may have been primarily psychological in origin, the key might be whether the person later relapsed into the same internal conflict which produced the symptoms in the first place. Fox, who lived to be sixty-seven, relates one relapse:

> I went to a meeting at Arnside [...] and I was moved by the spirit to say to Richard Myers: "Prophet Myers, stand up upon thy legs!" for he was sitting down: and he stood up and stretched out his arm which had been lame a long time: and said: "Be it known unto you all people and to all nations that this day I am healed."
>
> And after the meeting was done his father and mother could scarcely believe it was made whole [...] and (he) took off his doublet and then they saw it was true: and he came to Swarthmore and declared how the Lord had healed him.
>
> And after, the Lord commanded him to go to York with a message from Him: but he disobeyed the Lord: and the Lord struck him again so as he died about three-quarters of a year after. (Journal, 1653).

Leaving aside Fox's conviction that Myer's death was an act of God – the same sort of inference as fact which we may find in Mark – it may well be true that the relapse was due to internal conflict between the command which Myers felt that he had received and his unwillingness to obey it. On the other hand, the woman at Mansfield-Woodhouse appears to have had no further trouble lifelong. It may be that all Jesus' healings were permanent; but the short span of his working ministry means that there was little chance of any relapse becoming known, while later concepts of the nature of his supernatural identity may have meant that the question was never asked.

After his account of the Mansfield healing, Fox comments caustically on the unbelieving age he lives in, which, if he chose to instance particular cases, would be unable to accept 'all the great and wonderful things which were done through the power of the Lord.' Jesus, however, lived among people enthusiastic for signs and miracles; and indeed, to himself each healing showed the power of Satan being broken (3.26). Yet, although the inner compulsion, when it came, could never be denied, he tried his utmost to mitigate its effects on his principal task.

He would never let any cured person accompany him around the country. With the leper, sternly commanding him to say nothing, Jesus sent him off very firmly (*exebalen*, threw him out, drove him away) to go to the priest and make the proper offering. When the healed madman from the town of Gergesa (according to Mark) came down to the boat and asked to accompany Jesus, he was sent instead to proclaim in his own Gentile town how the Jewish God had healed him; which might do some good without hampering Jesus' mission to his own nation. After curing the deaf-mute, **he ordered [the local people who had brought him] to tell no one'** (7.36); Having already led the blind man out of Bethsaida, (*kōmē* is a settlement of any size but of less than 'city' status), he ended by telling him to go back to his own home without even re-entering the town.[9]

Least realistic of all, perhaps, is the command to Jairus and his wife to say nothing, since so many people already knew that their child had been pronounced dead before the prophet arrived. There was no chance that the parents could avoid giving some explanation to the ejected mourners and to their neighbours, even if they stopped short of speeches to the crowd. If Jesus, with his knowledge of human nature, really did give such an apparently naive instruction, it suggests an almost desperate wish to mitigate a major hindrance to his mission.

Particular Cases

Among the earlier healings, a salient point about the leper's cure is Jesus' own state of mind. He was overcome with anger (*orgistheis*),[10] but why and with whom is not clear until we give full weight to the human side of his action. Whatever type of skin infection this was, to call it leprosy implies visible, ugly, sores. Jesus – who had probably never been close to a leper before, since they had by law to keep their distance – was, I suggest, furious with *himself*; because his urge from the spirit told him to embrace the sufferer, but dread of contagion, perhaps a fear of the ritually 'unclean' and, above all, revulsion at the man's disfigured appearance, made him hesitate; and cost him a moment of fierce struggle before he could bring himself to comply. That he then did so is where we may so clearly see the love of God in him; but it is no wonder if afterwards his manner was more abrupt than usual as he ordered the leper to be off to the proper authority.

The actual cure of the paralysed lad, (Jesus calls him *teknon*, child), after his friends lower him through the hole they have made in the thatch,[11] is a clear case of release from a paralysis caused by guilt. It is usually claimed both by Christian and by other scholars that Jesus here claims to be able to forgive sins; which may indeed be the most obvious meaning of 2.10 as it stands now. Is it not more likely that Jesus made no such claim to God's privilege, but simply upheld his right, or anybody's right,[12] to assure a sufferer that *God* had forgiven him? And that 2.10 is a rider by Peter, preaching later from his developed Messianic theology, and later still included as words of Jesus by Mark? Such a development lies within those limits of accuracy outlined in the introduction.

So far as healing is concerned, this is the one cure explicitly linked to overcoming the sufferer's feeling of guilt, although there were probably others; reportedly, guilt may even sometimes be a cause of blindness.[13] Yet it is pointless to dwell too long on the technical details, if Jesus' 'technique' consisted solely of 'hooking up' to the Spirit and doing as he was then 'moved' to do.[14] That he healed a number of people with various complaints may be taken as fact; and it is the overall effect of this on his ministry which is important.

The healings turned Jesus from an unimportant person seeking a hearing into a well-known figure whom ordinary people in Galilee could regard as a prophet. He would no longer be ignored, even by visiting scribes from Judaea (3.22). Mark gives us no reason to suppose that these scribes had travelled north merely to see Jesus, rather than on business of their own; but while they were in Galilee, where Jesus was now a known teacher, they might well have been interested to learn what he was teaching.

Notes to Chapter Three

[1] See V. Taylor 1953, pp.237-242; Hooker 1983, pp.14-16, 34-43.

[2] Mark 5.14 shows that the swineherds made sure that they were first back to the town to tell their version. 'If this story were originally related of a Jewish exorcist in a Gentile country [...] it would contain nothing surprising' says Dibelius (1934, p.89); but that indeed is exactly what it is.

[3] James 1902, Lectures IV, V & appendices; Weatherhead 1951, throughout; also Dibelius 1934, p.80n; Hooker 1991, p.85.

[4] Buckman and Sabbagh 1993, although themselves certain that no such cures result from anything but chance, remission of symptoms, or temporary effect of mind-over-matter, list many cases which in earlier times could have been thought miraculous.

[5] John's paralysed man has been so for 38 years, his blind man was born blind, and his corpse is four days dead (John 5.5; 9.1; 11.39). These appear to be Marcan themes exaggerated deliberately in order to exclude rational explanation.

Mark 8.1-10, which does show uncharacteristic signs of exaggeration, may be a doublet and not directly from Peter.

[6] Gardener 1986 gives a careful examination of present day cures, many with independent medical corroboration, which parallel the range of cures in Mark. In many the link between a happier mindset and healing is patent.

[7] *NEB* renders *egeiren* (9.27) as **raised him to his feet**; but so weakens the sense of *kai aneste*, **and he got up**.

[8] *Hēpsato* can be used for 'touched' (eg. Lxx Jer.1.9); but the root meaning of *hapto* is 'fasten on, cleave to, unite.'

[9] Textual variants add phrases about not talking to anyone there, even if he did re-enter Bethsaida.

[10] *Orgistheis* (became angry) is the minority reading, but must be correct, with the less startling *splagchnistheis* (moved to pity) a later substitution; see Hooker, 1991, p.79.

[11] Luke says **tiles**; but see Reed 2002, p.159.

[12] Or possibly any *prophet's* right, if *'bar nasha'* can mean 'a man like me' here; see Lindars 1983, p.45.

[13] W. C. Handy, the jazz-musician, is said to have recovered from blindness on ceasing to feel guilty about wanting to play jazz.

[14] Fox did some inspired first aid on a rider whose neck seemed broken by a fall; whom he restored to breathing and health in ways recommended in modern paramedical practice (*Journal*, Appendix 2 in Penguin edition). The term 'hook up' is borrowed from the American therapeutic masseur, Dr. Milton Trager.

CHAPTER 4

The Teacher

The Gospel of Generosity

The words of Jesus were viewed in Capernaum as *didachē kainē*, new teaching (Mark 1.27), but Mark seems, naturally enough, to have heard little from Peter in urban Rome about new teaching intended for agricultural communities in Galilee; only controversies, parables and sayings whose point can be applied, or even misapplied, to the life, mainly the life of the poor, in the Gentile city.[1] In Rome, Peter probably had to spend much effort on the Ten Commandments, which Jesus had been able to take for granted: the best source for the original teaching of Jesus is therefore Q, that hypothetical collection of sayings, drawn on by both Matthew and Luke for the teaching of Jesus, which is probably even earlier than Mark.[2] The overall theme of both sources is, however, the same.

The message that comes through from the teaching and perhaps still more from the actions of Jesus is that he preached the gospel of Generosity – asking from us more than we, or his contemporaries, would consider sufficiently generous. If one had to choose a single saying to typify Jesus' teaching, one might think first of **Love your enemies**; which is found in Luke 6.35f, firmly linked to financial realities:

> **But love your enemies *and do them good and lend without despairing of anyone*;[3] and your reward will be great, and you will be the sons of the Most High; for he is kind to the ungrateful and wicked. Be compassionate, as your Father is compassionate.**

The same message can clearly be seen in Mark, and it asks for generosity of mind and heart as well as from the pocket. When asked which is the most important commandment, Jesus does not merely specify a whole-hearted, unlimited love for God, but proclaims, as second only to that, loving one's neighbour as oneself (Mark 12.28-34).

Generosity of mind is important in this, and nothing made Jesus more angry than mean and narrow interpretations of the Law (Mark 2.6-12, 18-20, 23-28; 3.1-6, 28-30; 7.1-15) such as would, for example, prevent someone being healed on the Sabbath. As a good Jew, Jesus lived by the Law of Moses; but he had no time for interpretations of it that were petty. Generosity of friendship is vital, as can be seen in Jesus' acceptance as family of all who want to do the will of God (3.35); in his embracing of the leper (*hēpsato*, he clung to him, hugged him hard, 1.41); in his happy response to the alien woman's telling retort (7.29), in his willingness that his name should be used to heal by someone not of his followers, and in the dictum that **whoever is not against us is for us** (9.39f). Yet the nub of the matter is parting with possessions, as generously as may be, beyond all bounds of prudence.

To say that the measure you give will be the measure you get, with something added (Mark 4.24), is not meant to encourage the giver to calculate, but rather to be generous in attitude, open hearted and open handed; the same attitude which accepts violence without retaliation, that gives the shirt as well as the coat, or goes the extra mile (Matt.5.39ff). The two people most commended in Mark's gospel are the widow who gave to the temple a tiny sum which she could not afford, and the woman who anointed Jesus' head with a whole jar of perfumed oil. In the first case the widow's two small coppers – all she had – are contrasted with the impressive but less truly generous gifts of those who have plenty to spare (Mark 12.41-44). In the second,

> **But there were some saying angrily to each other, 'What was the point of this waste of the perfume? For it might have been sold for three hundred *denarii* and given to the down-and-out.' And they told her off angrily (*enebrimōnto*). But Jesus said, 'Leave her alone. Why are you so hard on her? She has done a lovely thing for me. You have the destitute among you always, and you can help them whenever you like; but I shan't be here for ever. What she could do, she has done; she has anointed my body in advance for my funeral. Truly I tell you, wherever in the whole world the great news is spread, what she did will be remembered to her credit** (14.4-9).

It is immaterial whether or not the final sentence is the narrator's comment. To Jesus, the point was not that her action was wasteful or foolish – he could see as well as anyone that it was both – but that it was generous, the act of someone loving enough to defy criticism and expend something of great value so that she might do him honour. Indeed, if Mark's Simon whose nickname was 'the Leper' is the same man as Luke's 'Simon the Pharisee' (Luke 7.36-50), this may truly have been a woman of ill repute,[4] in which case it was even braver of her to enter the Pharisee's house at all.

The Kingdom of God

Jesus preached *metanoia,* changing one's attitude, to live in a new way, so as to be ready for the Day of the Lord, when the heavenly Son of Man would suddenly appear to judge and rule the earth. Some American scholars, Burton Mack, Robert Funk and the Jesus Seminar in particular, have argued that Jesus' meant no more than a new way of living by his 'Kingdom of God',[5] but this is a very shaky position, first assuming that Jesus could not make his teaching clear even to his closest disciples; secondly, interpreting all references to the Kingdom in Q either as secondary additions or, where this will not do, as having no apocalyptic meaning;[6] and thirdly, attributing the strongly apocalyptic element in the gospels to some of Jesus' disciples who had, they claim, first been disciples of the apocalyptic Baptist.[7]

That last, quite popular fallacy, depends on taking John as fact and Mark as invention; instead of, as argued in our introduction, the other way round. Furthermore, on closer examination the Q references on which Mack's non-apocalyptic Q1 is based, his '*Original Book of Q*', are also apocalyptic, looking forward to a world-changing future event: as examples, **Your kingdom come**, in the Lord's Prayer could only have been understood by Jesus' hearers then as referring to the apocalyptic Day of the Lord, and therefore a good teacher would only have used it so; again, **Lucky are the down-and-out; God's kingdom is theirs** (6.20) forms part of a triad:

> **Lucky are the down-and-out; God's kingdom is theirs.**
> **Lucky are the hungry; for they shall be full-fed.**
> **Lucky are those who weep; for they shall laugh.**

So, when the kingdom comes, the hungry will be fed, the sorrowful will laugh, and the destitute will walk right in. This is not only explicitly future, it implies a drastic changing of the world we know.

Scholars wishing to find a non-apocalyptic meaning for Jesus' 'Kingdom of God' (what C. H. Dodd called 'realised eschatology', the unseen reign of God in the heart) always turn to **the kingdom of God is within you** (Luke 17.21), but the use of *humōn*, the plural form of 'you', supports rather the New English Bible's **among you**. The context is that of Pharisees asking *'When* will the kingdom of God come?' Jesus' answer here, that the kingdom cannot be seen as it approaches, means exactly the same as the parable of the seed growing secretly in Mark 4.26-29; the kingdom is already here, growing invisibly among you until the day when, like the new crop, it will suddenly appear.

Yet the idea of God reigning in the heart, if not precisely what Jesus meant by God's kingdom, is exactly the way in which he wanted people to anticipate it. He called upon people to be open-handed, open-minded, open-hearted; to eschew violence, to forget grudges, to be good to the deserving and the undeserving alike, to trust in the great news enough to begin *at once* to live in the ideal world it foretold, freeing themselves from prejudice, envy and greed; loving and giving and sharing, rather than amassing and defending. It is above all his call to find the courage to live that generous life *now*, without waiting for a changed world to make it easy, which has made his teaching carry down the ages to challenge us today.

It might be asked, if Jesus, like the Baptist, preached the Coming of God's Kingdom, in territories ruled by Herod Antipas, why was he too not arrested and even beheaded? Was Herod simply superstitious, as suggested in Mark 6.16? Did he hesitate to add to the unpopularity accruing from his execution of the Baptist? Neither consideration would be likely to have saved anyone seen as a political threat; but probably Herod learned, from the Herodians noticed in Mark 3.6,[8] or otherwise, that Jesus advocated non-violence to the point of loving your enemies, which was not the route to revolution.

Levels of Discipleship

Albert Schweitzer had, in his *Quest of the Historical Jesus* (1910), described Jesus' teaching as an 'interim ethic', designed only for that short time before the Day of the Lord should come, and therefore less suited to a continuing world. Certainly it has its difficulties; but these result rather from the failure to distinguish the teaching given to different groups and at different times.

The prime distinction is between the teaching which Jesus gave for everyone, and the special demands he made of his disciples. It is the latter who must cut all ties in order to be wholly available as a trained taskforce, and to them he says, **If anyone comes to join me and does not reject his own father and mother and brothers and sisters and even his own life, he cannot be my disciple. Sell your possessions and give the money away to help others. Leave the dead to bury their dead, but you come and follow me.** (Luke 14.26; 12.33; 9.60; and parallels).

It is not realistic to suppose that Jesus wished that the 'multitudes' to whom he also spoke should cease to look after their homes and families: the kingdom of God would be brought no nearer by the total disruption of social and economic life in Galilee. Indeed, if all well-disposed persons immediately reduced themselves to voluntary destitution, as his disciples had done, where could the latter hope to find the hospitality on which they would depend when sent out on their own? Identifying the original target-groups for different teachings is important, and may resolve apparent inconsistencies better than do hypothetical stages in the development of the Christian cult.

There are three standards, best seen in relation to property. The many are not called upon to sacrifice all they possess, only to be very liberal with it. The saying **Give to everyone who asks of you; and if someone takes away your goods, don't ask to for them back** (Luke 6.30) presupposes that you will have something to give, or even to lose. The aim, in Bultmann's phrase, is not poverty but surrender.[9]

The disciples, however, *were* called upon to give up everything they possessed. To be a follower of Jesus meant more than physically leaving home, it meant making the same sacrifice which he had made, by disowning all family responsibilities and renouncing all property, thus to be completely free to follow the promptings of God in the heart. This was to embark on the big adventure of trusting God blindly, and it was rewarded with an exhilarated joy; which may be what that rich young man was hoping to find, until he learned its price (Mark 10.17).

Thirdly, when selected disciples were later sent out in pairs as 'messengers' (*apostoloi*), they had new instructions. Going out on their own was not only a way to spread the word more widely, it was also a training exercise and a testing for them, raising their reliance on God to a new level.

> **And he ordered them to take nothing for their journey except a staff; no bread, no bag, no copper in their money-belts; but to wear sandals, and not to wear an extra tunic** (Mark 6.8f)**.**

These orders, although more realistic than those given by Matthew (10.9f) and Luke (9.3; 10.4), who want the messengers to tramp the stony roads barefoot, without even a stick to keep off a dog, nonetheless go beyond the normal practice of Jesus and his disciples. Not that they ever stamped around armed to the teeth, but they did take along food and money (Mark 6.35-38; 7.14), even if to spend 200 *denarii* on bread for a crowd seemed unrealistic. Now, sent out on their own, without the support of those women disciples who did so much to look after the group (Mark 15.40f; Luke 8.2f), the messengers would naturally think to provide themselves against the needs of the road, like other travellers. This they were told not to do, not even to the extent of one copper coin; so that by adventuring boldly they would strengthen their own trust in God, obtain a more sympathetic hearing by visibly practising what they preached, and, most of all, discover the power and guidance that comes from trusting.

The Cynics

The Cynics have been invoked as a source or pattern for Jesus' teaching,[10] but this was very different from the Cynic way. The Cynics habitually went barefoot; practical enough in the paved streets of Rome or Alexandria, less so on a gravelled Roman B-road or a rocky track. The Cynic customarily wore only a cloak, with no tunic under it: merely eccentric in the Graeco-Roman world, but unseemly in Jewish communities. The Cynics begged; the apostles, as Crossan notes, did not;[11] they were reliant on hospitality, which is a different matter. They were to stay with their hosts, and to accept whatever food was set before them. The Cynic beggar stowed away in his food-bag whatever he could get and went off on his own; the apostles remained, entirely dependent on the resources, generosity and life-style of their hosts. Even so, those particular instructions were only for those journeys, and later were specifically cancelled (Luke 22.35-38). Indeed, neither the record of Mark nor the teaching in Q show any close affinity with the Cynics, since pithy aphorisms are characteristic of many oral teachers, not confined to any school.

New Teaching

It was not instructions to the disciples, but the teaching for synagogue and crowd, which was judged ‘new’: the social programme which Jesus expounded for everyone. Mark, hearing only teaching given in Rome, has little to say of the particular kind of generosity which Jesus had urged in the very different culture and social structure of agricultural Galilee; but John Yoder suggests that Jesus was asking for a full Year of Jubilee, in which all debt and bondage between fellow Jews should be cancelled, with land reverting to its original owner, according to the provisions of Leviticus 25 and Deuteronomy 15.[12]

Yoder perhaps relies too much on words attributed by Luke to Jesus at Nazareth, an overt claim to prophetic status which, like the over-dramatic ending of that visit, is unknown to Mark. What can certainly be said is that Jesus wished people to live every day in the spirit of Jubilee Year. To free their fellows from debt, which led to imprisonment, and from slavery, would truly be to **bring the bound and those who sit in darkness out of bondage and the prison** (Isa.42.7). Yoder’s basic thesis seems sound, however: for the general thrust of Jesus’ teaching is clear from Luke's startling, and therefore very probable, version of the Lord's prayer (11.4): **Forgive us our misdeeds** (*hamartias*), **as we ourselves forgive everyone who owes us money** (*panti opheilonti ēmin*).

Christians have usually avoided taking this literally, but there is no doubt at all about what it says. Granted that in Aramaic *hoba*, a debt, can also imply one's own short-coming, the literal meaning of the Greek is still the most obvious and not to be excluded; for why else use two contrasting phrases, making a clear distinction between what God will do for us and what we must do for others? If the meaning is indeed that we must write off what others owe us in money, then so daunting a suggestion can hardly be other than the original teaching of Jesus; and 'new' it would certainly have seemed. It appears already to be toned down in Matt.6.12, where the use of 'debt' in *both* clauses excludes the literal interpretation, in favour of the easier and more conventional idea of a reciprocal forgiveness, a mental or spiritual activity which stops short of actually parting with one's money.

Debt was a big issue in Galilee: as Matthew's Unmerciful Servant (18.23-35), Luke's Dishonest Bailiff (16.1-13), Jesus' words to Simon the Pharisee (Luke 7.41f), and the advice to settle out of court (Matt.5.25f; Luke 12.57ff), all show. Peasant farmers chronically need to borrow to bridge gaps between sowing and harvest, between harvest and sale, and, in every bad year, between income and expenditure.[13] As Yoder says, the problem of credit drying up when the sabbatical year approached must have been real, since it made the good rabbi Hillel devise, as the only possible solution, his famous *prosboul*, a legal fiction which ensured that credit could still be had, at the price of forgoing the sabbatical remission.[14] The reversion of land at Jubilee, if it was ever more than visionary, was based on the concept that land could not be sold in perpetuity, because the land was God's (Lev.25.23), an idea which may have faded under foreign kings who claimed all land as theirs; but Josephus, claiming that the sabbath year provisions are scrupulously kept (*Ant*.3.15.3), must mean at least the cancelling of debt and of bondage between fellow Hebrews.

That Jesus was indeed concerned about this problem is also shown by his criticism of prudent lenders:

> **And if you lend to those from whom you hope to receive, what credit does that do you? Even sinners lend to sinners, to receive as much again. But [...] lend, despairing of no man** (Luke 6.34f).

(The common version of the last words, **lend, asking for no return**, a dubious but intelligent rendering of a doubtful text, may have begun as an explanatory gloss: compare Matt.5.42.) The words cannot merely mean 'lend without hoping for interest', since that was already the law (Lev.25.35f) and scrupulously kept; they can only mean 'lend, even if you don't expect to see your money again'; which would apply particularly to lending as a sabbatical year approaches. For in any other circumstances, a loan is precisely money which is due to be returned; and if one does not expect it back, it is a gift, not a loan. In this particular context, however, with debts cancelled every seventh year, there was simply a big risk that money lent might never be repaid; and only in that context do these words of Jesus have a proper meaning.

Yoder took his argument much further, drawing heavily on Luke, who has much to say about the mighty being put down from their seat, and the rich being sent empty away. Yet, apart from Lucan rhetoric, there is no evidence that Jesus was hoping to bring about an egalitarian society;[15] only a just and kindly one, as envisioned in Deuteronomy, where the richer would help the poorer, restoring to them the means of living independently rather than exploiting for profit their financial weakness (Deut.15.7-18; 24.6, 10-22). All people should be treated as equally important, however unequal their means. The Jubilee provisions for the release of Jewish slaves, the cancellation of outstanding debts, or even the return of purchased lands to the extent that every peasant might have his own small strip, would not have reduced the rich to penury; but would have meant parting with possessions, with capital, markedly reducing one's own status and financial security, unlike safe giving from income. It was not a welcome message to the men of standing and substance, in whose hands lay any possibility of major change towards a kindlier capitalism, and they seem to have remained cool to this teaching.[16]

His message was only 'revolutionary' in as much as it called on the individual to change his or her ways. It looked for change at the grass roots of society; not in the political landscape, in which change from below could only be attempted by violence and war, which he wholly rejected. In today's world we must use proper political ways to bring reform and alleviate suffering; but we must not therefore neglect our responsibilities in the local community where we may often achieve more.

Show us a Sign

The Jews were much respected by the Romans for their commercial integrity and obedience to their Law; and, obeying the Torah, well-off Jews gave away a standard ten per cent of their income; and many, Pharisees in particular, were very scrupulous, reckoning their tithe even on garden herbs. They were fine examples of honesty, upright living and regular charity, liberal givers by any modern standard; but to Jesus a great disappointment, for they were not prepared to give up being men of substance.

To them this new prophet would seem a zealous young idealist, who would learn more sense as he grew older. It was, Jesus remarked somewhat bitterly, easier to get a camel through the eye of a needle than to lead a rich man into the kingdom of God (Mark 10.25); and his sense of what that kingdom demanded was, not necessarily to abandon all worldly goods – Peter and Andrew still owned, after a fashion, their house and their boat – but rather to hold them with no thought of ownership, no commitment to increasing one's wealth, but ready at any time to devote the whole to the work of God, at the sacrifice of one's own power, prestige, influence, comfort or security. He was asking a great deal of those who had much to lose. Living in a time of peace and prosperity, they would see no reason to reduce their wealth just because the prophet thought the kingdom was at hand; **the vision he sees is for many days hence, and he prophesies for distant times** (Ezek.12.27), they might have thought. So they asked for some sign that the Day was near (8.11); and there was nothing, no war, famine, pestilence nor natural disaster, to which Jesus could point.

The kingdom, he said, is like a seed in the ground, growing secretly, with nothing yet to be seen; it is like a grain of mustard seed, apparently negligible, but destined to grow enormously (Mark 4.26-32). It is like yeast in the dough, working invisibly toward its end (Matt.13.33; Luke 13.20f). The apocalyptic Son of Man will approach like a thief in the night, unheralded and unseen (Matt.24.43f; Luke 12.39f); until suddenly he will appear in the clouds of heaven with great power and glory, like lightning flashing right across the sky (Mark 13.26; Matt.24.27; Luke 12.29). So make ready now! This was the heart of his new teaching, that men should live now as though the kingdom were already here, not wait until it came.

The New Way

That social aspect of Jesus's new teaching is confirmed by the first Christians who

> **used to sell their possessions and goods and distribute them to all, according to need [...] praising God and finding favour with the whole populace** (Acts 2.45).

It was surely their social responsibility which attracted the favour of those who did not share their doctrines. [17] They made a general shift towards less possession,

> **for those who owned lands or houses used to sell them, and they would bring the money and would lay it at the apostles' feet and it was distributed according to need** (Acts 4.34),

but note that this programme is variously applied, as already suggested of Jesus' teaching. Giving away property was neither compulsory (Acts 5.4) nor, presumably, uniform, since Barnabas' generosity gets special mention (Acts 4.36). Most would have kept their houses and, no doubt, continued to earn a living; and perhaps much of the disbursement was in setting up unemployed folk to earn theirs also – in Jewish eyes the best of all ways of giving, and one which might truly have won general approval.

Quite possibly such a community could and did thrive, until the severe famine in the late 40s which, followed by ever worse and greedier government, produced surging terrorism and rampant inflation. The Christians, with little wealth in reserve, might then have been ill able to cope; but the history of Christian social practice is not our concern here. What matters is that their first practice must have reflected their understanding of the way which Jesus taught but which few had chosen; and if their experiment did not last for ever, it was a worthwhile pioneering attempt towards a more caring community.[18]

Jesus' lasting achievement, however, was a body of teaching, memorably cast into aphorisms and parables, which would be relevant for all time. The prophet's insight into the moral imperative comes from a deeper source than his understanding of world history; and while Jesus was plainly mistaken in believing that the kingdom of God, for which he was trying to prepare his people, was imminent, his particular teaching was no 'interim ethic', valid only for that short term scenario, but an enduring challenge to all that is good in human nature.

Notes to Chapter Four

[1] Eg., a dictum about hand washing now frees converts from Jewish dietary laws (7.19); a ruling on divorce is adapted to Roman law (10.12).

[2] John Drury holds that Luke used Matthew for a source, as well as Mark, and that Q is therefore needless (Drury 1985, pp.4f; also A. M. Farrer, 'On Dispensing with Q', in Nineham 1955.) This hardly simplifies, since a written 'sayings source' would still remain likely for Matthew's 'Q' material; especially since Papias says that at least one existed.

[3] Here again Matthew (5.44-7) seems to evade the financial implications in the teaching.

[4] Thus, a likely possessor of expensive cosmetics. We must ignore John, where the woman is identified as 'Mary', in a family which the evangelist has (as a novelist, quite properly) constructed at Bethany.
[5] 'The liberation of the non-eschatological Jesus of the aphorisms and parables from Schweitzer's eschatological Jesus is the fifth pillar of contemporary scholarship' (Funk 1993, p.4).
[6] Mack 1993, p.44f; p.124, 'none of these (Q1) references paints an apocalyptic view of the world [...] Neither do any assume an apocalyptic view of the world as a larger frame of reference.'
[7] 'The subtlety of Jesus' sense of time – the simultaneity of present and future – was almost lost on his followers, many of whom, after all, started as disciples of John the Baptist, and are represented, in the gospels, as understanding Jesus poorly' (Funk, 1993, p.137).
[8] That the Pharisees and these Herodians now plotted to kill Jesus can only be Peter's inference, probably from hostility displayed later – they would not have discussed this openly, if at all.
[9] Bultmann 1934, p.51f.
[10] Mack 1993, p.114: 'Q1 enjoins a practical ethic of the times widely known as Cynic.'
[11] Crossan 1991, p.xii; pp.72-88 give a useful survey of the Cynics.
[12] Yoder 1972, pp.34-77. The release of enslaved Hebrews was once attempted, by Zedekiah (Jer. 34.8-22). Rescue from poverty and bondage belong in the context of the Lord's coming (Isa.58.6—59.20).
[13] The charity *Shared Interest* seeks funding to help Third World farmers with their cash-flow problems.
[14] Yoder 1972, pp.69-72. Crossan, 1991, pp.221ff, argues that the new factor was the wish to invest capital in loans, rather than a new dearth of credit: either way, money would not now be lent at risk.
[15] Hengel 1974, pp.23-30.
[16] This part of Jesus' programme broadly fits the social-science reading, that Jesus wanted the wealthy elite to resume their neglected role of patronage and succour their poor dependants); but Malina rejects the idea that Jesus called his disciples to a new way of life (Malina 2001, pp.141f; 149.
[17] cf. 'Justices and captains had come to break up this meeting, but when they saw Friends' books and accounts, how that we did take care one county to help another, and provide for our poor that none of them should be chargeable on their parishes [...] the justices and officers were made to confess that we did their work

---

[…] And so they passed away lovingly and commended Friends' practice' (G. Fox, *The Journal,* for 1660; (Penguin Books 1998, p.283).

[18] Like William Penn's Pennsylvania, far ahead of its time in justice and human rights

CHAPTER 5

His Parables

Phases of Ministry

In his reconstruction of the narrative outline C. H. Dodd discerned a three-phase early ministry. In the first, Jesus teaches in the synagogues all over Galilee Then, when his healings attract great crowds, comes the second phase, teaching beside the lake, or 'sea' as Mark has it; before, thirdly, withdrawing to the highlands to train his disciples in peace and send them out.

This, as far as it goes, is logical. The synagogue, whether meaning simply a Sabbath meeting for worship, or a specific room or building, was the obvious place in which to deliver God's message. But Mark is also quite emphatic about the teaching by the lake, for he says it three times:

> **And he went out [of the town] again, beside the sea, and all the crowd used to come to him, and he would teach them** (2.13);

> **And Jesus with his disciples withdrew towards the sea, and a big multitude from Galilee, and from Jerusalem and from Idumaea and TransJordan and around Tyre and Sidon, a huge multitude hearing what things he was doing came to him. And he told his disciples that a small boat is always to be handy for him because of the crowd lest they should crush him. For he healed many, so that all those who had diseases press upon him in order to have touched him** (3.7ff);

> **Again, he began to teach beside the sea. And a great crowd gathers round him, so having got into a boat he sits in the sea, and all the multitude was on the land close to the sea** (4.1).

The last passage introduces the story of the storm on the lake following a day of teaching, an anecdote into which Mark has put his section on teaching in parables. This is not inappropriate, since he also knows that Jesus particularly used parables when teaching the crowds.

Jesus' Use of Parable

The word *parabolē* can cover anything from riddles to elaborate allegories (Drury 1985, pp.7-20); but here the term will be used in its commonest sense of little stories or vignettes. Now the story of the vineyard (Mark 12.1-9) is a true allegory, a story in which the characters represent real people; the riddle about **How can the Messiah be David's son, if David calls him 'Lord'?** (12.35ff), which does not teach anything, is simply a riposte – if people want to ask silly questions, let them answer this one. (It seems mistaken to suppose that Jesus here is claiming Messiahship, because he does not in any way relate his question to himself.) But those two instances apart, Jesus uses neither riddle – his other questions, like those of Socrates, demand their obvious answers – nor allegory; although, if a story relates to a theological proposition like the Coming of the Kingdom, it is always easy to read allegory back into it, more on less inappropriately.

The parables, whether one-line vignettes like the Camel and the Needle's Eye, or more detailed stories like the Sower, are used like visual aids; they are analogies (the basic meaning of *parabolē*) used by Jesus to make a point, in preaching or in argument. Thus, when scribes from Jerusalem accuse him of sorcery, of healing folk through the power of Beelzebub, he refutes them with three short analogical questions; *not* riddles, for they elucidate, they do not puzzle. Can a divided kingdom survive? Can a feuding family prosper? Then, if Satan decides to attack the disease which he himself creates, how long can he last? Finally, the positive analogy: no one can enter a strong man's house and plunder his goods without first tying up the strong man (3.22-27): just so, if Satan's victims are being set free, it must be that Satan has been overcome by the greater power of God.

The advantage of such a method is that the scene pictured is understood perfectly well by ordinary folk, holds their interest and stays in the mind; and it is these plain folk who seem to become Jesus' principal concern. From the first, the house in Capernaum was likely to attract a crowd whenever he was there (Mark 1.34, 37; 2.1f; 3.20; also, we suggest, 9.14, 25); and while Mark gives no account of what Jesus taught in the synagogue, other than that it was novel, he gives many examples of teaching aimed at, and therefore adapted to, *ho ochlos*, the folk in the street.

When the **scribes of the Pharisees** criticise Jesus for consorting with **taxmen and sinners**, everyone present can appreciate Jesus' answer, that you do not need the doctor if you are well, only if you are sick; but on this occasion he spells it out for them (2.16f). However, when the 'Pharisees' (probably meaning, in Peter's idiom, anyone noticeably strict and pious) and, again, **the scribes from Jerusalem,** raise the matter of hands not washed before eating, Jesus condemns their elaboration of the law and shows how some use finicky interpretations to defeat the law's true purpose; but then, calling the crowd to him, he gives them the little parable which Drury names 'of the Digestion', which says that it is not what enters the body but what comes out of it which is unclean; whose meaning his disciples wish expounded (7.1-23). This is his most characteristic use of parable for the ordinary folk: give them the analogy, but let them work out its application, for no truth is as compelling as the truth you find for yourself.

Throughout Mark's gospel Jesus seems little concerned to convince the 'scribes and Pharisees', the precisians, sticklers for the letter of the law worked out in minutest detail; probably he knew that he would waste his time if he tried, so, let the dead bury their dead. Jesus simply dismisses their complaints and accusations, while putting his real effort into showing the ordinary people that they need not feel bound by such restrictiveness.

Thus, in the cornfields on the Sabbath, with only his disciples present, Jesus merely dismisses 'Pharisaic' criticism by pointing out that David once ate the sacred shewbread; a much more serious infringement than a relaxed interpretation of the fourth commandment. But usually his replies to critics are meant primarily for the common folk, *ho ochlos*: accused of using sorcery, he calls the 'scribes from Jerusalem' over to join him (3.23), because he is, presumably, already engaged with the *ochlos* and wishes them to hear his response. Even when the critic is Peter, again Jesus calls the crowd to him to hear the proper view ruthlessly expounded (8.34).

The Context Shapes the Form

But it is in the lakeside context that Mark specifically emphasises that Jesus always used parables when teaching the ordinary people (4.33f); and it is in that context that we should consider their form. Any one who has needed to communicate orally with several hundred people out of doors, without microphone or loudspeaker, will know that the medium shortens the message; the situation is quite unlike telling a story to one's children, yarning with a friend over a drink, or preaching to any indoor gathering. At the lake, although water does help to carry one's voice, it would be vital to speak simply and slowly from the boat in order to be understood.

Nor would it have been much easier when teaching in the temple – which is the setting of the Vineyard allegory and perhaps the original setting for the Good

Samaritan.[1] The repeated references to that crowd, large enough to stand off the temple authorities (11.18b, 32; 12.12, 37b: *RSV* and *NEB* vary their translations, but the Greek noun is always *ochlos*), mean large audiences; and although the temple is enclosed by colonnaded walls, it is greatly busy, with the roar of an overcrowded city as background. Similar acoustic difficulties would apply; yet, if **the great crowd heard him gladly** (12.37b), presumably they could hear what he said.

One reason for using stories would be that they hold attention, and have an internal logic which helps the hearers correctly to interpret the half-heard phrase. (In much the same way, Hebrew parallelism helps the hearer by giving repeated variations of a short saying: **Do not give what is holy to the dogs, nor toss your pearls to the pigs,** or, **Ask and you shall be given, seek and you shall find, knock and it shall be opened to you**.) The original parables must have been straightforward, simply phrased, without unnecessary detail; for the hearers needed a story which, even spoken slowly, was neither long nor complex, and it is evident from many sayings that Jesus was a master of brevity. Luke's carefully crafted stories would have been lovingly worked up for his readers.

Much of the crowd would be unsophisticated and largely uneducated. While uneducated need not mean unintelligent, yet the sinister subtleties which Crossan (1991 pp.276-82) detects in yeast or tares or mustard trees, would, even if they were valid, have been wasted on *ho ochlos*. These are the *vulgus*, the proletariat, the masses, in classical Greek *hoi polloi*; they would hardly detect, as Crossan does, 'ritual impurity' in the daily task of a woman making bread, nor find God's Son of Man allegorised in the malicious neighbour who tries to spoil a man's cornfield by sowing weeds. Concepts and images needed to be clear, simple and sensible; the quick-witted get there sooner, but in time the slowest can see them, too.

Each parable is designed to highlight one salient aspect, minor details being irrelevant; thus, Crossan's concern, that the Pearl Merchant cannot profit from his pearl unless he resells it, is of no importance: the *point* was that to attain the kingdom of God one must want it more than anything else on earth. The Dishonest Land-Agent shows the need to be practical in pursuit of *any* aim, good or bad; the Prodigal Son with the Virtuous Brother, like the Pharisee and the Publican in the Temple, shows that conscious virtue can be a bar to that generous open-heartedness which Jesus asks.

The Original Versions

It is then proper to suppose that when a parable of Jesus has been reduced to its simplest form, it will be very close to the way Jesus told it. Drury (1985, p.36) holds that it is impossible to recover the original version of any parable, for lack of an incontestably genuine original with which to compare it; but his analogy with the validation of an Old Master is not wholly apt. Rather, we have a large number of pictures all attributed to the same person, but badly in need of cleaning. When all the overpainting – for which Drury has a sharp eye – has been removed, there should be a number of works whose consistency with each other, and with other sayings of Jesus, will allow us to come close to their original presentation.
Take, for instance, the Good Samaritan (Luke 10.25-27). Luke tells it with the extra colour that makes a good story – he is, as E. V. Rieu said, a poet – but Jesus would have used a simpler version. Perhaps, I would suggest:

> *A man was set upon by thieves and left by the roadside, half dead. A priest came by and left him lying; then a Levite came, saw him and hurried away. But a Samaritan came along, and felt sorry for him. He bound up his wounds, carried him to an inn, and even paid for him to be cared for. Which of the three, would you say, was a neighbour to that man who was robbed?*

That gives the essential story in a form suitable for a large outdoor audience; although, in the circumstances in which the parable is usually heard today, Luke's retold version is a delight not to be forgone.

Consider next the parable of the Sower, which Mark places first in his lakeside teaching section. Matthew copies Mark's version almost word for word; but Luke, who can be concise where there is no human drama to exploit, trims that superfluous verbiage which suggests some slight expansion of the story in its retelling by Peter, who in Rome was not preaching to immense crowds. Peter may also be responsible for the rather laboured allegory which now offers an explanation. At its simplest, if a sower is concerned to sow all his field thoroughly, it is unavoidable that some seed will fly too far and be wasted, as anyone who has sown even a lawn will know;[2] but the alternative is for good ground to be left unseeded. To a sensible farmer the wasted seed is irrelevant; for his concern is to sow lavishly and thus maximise the return from the fertile land.

As told to the crowd, however, the point is that the seed is falling on everyone – but think, are you the kind of soil where it will grow? Listening to me will do you no good until you put my teaching into practice. It is the lesson of the houses built on rock or sand (Luke 6.46-49; Matt.7.24-27), which Jesus teaches also in Mark 3.35: **Whoever does the will of God, he is my brother and sister and mother**. There, Luke has seen the parallel, and elaborates, **My mother and brothers are those who hear the word of God and do it** (Luke 8.21; cf. also Matt.7.21). The lakeside crowd, however, are not given the message in clear, but left to work it out for themselves, so that they may then take it to heart. **If your ears work, listen.** Perhaps Peter felt that when using the Sower parable in Rome he needed to spell it out for his urban audience.

Meant to Baffle?

That rather baffling remark about the reason for using parable being to prevent understanding, which not even Matthew or Luke accept in the brutal form of explanation withheld from the masses **in case they should understand, repent and be saved** (Mark 4.11), probably owes its present form to Peter's own conviction that, since the nation as a whole *did* reject Jesus, it must have been God's plan that they should do so. This is one instance of Peter's concept of the 'Messianic secret'. It cannot, he thinks, have been Jesus' fault that he did not persuade the nation; so God must never have intended that they should accept the 'great news' that Jesus preached, and Jesus rightly wrapped his teaching, and his identity, in mystery, so that God's purpose might be fulfilled. Anyone holding a belief that all that happens must be according to the will of God is liable to draw similar conclusions.

J. D. G. Dunn (1983, pp.116-31) has shown serious inconsistencies in Wrede's thesis of the 'Messianic Secret' and claimed them as the theological inventions of Mark; but if that 'secret' is Peter's amalgam of Jesus' commands used in exorcism, demands for silence about healings, and teaching in parables – by which the apostle has explained, at least to himself, the non-acceptance by his people of Jesus as Messiah – then even those inconsistencies seem all too likely. It is only when Mark is supposed to be a serious theologian and talented author that the difficulties arise.

Yet, as Vincent Taylor said, there is surely here the misinterpretation of a genuine saying. We may note the Septuagint version of Isaiah, which gives:

> **And (God) said, Go and say to this people,**
> **In hearing you shall hear, and not understand,**
> **and when you see you shall see and not perceive.**
> **For the heart of this people has become gross,**

and their ears are hard of hearing,
and *they have shut their eyes*
on purpose not to see with their eyes
nor hear with their ears
nor understand with their heart
in case they might repent, and I should heal them (Isa.6.9f).

This is the version which Matthew quotes; and whether or not this was the one which Jesus knew, it probably represents his thinking. The Greek text makes clear that it is the people themselves who choose to be deaf and blind to what Quakers would call 'the promptings of love and truth in the heart'; while God asks nothing better than to heal them, if only they will 'turn to the Light'.

Reading it so, Jesus is shown as longing to bring the whole crowd to the Truth, but with no illusion that he is likely to succeed. Parables are the best way of interesting his listeners; Jesus can hope that some will puzzle out the application and accept the lesson, but the Sower story is a wry acknowledgement that many of his hearers will fail to grasp what he is trying to tell them – that is its negative side. Teachers may recognise that end-of-a-hard-day feeling, when we wonder whether we have actually succeeded in teaching anything at all.

Mark is clear that Jesus did not explain his stories to the hearers, leaving them to find the meaning for themselves, but he is equally explicit that Jesus did explain them to the disciples; and with the Sower parable at least it is easy to see why. What the disciples needed to see, if they were to be sowers themselves, was the other side of the picture, and to adopt the farmer's philosophy: sow generously and never mind what is wasted, the good soil will bear you a fine harvest.

Laboured though the explanation now found in Mark may seem, it could well go back essentially to Jesus, attempting to make this point to those whom he would later send out in pairs to spread the word. It is hard, however, to read Mark's gospel as the testimony of Peter without coming to feel that the apostle was none too quick in the uptake: Jesus, perhaps, did not call him The Rock for nothing. It may be that he was the one who, like a person who cannot see the point of a joke, always had to ask for an explanation; and then Jesus, valuing him for his other qualities, would patiently explain. In the case of the Sower we may have one such explanation, as it has emerged from repeated retelling.

Realistic?

The realism of the parables is much debated; but this is partly a question as to how the term is used. They are analogies from real life, but some, as with the sower or the woman kneading yeast into her dough, tell of everyday tasks; others are occasional incidents, like losing a sheep or a valuable coin; yet others are unusual twists to a normal situation, like the foolish bridesmaids who miss the feast, the wounded man rescued by the despised alien, or the man who forgives his defaulting debtors. A king going forth to war was not an everyday occurence, but it was a real possibility – in 37 AD, for example, Herod Antipas came off badly when attacked by Aretas IV of Nabataea, and in 39 AD he was deposed on evidence of his stockpiling armaments to a level suggesting independent reprisals (Josephus, *Ant.*18.251f). Even the Last Judgement parable (Matt.25.31-46) turns on the behaviour of ordinary people in real life.

There is no need for the storyteller to limit himself to customary or even probable behaviour, however, so that it is irrelevant to assert that a rich man journeying would probably advise his household as to when to expect his return: this one did not, and they were caught out, which is the point (Mark 13.34-7). The one-liners are sometimes fantastic – a man gets a plank stuck in his eye (Matt.7.3ff) or, after carefully straining the gnat out of his soup, absentmindedly swallows a camel (Matt.23.24). Whether unjust judges or importunate widows (Luke 18.2-5) are anything out of the ordinary may be a matter of opinion. The sower's hundredfold return on his seed might be hyperbole, but the soil of Galilee was certainly remarkably productive.

Parables and Ministry

Taken together, the parables in Mark, both the one-liners which are the majority, and the longer ones like the Sower, are almost a microcosm of Jesus' ministry. He comes preaching the imminence of the Kingdom, already advancing invisibly like a seed growing in the soil, and due to produce great growth from an insignificant seed, like mustard. But, preaching in the synagogues, Jesus encounters the opposition and hostility of the rigidly religious, particularly the 'Pharisees', devoted to keeping the Law in minute detail, whereas Jesus appealed to the great principles which the Law embodies. He challenges their negative interpretations of Sabbath observance: the minor grumble that rubbing a few ears of corn amounts to preparing a meal is shrugged off with a reminder about David breaking a more serious taboo, but the objection to his healing on the Sabbath is more rigorously countered by asking whether the law tells you to do good or harm on the Sabbath; and he is angry when they will not answer. Again, Pharisaic concern for fasting is shrugged off by asking whether the bridegroom's friends can fast during the celebrations; but over-insistence on ritual washing, a real difficulty for the 'have nots', provokes a denunciation of ways in which the tradition is used to twist the law and serve self-interest. This Jesus follows up for the benefit of ordinary hearers with Drury's 'Parable of the Digestion', to show that one is not befouled by what comes into one's body, or one's mind, from outside, but by what comes out from inside.

We may note that Jesus seems most concerned to make sure that the ordinary people, bystanders at any controversy, are not taken in by the misguided views of his opponents. In the Beelzebub controversy, when scribes from Jerusalem accuse him of healing through sorcery, there could be little hope of persuading those already so prejudiced: what was important was to refute the charge for the sake of those who might then listen to him. So Jesus poses his questions, as we have seen, and adds the analogy of the strong man, who cannot be robbed until the burglar has overpowered him. Jesus is claiming, as he does specifically in Luke 8.20 (cf.Matt.12.28) that he heals **by the finger of God**.

The scribes from Jerusalem, the 'Pharisees' and rulers of the synagogues, the older men, all these, Jesus soon realised, were too set in their ways to be persuaded: like old wineskins that cannot stretch to hold fermenting wine, old cloth that will be pulled apart by a patch of new stuff. He needed the young, ready to think radically.

Men of property, too, whether Pharisaically inclined or not, were little help; even the enthusiastic one, of whom Jesus had great hopes because he was so young (as Matthew correctly infers, from that impetuous approach and Jesus' affectionate welcome) could not bring himself to give up his wealth; and the comment that a camel would find it easier to get through the eye of a needle sums up a long disillusionment about how much could be achieved through appealing to men of substance (Mark 10.17-31; cf. Matt.19.20).

But the poor, the mass, the many, could at least hear him without the inhibition of wealth, and he taught them in parables. We may note that The Seed growing Secretly, used to explain the invisible approach of the Kingdom, cannot well be allegorical, with God as the farmer who will harvest his crop; for the very point is the ignorance of the farmer himself, who has no notion why or how seed grows and just gets on with his life and work; but he knows a crop when he sees one, and reaches for his sickle. In the Mustard Seed there is even less room for allegory, since that insignificant seed has the only role.

Instruction to the disciples when Jesus had withdrawn with them into the hills, and was preparing them to go out in his stead, might be the context for Not Hiding your Lamp but placing it where it can light the whole house (Mark 4.21): **Let your light so shine** as Matthew has it (Matt.5.16). It is they, too, who must assert themselves, have a bit of bite, like salt (Mark 9.50); but the argument as to which of them was most important, and the ill-feeling created by the Bar Zebedees' bid for special favour (9.33ff; 10.35-45), illustrate why Jesus also says **Have salt in yourselves, and be at peace with one another** (9.50).

Early on, Jesus had asserted his right to mix with all kinds of people: it is not the healthy who need a doctor, but the sick (3.17). Yet his mission was necessarily directed to his own nation, for the Gentiles would only be brought to the worship of the true God through the agency of a redeemed Israel: as the prophets had said (Isa.46.17, 22f; 56.6ff; 60.3; Jer.7.11; Zech.14.16). This is almost explicit in Jesus' initial response to the Syro-Phoenician woman, that one must not take the children's food and toss it to the puppies (Mark 7.27): he must not turn away from his mission to Israel to do favours for strangers. He may have been torn between natural compassion for the suffering, and doubt as to whether it was right to invoke God's healing power at all when outside the land of Israel, or on behalf of a heathen foreigner; but the woman's deft retort seems to have resolved his doubt, and he felt happily free to give her the help which she was asking.

To that period of wandering outside Israel belongs also the analogy of the would-be follower having to carry his cross with him (8.34). The placing of the rich young man during the Peraean ministry (10.25) is probably quite arbitrary; but the one-liner about telling the mountain to go and jump in the sea (11.23) could, with its stress on trusting God, well fit the increasing tension of the final week in Jerusalem, as most certainly does the Vineyard allegory with which Jesus challenged the authority of the chief priests (12.1-9).

That final week is also appropriate for the instruction to observe the warning signs when the troubles are coming, as come they must before the Kingdom arrives (14.28f); and for the reminder to be always ready, in the story of the man who came home and caught his servants napping (14.32-37). Finally, at the Last Supper, the words **This is my body [...] This is my blood [...]** are clearly parabolic in form, however we may wish to understand them (14.22-24). The final challenge to the High Priest and his fellows is, however, neither parable nor allegory but a last proclamation of the prophecy which had formed the basis of Jesus' whole mission; **And you shall see the Son of Man seated at the right hand of Power and coming with the clouds of heaven.** That, as Jesus believed, was the simple truth.

Notes to Chapter Five

[1] It would reconcile Mark 12.28-34 with Luke 10.25-37 if 'But who is my neighbour?' was a follow-up by another questioner, and that it was after *his* put-down that no one dared ask any more questions Mark (12.34b). Yet these might be two separate incidents.

[2] Drury 1985, pp.55-58, properly disposes of the explanation (by Jeremias, 1966, pp.9f) that the path and thistles are ploughed up later; nonetheless, the Sower remains a simple example from daily life, not an allegory.

CHAPTER 6

His Disciples

The Four

It was argued above (Chapter 2) that the four fishermen had met Jesus, and learned something of him, before the day when he called them to leave their nets. Jesus, demanding total commitment from those who joined him, always insisted that new disciples must reckon the cost beforehand;[1] for he could not use the feckless and irresponsible, any more than the semi-committed, to whom he offered daunting challenges (Mark 10.21; Matt.8.18-22, Luke 9.57-60). Since it seems that they were expecting his summons, and had already promised to support the new prophet, Jesus must have met these four at some time between his call and his return to Galilee; very likely as chance-acquainted Galileans in Jerusalem, since the fishermen would probably not leave their fishing except to attend one of the major feasts. It seems unlikely that a builder from Nazareth would have met fishermen at Capernaum otherwise than at a feast, or on the roads to Jerusalem; but then, folk were on holiday, with time to talk at length. That Mark had never heard of such a meeting is likely enough, for there was no reason why it should ever have been included in Peter's preaching, nor among his random reminiscences.

When Jesus first entered Capernaum he had these four as his only disciples; very committed disciples, who had made the decision to give up their work and leave homes and families, trusting, as Jesus did, that God would provide for them all. Many dedicated people have done the same, and the Quaker Marmaduke Steventon records a specific experience of such assurance:

> for the Lord said unto me, immediately (ie. *directly*) by His Spirit, that He would be as an husband to my wife and as a father to my children, and they should not want in my absence, for He would provide for them when I was gone. And I believed that the Lord would perform what he had spoken.[2]

Neither Peter nor Marmaduke were leaving their families destitute; indeed, we may reasonably suppose that each family had not only a house but a small plot of land or some other means of supplying basic needs. Yet a marked drop, probably from working-class prosperity to poverty, is implied, and all the disadvantages of living without one's man to help. It cannot have been easy to leave them, nor to be left, so.

Assuming the four men to be friends all much of an age, these first disciples were perhaps in their early twenties; given that Peter, and very likely Andrew too, were married, and one of them probably the father of at least one child, the toddler (*paidion*) in the Capernaum house (9.36). Only the reference to a mother-in-law assures us that Peter was wed; and of the sons of Zebedee we know only that they worked for their father, so probably still lived at the family home, and may have been a year or two younger than Andrew and Peter. All four, however, were probably full-grown young men, not adolescents.

Josephus (*Life*, 11-12) records that when he spent three years as disciple to Bannus, a desert ascetic, he was nineteen at the finish; and between fifteen and nineteen or so would certainly be a natural age for such a venture, while one was old enough to have some adult status without having full adult responsibilities. If, then, the most of Jesus' disciples were in their later teens, as seems likely, the position of leadership enjoyed by the first four may have owed something to their being the eldest, as well as the first.

Throughout, these four have a special position. Peter, James and John are witnesses to the healing of Jairus' daughter, and to the Transfiguration. That Andrew, still one of the inner circle at the end (Mark 13.3), is left behind on these occasions suggests that he was the most mature, quite likely the oldest, the one whom Jesus could best trust to take charge of the younger men during his absence.

It seems probable from the episode where Jesus heals Peter's mother-in-law that he was already a guest at the house of Peter and Andrew: the phrasing **And next, leaving the synagogue, they went to the house of Simon and Andrew with James and John** includes Jesus in 'they', the hosts; and from then on, that house seems to have been his base whenever he returned to Capernaum. Whenever Mark speaks of Jesus being 'at home' or 'entering his home' (2.1; 3.20; 7.17; perhaps 9.28, arguably mislocated) the phrase would be Peter's, referring to his own home.

The Twelve

These four, and perhaps no others, would have accompanied Jesus around the synagogues of Galilee; but many other young men may have **followed him** and **sat round him in a circle** to hear him teach in one place or another. By the time that Jesus was becoming disillusioned with the over-religious (2.8, 17, 27; 3.5), and starting to teach **all the common people** (*pas ho ochlos*, 2.13) at the lakeside, his following could block access to the house if he taught indoors (2.2).

In this gospel, the taxman whom Jesus invites to join him as he passes the customs point is Levi, son of Alphaios;[3] he might or might not be related to James, son of Alphaios, one of the twelve, but Levi is not Matthew, nor is he listed anywhere amongst the Twelve. The Synoptics are unanimous about eleven – the original four, then Philip and Bartholomew, Matthew and Thomas, James the son of Alphaios, Simon 'the Caananite' (in Luke, 'the Zealot') and Judas Iscariot. The twelfth is Thaddaeus, in Mark and Matthew (in some texts of Matthew, and a few of Mark, Lebbaeus) or, in Luke, Judas, son of James. Since Peter would hardly have forgotten the names of the other eleven, whereas one name in a list of unknowns is easily mislaid, it is best to accept Thaddeus with Mark (Matt.19.1-4; Mark 3.13-19; Luke 6.12-16).

In Dodd's reconstructed 'framework', lakeside teaching forms the second phase of Galilean ministry, and then the third phase is a single period of withdrawal to the hill-country, starting with the choosing of the Twelve and continuing until their commission and dispatch as *apostoloi*, messengers. The reality, as Dodd would probably have been first to acknowledge, was perhaps not so tidy; for since Jesus, in a story apparently related to lakeside teaching, already has many disciples (2.15), the need for some organisation would have become apparent.

The explanation of the Sower parable, which may indeed have been told anywhere, is set in a context where Jesus is with both the Twelve and other disciples for **when he was alone, those around him with the Twelve** (4.10) must mean by **alone** that the crowds had gone. The same episode – in Mark's arrangement – shows one reason why there needed to be a special group:

> **And he said to them that day in the evening, 'Let us cross to the other side.' And leaving the crowd they took him with them just as he was, in the boat, and other boats were with them** (Mark 4.36).

No more is heard of the other boats, which may therefore be disregarded; probably they had simply drawn near to hear the prophet, and now went about their business. The point is that one boat can only hold a limited number of people.

The vessel, *to ploion*, is a full-size fishing boat. The outline mentions Jesus asking for a *ploarion* (3.9), which suggests something smaller, but as things developed the *ploion* became more practical. Such a boat could accommodate Zebedee, his sons, and some hired men, with enough room to mend fishing-nets

(1.19f). This one, in a later story, carries Jesus and twelve disciples when he takes them off for a quiet day after their preaching tour (6.30ff).

Archaeology now possesses a specimen: the so-called 'Jesus boat', discovered in 1985, nearly 27ft. long and over 7ft.6ins. wide; such a vessel *could* carry a dozen or more, but at the cost of little freeboard (4.37) and deeper draught – hard work against a headwind, and Jesus walks out to the boat to save it from grounding in the shallows (6.48). But the size of boat was only one parameter for the size for this cadre; that twelve were chosen, rather than ten or fourteen, was surely symbolic, relating to the Twelve Tribes of Israel;[4] hence the need to restore the proper number after the loss of Judas (Acts 1.15-26).

It is likely, therefore, that, before Jesus had done much teaching of crowds by the lake, or possibly before he even started,

> **he went up into the hill country and he summoned those he wanted, and they went off to join him. And he appointed twelve so that they would be with him and so that he might send them off to preach** (3.13f).

The hill country (*to oros*) hardly seems a helpful phrase, since so much of Galilee is hilly; but for that very reason 'the hill country' almost certainly means the northern part, known as Upper or Upland Galilee because it was higher and more mountainous than the rest. It was also much less populated or cultivated, having no recognised cities at all,[5] which would make it an obvious place in which to get away from crowds; an aim which could not have been well served by collecting the disciples on top of those conspicuous hills in Lowland Galilee which have been suggested – Mount Tabor, or the Horns of Hattin.

Matthew's Sermon on the Mount, attended by crowds (Matt.7.28; 8.1) gives a slightly more realistic picture than Luke's version, in which the crowd docilely wait in the plain below until Jesus descends (Luke 6.17), but both seem simple adaptations of Mark; for linguistically, *to oros* could equally mean a single mountain. It is Luke who has devised the traditional scene in which Jesus calls out from the assembled company of his disciples the twelve whom he wants for special duties (Luke 6.12). Mark's wording suggests that Jesus went up into the hill country alone, and then sent for twelve to come and join him there (3.13).

A likely possibility is that he shed all his disciples except the first four, and disappeared with these, leaving no address. Having found suitable shelter in the highlands, Jesus could send the four to fetch another chosen eight. Then, free from distractions, he would have grounded them thoroughly in the good news of the kingdom and the *metanoia* it demanded. When he went back to spend much of his time teaching the crowds, the Twelve were kept by him for special training: it was for them to understand fully what lay behind the parables he told, the mystery of the kingdom, and when they were alone he explained all things to his own disciples (4.34).

The time came when Jesus stopped teaching by the lakeside and withdrew again: **And he made a circuit of the villages, teaching** (6.6b). This sentence introduces the sending out of the twelve in pairs to preach, and probably 'the villages', although Mark does not catch the allusion, refers to *Tetracomia*,[6] the Four Villages, the Greek name for Upland Galilee. Such a region would have offered a welcome respite from the crowds, and while touring the little townships Jesus could continue the training of the Twelve. There he could indeed find a quiet hilltop when he needed to be alone with them; and Luke's tradition is probably correct, that the commissioning of the disciples, and their, perhaps earlier, enrolment as the elite Twelve (with suitable nicknames to distinguish, eg., Simon the Rock from Simon the Caananite),[7] took place on a hill-top site; for the top of a hill is a most natural place to be away from men and feel close to God, as the stories of Moses and Elijah confirm.[8]

The Messengers (Apostoloi)

So now the Twelve were commissioned to preach and to heal:

> **And going forth they preached that men should change their hearts. And they cast out many demons, and anointed with oil many sick people and healed them** (6.12f).

They must also have been told when to return and where to foregather; the obvious rendezvous being the house in Capernaum, their only permanent base. For how long they went out can only be conjecture, but bearing in mind that this was a training exercise for them as well as a wider spreading of the message, it could hardly have been less than a month; yet two, three at the very most, seems quite long enough for inexperienced youngsters to be away on their own. Six weeks might be as likely a period as any.

Mark can only fill the gap, between the dispatch and the return of the apostles, with the story of Herod and the Baptist; knowing nothing, apparently, of where Jesus spent this time; which was probably still somewhere remote in Upland Galilee. As soon as he came back and met the returned disciples, the house was once more besieged (6.31b). Not even by leaving early, by boat, could Jesus escape the crowd; and during that day, as he gave to the crowd the time which he had wished to devote to the disciples, and then gave away their food as well, it became clear that if he was to build further on the disciples' missionary experience, it could not be in Lowland Galilee.

In the event, he left the country, taking with him the Twelve,[9] which gave him the opportunity, as they wandered, to consolidate what they had learned and to teach them further; but of what he told them at that particular stage we know nothing until, near Caesarea Philippi, he began to prepare them for the death which he now clearly foresaw for himself.

The Followers

The Twelve were not the only disciples, however. Out of many others, the names of at least five are known: Papias records John, later called 'the Elder', and Aristion; Acts has Joseph Barsabbas, nicknamed Justus, and Matthias; Luke's Emmaus story gives Cleopas, with his unnamed friend, or wife. If Little James (*Iakōbos ho mikros*) was, as his nickname suggests, a convenient way of differentiating James, son of Alphaios from James, son of Zebedee, his brother Joses, whose name was known to Peter and whose mother belonged to the inner circle of women followers (Mark 15.40), was probably one more such disciple.

The phrase, referring to Jesus' disciples,[10] **For they were many and they used to follow him** (2.15b), suggests that around Capernaum, 'follow' is to be taken literally. Yet this cannot always have been the case. It is unsure whether Jesus called to the hill-country only twelve on whom he had already decided, or a larger group from whom he finally picked the most promising (3.13). Other disciples appear as **those around him with the Twelve** (4.10); but whenever the boat was used for transit, it would seem likely that only the Twelve could accompany him. It is reasonable to suppose that these other young men came to listen to Jesus whenever he was teaching in Capernaum, or anywhere that they could; and were dismissed when Jesus thought best. When he withdrew into Upland Galilee to prepare the Twelve for their mission, he probably sent the others home, like mediaeval university students released to help with the harvest.

However, if there is, as common sense suggests, substance in Luke's tradition that before setting off towards Jerusalem Jesus sent disciples ahead to places he would visit on his way (Luke 9.51; 10.1), those could not then have been the Twelve, who were travelling with Jesus and whose mission Luke records separately (9.1, 6), but others. The figure of seventy need not be reliable; but it would have been sensible both to train these others further while there was time, and to prepare the way for Jesus' necessarily short visits to Peraea and Judaea (Mark 10.1).

The distinction between the Twelve and others recurs in 10.32:

> **And they were on the road going up to Jerusalem, and Jesus was walking ahead of them, and they were puzzled (*ethambounto*),**[11] **and those who followed were afraid, and gathering the Twelve round him again he began to tell them**

which is easily seen as Mark's rendering of Peter's, 'Jesus was walking ahead of us, and we (*the Twelve*) were puzzled, and the followers (*other disciples, perhaps Luke's seventy*) were afraid'. The presence of a numerous band of other disciples would also explain Luke's **the entire multitude** (*hapan to plēthos*) **of the disciples** (19.37) at the entry to Jerusalem. This larger body of disciples explains too why the money-changers seem not to have resisted their eviction (Mark 11.15); and how Jesus can send two disciples to prepare a dining-room, yet himself arrive later with the Twelve (Mark 14.13, 17). Probably it had been two of those 'followers' who fetched the donkey, and returned it promptly as promised; and Mark's account of the ride may be repeating the distinction between **those going ahead** – the Twelve would naturally take it on themselves to lead the way – **and those following** (11.1, 3, 9). Justus Barsabbas and Matthias are chosen from

> **the men who have accompanied us during the entire time that the Lord Jesus was going in and out amongst us [...] until the day he was taken up from us** (Acts 1.21f).

This can hardly mean that any of these others was always present throughout the ministry, but must certainly mean that they had witnessed the crucifixion. Other disciples, then, had also been with Jesus frequently throughout his ministry and had come to Jerusalem with him.

Women disciples

We also have the names of some of the women followers: Mary Magdalen; Mary the mother of Little James and Joses; and Salome, whom Matthew equates, plausibly enough, with the mother of John and the older James (Matt.27.56; Mark 15.40, 16.1). Luke, who names two more, has been taken to mean that many women went with Jesus around the country:

> **And it happened subsequently that he also was travelling round towns and villages, preaching and bearing the good news of the kingdom of God and the Twelve were with him, and there were certain women who had been cured of evil spirits and diseases, Mary nicknamed Magdalen, from whom seven devils had gone out, and Joanna, the**

> **wife of Herod's steward Chuza and Susanna and many others, who provided for them from the means at their disposal** (Luke 8.1-3).

In the Greek this is one sentence, so translators punctuate it variously; but Luke appears to say that many women were accompanying Jesus on his travels, which seems unlikely. It is hard to envisage the prophet travelling with a crowd of women companions, for that must have brought discredit to himself and to his teaching; the women, too, would more likely have been removed by their menfolk, and then denied further opportunity to support the prophet's work, even from their own resources. Jesus was at times accused of sedition, blasphemy and sorcery, but the worst ever alleged against his private life was to call him, as he says, a glutton and a drinker, a friend of taxmen and immoral persons. That he should allow a sinful woman to approach him, let alone accept with kindness her ministrations, caused criticism enough (Luke 7.36-50; cf. Mark 14.3-9); it would have been extremely foolish to give the malicious any stronger ground for attacking his reputation, for when a man preaches strict chastity, many will be eager to believe the worst. Yet not even when the High Priest is trawling for possible accusations, or when the crowd deride the fallen hero on the cross, is there any suggestion that Jesus' sexual morality could be impugned; and all that any rabbinic source alleges is that Jesus himself had been a soldier's illegitimate offspring.

Mark, too, says that women followed Jesus in Galilee, but offers the more credible picture of just three: of these, one Mary apparently has a son amongst the Twelve, Salome probably has two, and Mary Magdalen, who may have lost touch with her own kin during the serious mental illness implied in Luke 8.2, could be chaperoned by the two mothers. These three in Galilee had followed him and looked after him (Mark 15.40f); their performance of domestic tasks might allay patriarchalist concern at their inclusion amongst the disciples, while the presence of their sons would check the obvious slanders. They seem to be distinguished by Mark from the other women looking on from afar (15.40), and also from the many others who had simply come down with Jesus to Jerusalem (15.41); these three, it is clear, had at least often travelled around Galilee with Jesus.

Mark was probably Luke's only authority for saying, as Luke seems to say,[12] that *many* women followed Jesus around Galilee; Luke perhaps misunderstood Peter's habit of making a statement before expanding it almost tautologically.[13] As the apostle recalls the crucifixion scene, he remembers the group of women there, which included the special three who had followed Jesus around Galilee – and who would prove sufficiently resolute to sally out to Jesus' tomb in the early hours of Sunday morning.[14] The remainder he redefines as **many other women who came up to Jerusalem with Jesus**.

Such other women, we may suppose, came to listen in the crowds, and found opportunities to give in proportion to their means; but lived at home, for theirs was a far from broad-minded milieu. Yet if it was impossible for them to traipse around the country with Jesus, there was nothing to stop them going south for Passover, travelling with husbands or sons or in the company of other women. It is clear from Mark that many had done so, and were present in Jerusalem, and saw Jesus crucified.

In sum, Jesus had gathered in Galilee a number of male disciples, probably for the most part in their later teens when they joined him, from whom he selected twelve, a number both symbolic and practical, as a special cadre. These twelve he trained specially; and apparently, after their return from their preaching tours, kept with him all the time.

Travelling in Galilee, the party might at times have numbered nearly twenty; Jesus, the Twelve, three women, and perhaps some others closely linked to the main body; like Little James' brother Joseph, whose mother was there. Outside Galilee, it may have been the size of the group which prevented Jesus from remaining *incognito* (7.24); but the Twelve had to be there, to receive further training, for which Galilee had now become impracticable.

Jesus probably arrived at Jerusalem with his usual party and a substantial group of other disciples, with many sympathisers also amongst those who had come up for the feast; even before the crowd took his side, a quick arrest was not feasible by day, and he was not in the city at night – nor, it seems, at siesta time either (13.1, 3).[15] When his arrest had been accomplished, and the crowd manipulated against him (15.11), his disciples were present, perhaps to glimpse his public trial, definitely to see him die; for the emphasis of the double conjunction in *ēsan **de kai** gunaikes, **but also*** **there were women watching from a distance** (15.40) would imply that the men were there watching too, and probably nearer. After Jesus was dead, however, it was left to the women disciples to stay to observe what followed.

Notes to Chapter Six

[1] Luke 14.28-35; also 14.26f; 9.23. Cf. Matt.10.37f; 16.24; Mark 8.34.

[2] J. Besse, *A collection of the sufferings of the people called Quakers*, 1753, pp.201f. Quoted in *QFP* sec.19.17.

---

[3] Mark 3.18; 15.40. *Halphaios*, in the Aland Greek New Testament, 4th ed; but *Alphaios* or *Alphaeus* are common usage.
[4] Some scholars claim that the evangelists created the Twelve for the sake of symbolism; it is perhaps more likely that Jesus did so. Matt.19.28, Luke 22.30 express the symbolism explicitly.
[5] A city (*polis*) had its council and a measure of self-government, something like an English borough.
[6] Perhaps Safed, Gischala, Meron and Jamneith; all sizeable settlements, but with no self-governing status. For *Tetracomia*, see *Times Concise Atlas of the Bible*, 2000, pp.113 ff.
[7] 'Canaanite' means 'trader' in Lxx Prov.31.24 and, probably, in Zech.14.21; Luke's 'Zealot' is also plausibly a translation of Syriac '*Kananitis*' (v. Liddell & Scott's Abridged Greek-English Lexicon, OUP 1958). It is perhaps more likely that this was another of Jesus' little jokes – Simon the Salesman, for a voluble enthusiast – than that the disciple was linked to an extreme nationalist body probably non-existent, certainly not active, during Jesus' lifetime.
[8] Moses: Horeb, Sinai, Hor, Pisgah/Nebo. Elijah: Carmel and unnamed (1 Kings 19.3). Cf. Abraham (Gen.22.2), George Fox on Pendle Hill (*Journal*, 1652).
[9] An obvious inference from Mark 7.24-37, specific in 8.27-34.
[10] It can hardly mean the taxmen and sinners; Levi possibly excepted, they surely did not leave their work to follow Jesus *habitually*, as the imperfect tense implies.
[11] *Thambeō*, to be astounded, gathers a nuance of terror in later Greek: 'worried' may best express both puzzlement and apprehension here.
[12] Luke 8.3. *NEB* adds commas to differentiate the three from the main group; but using 'several' rather than 'many' seems weak for *allai pollai*.
[13] Eg. **Everywhere into all the region** (1.28); **The leprosy left him and he was cured** (1.32); **And on the first day of unleavened bread, when they sacrificed the Passover lamb** (14.12).
[14] **Very early** (*lian prōi*) meant, in those times, long before sunrise; cf. Mark 1.35; **The sun having risen** is incompatible, and in some texts amended or omitted. Major's suggestion that a **not** (*ouk*) is missing could explain the error.
[15] Luke 21.37 says that Jesus spent every night there; but his custom was probably to pass every afternoon, after his day's teaching, at Gethsemane, but to sleep at Bethany (Mark 11.11f, 19f), on the far side of the Mount.

CHAPTER 7

The Wonder Worker

Hard to Believe?

The belief that Jesus could not only heal but also work miracles, in the sense of overcoming the laws of nature, rests primarily on Mark's two linked incidents of Feeding Five Thousand People and Walking on the Sea; both often quoted to show how impossible it is to believe the gospels. The timely Stilling of the Storm, or the wanton destruction of the Gadarene Swine and later of the Fig Tree, are easily seen as coincidence misinterpreted; but no obvious reconciliation of the Multiplication of Food and Walking on Water stories with the world we live in offers itself: either the record or the laws of science must be wrong.

The intention here is not to dissuade those Christians who accept the occasional arbitrary overriding of the laws of the universe; nor those scholars who, rejecting the validity of the record, consider 'symbol' or 'parable' as satisfactory explanations; for neither group has a problem. But, for all those who cannot accept that God will overrule God's own laws of nature, and in matters trivial when compared with the many appalling evils in which God never seems to intervene directly, there is no easy way round the problem which these two unlikely stories pose. To find proper sense, the text of these episodes must be examined in detail.

Feeding the Crowd

We may begin by noting that nowhere does Mark actually state that Jesus made food multiply: that, it would seem, he had not heard Peter say, although Mark's account suggests that that is what he himself believed. (Hence his application of the remark about not understanding about the loaves, 6.52.) The statement about Jesus walking on the sea, however, is quite unambiguous, and old explanations as to how the preposition in Mark's text might have been altered must fail for lack of any support in the textual record. So far as we can tell, *epi tēs thalassēs*, 'on the sea', was what Mark wrote; and while this might also mean 'beside the sea' (John 21.1), in this story that translation makes no sense of the disciples' mistaking Jesus, whom they had come to meet, for a ghost, nor of their subsequent 'amazement'. Our task is to discern what really happened, and how valid the record then appears.

The whole episode begins when the Twelve return from their preaching tours. Jesus too, we may safely assume, returns only now from Upland Galilee, to which he withdrew when crowds hoping for sensational healings made it impossible for him profitably to continue working in Lowland Galilee: he could hardly have returned to lodge with the womenfolk in the Capernaum home while Andrew and Peter were away without giving rise to scandal. It is suggested in the introduction that the healing of the Epileptic Boy (9.14-29) happened here, in Capernaum, after some of the returning disciples had arrived back slightly before Jesus; but, whether because there had just been a notable healing, or for whatever reason, we are told that:

> **there were crowds of people coming and going, so that there was never a time when they could eat. And he says to them, 'Come away by yourselves to a lonely spot, and rest a little.' [...] And they went off in the boat to a lonely place on their own. Now a lot of folk saw them as they were leaving and recognised them and ran together on foot from all the towns and got there ahead of them. And when he left the boat he saw a huge multitude, and he felt sorry for them; because they were like sheep with no shepherd, and he began to teach them many things** (6.31a, 32ff)**.**

Nowhere are the strength and the compassion of Jesus better shown than in his ability to give up the pleasant day he had planned for himself and his friends, in order to answer the real need he could sense in this tiresome but pitiful crowd; and later, when after hours spent teaching, he converted a social problem into an epitome of his gospel of generosity, that truly was genius.

A Social Difficulty

> **And now time was getting on, and the disciples come to him and they were saying [...] send them away so that they can go into the farmland and villages around here and buy themselves something to eat** (6.35f)**.**

What they really mean is 'Send them away, so that we may be free to get out our own food and have our own meal.' The key to the whole episode is, I suggest, that in the Mediterranean culture one does not eat in front of others, known or strangers, without asking them to share one's food – a convention which survived, in some countries, into the twentieth century at least.[1] That was why the continual going and coming of many people at the house had made it impossible to find a time for a proper meal; and the disciples and Jesus cannot eat now without offering to share their food with this equally hungry crowd and watching it all disappear. But Jesus realises that the unwanted crowd are in exactly the same quandary: the first proper meal of the day was usually an hour or so after noon, so he could expect that they, like his disciples, had mostly packed up some food before going out for the day; but were equally afraid to bring it out to share with so many.

Having found out what food he has at his immediate disposal, five loaves and two fishes, Jesus organises the crowd, moving them back from the sand and shingle of the beach onto the grass,[2] where he can get them spread out and broken up into convivial clusters (*sumposia*),[3] seated and at ease. Freed from the pressure and the anonymity of being in a great crowd, they might be able in these smaller social groups to act and react more normally and perhaps, amongst this lesser number, to risk bringing out their food to share, if given a lead. So Jesus gives them one:

> **And taking the five loaves and two fishes; having looked up at the heaven he asked a blessing and broke the loaves and gave them to the disciples to offer to them (*the crowd*) and he shared the fish out to everyone (*the crowd*)** (6.41)**.**

The text seems to mean that Jesus himself took round the fish, while the disciples, following his example, distributed the bread. This catalytic action worked, and since, although some might have brought nothing, those who had would mostly have brought plenty, **they all ate and were satisfied**.

A Lesson, not a Sign

The purpose of our detailed scrutiny is not merely to show how closely this not altogether original explanation follows the text, without need of miracle; but also to show how little there is to suggest that the action was in any way contrived, or Messianic. The Messianic idea derives only from the fourth evangelist, who wishes to give his reader a reason for Jesus to part from the disciples (whom, he will next aver, Jesus rejoins by walking *three or four miles* out across the water) and who loves to devise dramatic escapes from crowds. Plainly Jesus did not deliberately plan a great communal meal, since he had intended a day away from the crowd; but he used the occasion to demonstrate the need to share willingly whatever one has. The little boy in John, coming forward with his own food, is a charming explication of Jesus' point about sharing; although in John that voluntary act is followed by an explicit piece of magic (John 6.9, 11-14); for the fourth Gospel would, taken by itself, fit the opinion that the story is a later invention, to support Jesus' teaching of 'commensality' (Crossan 1991, pp.320, 398-204).[4] In Mark, however, there is no claim that this was recognised by the crowd or the disciples as a miraculous, nor as a symbolic, act; only an implication in the wording of verses 43 and 44, which may be either what Peter later said or what his hearer understood. It is because Mark 6.35-44 does *not* proclaim a miracle that most gospel retellings of the story, starting with the doublet which appears later as the Feeding of the Four Thousand (8.1-10), have improved the details to make it one.[5]

Walking on the Water

While Feeding the Crowd may be considered as a memorable and important piece of teaching, the alleged Walking on the Water is not in any way significant, except as an example of how oral transmission from Peter to Mark could transform a slightly comic incident into a fabulous miracle. It is a classic example of the Inexplicit Narrative, in which the teller fails to see the need to explain details or to include background which to himself is perfectly clear: such as that the disciples, having given away all their food, needed to buy more. Rewritten as what Peter could have said, plus what he failed to say, Mark 6.45-51 might run:

> **And straightaway he made us disciples get into the boat and row across to the other side near Bethsaida (*to have a meal and buy new supplies)* while he dismissed the crowd. And when he had sent them away, he went up on the hilltop to pray. And as it was starting to get dark (*6pm? 8pm?*) the boat was well out to sea and Jesus was by himself on the land. And (*on our way back)*, at about three o'clock in the morning,[6] seeing us struggling to make headway, for the wind was against us, he comes towards us (*along a spit of sand)* walking (*it seemed*) on the sea, and he was aiming to go out beyond us (*to the end of the spit*). But we, seeing him walking along on the sea (*as we thought*), took him for a ghost, and we cried out. For we all saw him and were terrified. But he spoke to us at once and said, 'Cheer up, it's me. Don't panic.' (*So now he made straight for us, through the deeper water*) and he hove himself up into the boat with us, and the wind dropped. And we were absolutely dumbfounded (*at having been so foolish*).**

Such a rendering of the story fits all the obvious circumstances. Many commentators have created problems with the geography by siting the Feeding of Five Thousand on the east side of the lake: but this is wholly improbable. The apostles, back from their travels, must be assumed to have reported to Jesus (6.30) at Capernaum, their usual base, where the boat would have been: Jesus then takes them by boat to some lonely (prime meaning of *erēmos*) spot on the coast, not many miles, not indeed far enough, from Capernaum. The ever-inquisitive Capernaum crowd follow by land, joined by folk from every place they pass, if we allow 'towns' to be the raconteur's exaggeration for 'villages' (6.33); but, since they outran the boat, the distance cannot have been huge. Afterwards, having given away all their supplies to the crowd, the disciples' urgent need is for food; but for Jesus, whose work is being frustrated by intrusive crowds, a time alone to seek guidance is more urgent. Dispatching the disciples in the boat, with instructions to get food, get some sleep, and return a few hours before dawn, would serve both purposes.

Time Factor

It had already been past the normal mealtime (6.35f) before Jesus had insisted on organising a shared meal with the crowd; after that every one probably slept on the grass, not attempting the walk home until the sun was lower and the heat of the day past. Allow for some leisurely leave-taking, for gathering up of their traps and families, for the disciples to collect up scraps and rubbish (which again, they would hardly have done during the noonday heat), and it is not surprising that by the time the disciples have finished, received their new instructions, and probably tried to convince Jesus that he would do better to come with them, it is so late that darkness comes before they have rowed very far. *Opsias genomenēs* need not mean as late as dusk, but the time-scheme suggests it, and this reads like the teller's viewpoint: 'And the last we could see, he was still up on the hill, when we were well out on the lake'. (**In the middle of the sea** seems better not taken literally, but to Bethsaida from any likely spot on the coast south of Capernaum would be no more than five or six miles.)

When they reappear in the small hours of the morning (6.48), plainly they are returning after a long interval; the timing makes no sense unless they have crossed to Bethsaida, spent some hours there, and are now coming back; and to collect Jesus is not only the obvious reason, but explains why eventually they all disembark a little further down that same west coast (6.53). Jesus sees them coming, and intends to use a handy sandbank as a jetty, so that they need not beach the boat, nor need he get soaked by boarding her in deeper water. Perhaps he pulls his long outer garment up around his neck to keep it dry, or bundles it onto his head, so appearing, in his shirt, as a pale, grotesquely shaped figure, flitting along the surface of the sea. Be that as it may, the result is clearly stated – **they took him for a ghost** (6.49). When panic ensues, Jesus, who **wanted to go beyond them** (6.48), abandons his sandbank before reaching its end, where he had hoped simply to *step* aboard, wades straight to the boat and has to 'climb up' into it from deeper water. The disciples, having made such fools of themselves, are struck dumb and hardly know where to look.

Again, there is little original in this explanation, except perhaps the attention paid to times of day. It is merely common sense applied to Mark's actual words: but it shows that there is no need to suppose that the tale was distorted by 'homiletical or doctrinal interests', as V. Taylor suggested. The distortion occurs quite naturally through Peter telling the story, as people do, without seeing the need to explain what is perfectly clear to him; and Mark sets it down, too late for checking, as he had remembered but partly misunderstood it. Here the errors come from the evangelist, not the apostle.

The Sequel

There was nothing so very important in this episode, except for whatever decision Jesus reached on the hilltop – which we are not told. However, that day had made obvious that there would be little opportunity to train the disciples further while he was anywhere near Capernaum. It may be that, in his weeks of relative solitude, probably in Upland Galilee, while the Twelve were out on their journeys, Jesus had already begun to sense that he was being called to extend his mission to the south and to Jerusalem itself; which could only have one ending. For every reason, the further preparation of the apostles, who had completed their 'basic training', had to be his priority now.

When Jesus rejoined his disconcerted disciples in the boat, they went on (taking **crossing over** (*diaperasantes*) as being from Peter's point of view, so meaning 'completed our crossing back to the western shore') and landed further south, in the notably fertile region called Gennesaret. Here, less well known, he might have hoped that he could pursue his mission, or at least pass through, free from crowds obsessed with miracles. But no:

> **And when they had got out of the boat, people recognising him ran all over that district and they began to bring along on beds those who were afflicted to wherever they were hearing that he is. And anywhere at all that he came, into villages and towns and fields, in the**

> **market-places they laid the sick and begged that they might touch even the hem of his robe; and all who touched it were made well** (6.54ff).

We cannot tell what guidance Jesus had found in prayer on the hilltop, but he must have faced the choice between further teaching for the people and further instruction for his disciples; and clearly he understood that the latter were now the priority. Very soon he left Galilee, never to teach there again.

The story need be followed no further. Both 'miracles' in Mark 6 can be seen to have sensible explanations without rejecting Mark's text, merely examining it more carefully; its mistakes are clear examples of the pitfalls of oral transmission. The way is open to accept Mark's record as sound history, provided the possibility of errors of this sort is always kept in mind.

Notes to Chapter Seven

[1] In the days of compartment-trains, for example, Spanish travellers would never start eating without first offering to share their food with others; and I have seen it willingly shared, although a polite refusal is customary.

[2] *Epi to chlōrō chortō* means simply where the grass grew; *chlōros chortos* is the Septuagint phrase for any growing grass or vegetation (AV 'green herb'); the new grass of spring is *chloē* (Heb.*deshe*), eg. Ps.23.2). *Chlōros* ranges from pale green to the yellows of gold, honey, sand and egg-yolk, and is used of the 'pale horse' of Death (Rev.6.8).

[3] Luke 9.14 renders Mark's **by hundreds and by fifties** as **in parties of fifty**; but the numbers can only be rough estimates.

[4] Crossan 1991, pp.320, 398-404.

[5] Stories so similar are always likely to be two versions of one event; in this second version the details are all implausible, from Jesus going near the lake, or the boat, while he was abroad, trying to escape notice; to his allowing a crowd, even if they wished to, to stay with him for three days where they are bound to run out of food. Luke sensibly omits this second Feeding, as too he omits the Walking on Water.

[6] **About the fourth watch of the night** probably means, approximately, around 3am, when the fourth watch of the (Roman) night began. It was still too dark to see properly.

PART TWO: AWAY FROM GALILEE

EXCURSUS

BETWEEN THE LINES

Jesus' Travels

Although this study aims to work solely from the text and direct inference from that, in order to make any coherent story of Jesus' movements prior to his arrival at Jerusalem some reading between the lines is needed. What follows, italicised to distinguish it from the main study, simply suggests a possible sequence of movements which would make sense, of what is, and is not, said in Mark's text.

So far we have said little about Jesus' travels, beyond speculating that he was probably on his way to celebrate one of the major feasts at Jerusalem when he digressed to hear the Baptist and received his own call to service; and that after his time of solitude, he probably went on to Jerusalem, where he could at least explain to his acquaintance why he had failed to appear earlier. From the Passion story it seems probable that Jesus had friends at Bethany and in the city; probably people long known to his family, with whom he might have arranged to stay any time that he was coming up for a feast; and the temple could have seemed a good place to 'wait upon the Lord'. If he had spent as much as six weeks in solitude, it would have been close to Pentecost when he reached Jerusalem and the four fishermen might have come for that feast. The story certainly implies that he must, in any case, have met them somewhere, before he called them to follow him, and that is one obvious possibility.

In Galilee

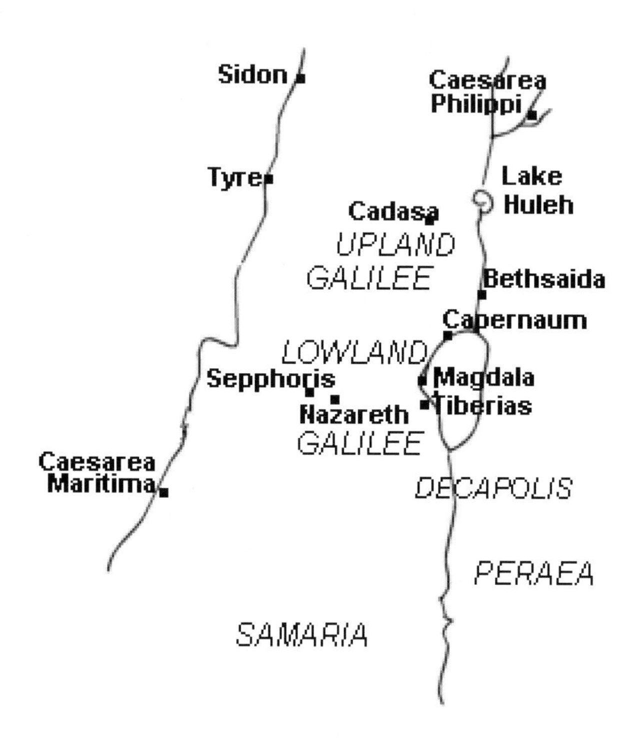

Of his next movements we know that, after John's arrest, Jesus came into Galilee preaching the great news that God's kingdom was soon to begin and that people must change their ways; and, having come, probably sooner rather than later, to Capernaum, he stayed there a short while with his first four disciples until the attention attracted by his first healings prompted him to leave on a tour of the other towns. At this time he would regularly have delivered his message at a synagogue every Sabbath.

After touring the country he comes back to Capernaum, and teaches indoors (2.1f). Why, when teaching was commonly done outdoors, and indoors meant such poor access for many? The answer must be that it was winter, the short season of cold and wet against which tourists today are always warned. As the people shivering in the open square in Jerusalem once shouted to Ezra, **'It is a season of heavy rain; we cannot stand here in the open'** *(Ezra 10.13). So we have here a first indication of time. If it is winter now, Jesus has had some months of summer and autumn to travel over Galilee, which would fit with the possibility that he originally set out to go to Passover in Jerusalem and in the end stayed there for Pentecost; if he came earlier to see the Baptist, his work in Galilee may have started soon after Passover. What seems sure is that after preaching around Galilee, Jesus had returned to spend the short winter at Capernaum, a clear inference from the text.*

(It seems that this was also when his family sought him out, since they also found him teaching indoors, with access difficult. If they had heard that he was wintering in Capernaum, instead of travelling around, that would have seemed a good opportunity to catch him. The visit to Nazareth probably followed once the rains had ended.)

Mark's outline twice mentions Jesus withdrawing to the highlands, and that is probably correct: choosing the Twelve the first time, during or before a spell of teaching the ordinary folk by the lakeside, but the second time concentrating on the training of the Twelve, perhaps taking them with him on a tour of the highland villages, before sending them out in pairs to proclaim the message themselves. He had the chosen Twelve with him during some of his lakeside teaching (4.10), but later gave up teaching the crowd so as to concentrate on the Twelve by themselves.

We have surmised that it was because his healings had attracted so many sufferers, and so many sensation-seekers, that he withdrew to Upland Galilee for a substantial time, while he first taught and then sent out his disciples; but as soon as he returned to Capernaum, throngs of people first made peace impossible even in the house, and then frustrated his plan for a quiet day with the Twelve.

It was now obvious that there would not, in Lowland Galilee, be any chance of peace and quiet; for not only at Capernaum, but now in Gennesaret, crowds immediately gathered: and **everywhere he went, into villages and towns and even out in the country, they set out the sick and begged him just to let them clutch the hem of his robe. And all those who clasped it were healed.** *Once more, healing was obstructing his proper work; and whereas previously he had withdrawn no further than Upland Galilee, now, even if he camped out with the Twelve in the remotest hills, that might not be enough. It is probable, too, that the short but cold and wet winter was again approaching, since he sought accomodation in a Gentile town, rather than wandering at large as he appears to* *have done both before and later. In that case he would have spent over a year on the various stages of his teaching in Galilee. The* ***incidents*** *Mark records do not, if totalled up, require so long; but there still remain periods of wandering in Decapolis and Iturea, the journey south, and the ministry in Perea, all to take place between, at most, early January and the beginning of April; hardly three full months. It seems impossible to include also the lakeside teaching, the training of the Twelve in Upland Galilee, and their mission, in that same period. If we accept that* ***two*** *winters may safely be inferred, the whole ministry of Jesus would seem to have spanned something between eighteen months and two years.*

The Sign of Jonah

Since the Feeding of Four Thousand (8.1-10) is surely a doublet for the Feeding of Five Thousand (6.35-56), and the unknown 'Dalmanutha' or 'Mageda' probably a mistake for Magdala, a fishing town in Gennesaret, then Mark 8.11-13, the sequel to the doublet, should follow the original story. We may suppose that Jesus and the Twelve returned, as sooner or later they surely would, to the boat left moored not far from Magdala (6.53):

> **The Pharisees came out [*from the town*] and began to argue with him, asking him for a sign from heaven, testing him *(ie., to prove his credentials)*. And having breathed out a great sigh, he says, 'Why does this generation want a sign? Truly I tell you, no sign shall be granted to this generation.' And having left them, having embarked again, he went away to the other side** (8.11ff).

Now, the verbal similarities between Matt.16.1-4, Matt.12.38f, Luke.11.29, and these three verses of Mark are considerable; but the last pair, from Q, have a longer version of the saying, in which no sign will be given to this generation ***except the sign of the prophet Jonah****. (Probably the evangelist added Jonah into Matt.16.1-4, which otherwise appears to be taken from Mark). Many conjectures have been made about this enigmatic phrase; starting with Matthew 12.40, that it was a reference to Jesus' burial and resurrection. However, it is possible to imagine Jesus, in the context suggested here, although already feeling himself urged by the spirit to go and preach in the south, in fact about to quit Galilee, going north; just as Jonah, called to prophesy in Nineveh to the east, fled westward, making for Tarshish. In any event, it sounds like a reference to a prophet leaving his own country.*

In every setting it is a disillusioned comment, which might well have sprung from Jesus' frustration at no longer being able to minister effectively in Galilee;

with perhaps a nagging doubt as to whether he was right to give priority next to further preparation of the Twelve to carry on his work, or whether he was simply, like Jonah, trying to evade the dangerous adventure set before him. Since he could be beset by doubt and fear in Gethsemane, so too he may have been puzzled and distressed when he first saw that his way was leading to a cross. To risk the possibility of beheading by Herod, as he had done from the start, was one thing; to face certain crucifixion if he carried his mission into the Roman prefecture of Judaea was another, and his mission might easily die with him.

Abroad

But with or without that final caustic comment, and whether as suggested here or in some other way, we are faced with the unusual case of a prophet apparently abandoning his task. **He arose from there and went away to the territory (ta horia**, *the boundaries)* **of Tyre** *(Mark 7.24a). By what route? A practical itinerary can at least be surmised.*

In Gennesaret, near 'Dalmanutha', the boat is again used to break contact with the crowd (8.13), and probably brought back to its normal place, on the shore near Capernaum. If they reached Capernaum at dusk, they could hope to leave the town that night, or early next morning, and make north into the highlands without attracting notice. They would surely have visited the house, for a meal and probably a night's sleep, and told those long-suffering women where they were going.

Since the Twelve are specifically present at Caesarea Philippi (and Peter, viewed as Mark's source, seems well informed about healings in the foreign places which Jesus had just visited) it is clear that Jesus took them with him when he left for Tyrian territory. He still needed to hear at leisure about their mission, to train them further, and to try to make them a cohesive, single-minded group. Probably he himself needed time and peace, now unattainable in his own country, to rethink his own mission,. Some Gentile town which might accommodate thirteen strangers without taking any great interest in them was indicated.

Tyrian territory was easily reached. Every city on the Greek model owned its own hinterland to supply its markets, and Tyre, being huge, had a territory stretching at this time from the coast eastward along the entire northern boundary of Galilee, to Lake Huleh and the marshes of the upper Jordan. It is not likely that Jesus needlessly went twice as far, to Tyre itself, when the much quieter town of Cadasa was less than twenty miles from Capernaum and only a few miles over the border.

And entering a house, he wanted nobody to know him, and he could not be concealed *(7.24b). Clearly, it got about that this was the healer from Galilee, and the Syro-Phoenician woman found him and made her plea. The successful healing of her daughter may have given Jesus not only satisfaction but reassurance, as a sign that God's power was still with him in these foreign parts. Nonetheless, he could not stay there, or the whole town would have been bringing its sick for him to heal, and quiet time with the Twelve would once again be impossible; whereas the priority, if he now foresaw his own death at Jerusalem, was to train them as replacements. So, as soon perhaps as there was a spell of decent weather – assuming that it was indeed winter when they went to 'the boundaries of Tyre' – Jesus set off to another Gentile area, on the east side of the Lake of Galilee: the Decapolis, the ten Greek cities strung out south and east of the lake to protect that area against raids from the desert.*

This is, notoriously, where Mark reveals his total ignorance of Near Eastern geography. **And leaving the territory of Tyre again he went through Sidon to the Sea of Galilee in the midst of the territory of the Ten Towns** *(7.31). Even if Jesus had gone much closer to the city of Tyre than is here suggested, Mark's assertion that he travelled from* **the boundaries of Tyre** *to the Sea of Galilee and Decapolis by way of Sidon is preposterous: Sidon being some twenty-five miles north from Tyre, its best route to Decapolis ran through Damascus!*

The conjecture by Wellhausen that the word should be Saidan, a version of Bethsaida, is the one that makes sense.[1] *Because of the impassably swampy Huleh valley (not drained until the 1950s), the practical route to the Decapolis from Cadasa, or even from Tyre itself, was to steer south-eastward and cross the upper Jordan near Bethsaida; officially renamed Julias when Philip had enlarged it to make a new 'city', the town would naturally still commonly be known by its old names.*

Mark 7.31 should therefore be read as: ***And leaving the territory of Tyre again he came through Bethsaida on the sea of Galilee and right on into (ana meson,*** *through the midst of* ***) the territory of the Ten Towns****; which would imply beyond the Golan hills, perhaps twice as far east and south of Capernaum as he had been north before. The lie of the country would make sense of returning later the same way, from the Decapolis as far as Bethsaida, before turning north along the upper valley of the Jordan towards Philip's other new city, Caesarea Philippi.*

The healing of the Blind Man is set in Bethsaida and belongs well enough where we find it; the healing of the Deaf-Mute might have taken place anywhere, but might possibly be a reason why Jesus, although not yet ready to re-enter Israel, came back from the Decapolis to Caesarea Philippi in Iturea.

Feeding Four Thousand?

Having got Jesus back near the Sea of Galilee in 7.31, Mark was able to insert next his Feeding of Four Thousand (8.1-10). Since there is later found the apparent insertion of a short document (13.14-20), probably because for one reason or another it was thought to have Peter's authority behind it, this story of Feeding Four Thousand might have been included similarly, because some senior Christian at Rome truthfully swore that he had heard it from Peter himself – and was unaware that he himself had improved on it.

However well the original crowd had been organised, its number would only have been guesswork, so very likely Peter said 'maybe five thousand' one time and 'four thousand or so' at another, and mentioned Magdala instead of just the region; but the less plausible details already mentioned suggest another tongue in the telling. Peter was no longer alive, to be consulted; and Mark, whose priority was 'to omit nothing', decided that he should include the tale.

Mark was quite prepared to believe that Jesus had walked upon the sea, so his critical sense would not have balked at the idea of a crowd being allowed to stay with Jesus for three days while they ran out of food; nor suspected that the 'Miraculous Food when Starving in the Desert' theme (8.3f) might have been suggested by Exodus 16. Nor would he know that there was no such place as 'Dalmanutha'. Today this episode may be disregarded as a mere doublet; but that, for Mark, was not an option, so he conscientiously included it and then, rather neatly, used the story of the Pharisees asking for a sign – which in his version ends with Jesus crossing the lake **to the other side** *– to move Jesus back to Bethsaida again and heal a blind man there (8.11ff).*

The obviously genuine story of the disciples naively taking Jesus' comment about the yeast of the Pharisees to refer to their omission to lay in bread (8.14-21) is probably a true sequel to the request for a sign (8.11-13), with criticism of over-sceptical Pharisees arising during the crossing (8.14, 21). However, both the request for a sign, and the available boat, would fit better before the withdrawal from Galilee, shortly after the Feeding of **Five** *Thousand, as suggested above. Jesus seems to be telling them not to be so silly as to suppose that he is making a fuss about the absence of food; was he not the one who had, a few days before, made them give their food away?*[2]

Caesarea Philippi

From Bethsaida, Jesus now went north again; but in Ituraea, east of the Jordan, not through Upland Galilee to the west. And he went off to the villages near Caesarea Philippi, **and on the road he was asking his disciples, saying to them, 'Who do people say that I am?'** (*The point of the question was not a wish to be hailed as Messiah, for that claim he promptly suppressed, telling them not to say it about him to anyone (8.30), but rather to lead into his explanation of the role and the fate which he saw before him as Son of Man.*

Notes to Excursus

[1] Cited by Taylor, 1953, p.353; Wellhausen conjectured a misreading; mis*hearing* is an even commoner source of error.

[2] The addition of the details from the second version of the Feeding -- seven brimful baskets of fragments as well as twelve good hampers (8.19f) – might mean that all of 8.14-21 came with the main Four Thousand story from that conjectural less reliable source; but possibly Mark is being editorial, trying to put down what he thinks must really have been said, or implied.

CHAPTER 8

The Son of Man, the Servant of God

Son of Man

If Jesus had left Galilee in order to find time and peace to reconsider his own mission as well as to teach his disciples, how did he now see himself and his task?

In Mark's gospel there are just two occasions when Jesus makes any statement about his own identity or role, as opposed to his purpose. Usually he may say that he has 'come out' to preach the gospel, or to call sinners, or to serve rather than to be served; but nothing about himself. Now, however, in a foreign land, near Caesarea Philippi in Iturea, he actually invites the disciples to tell him who people say he is, and then what they themselves think.[1]

The historicity of this interchange, as also of the second instance, when Jesus admits to the high priest that he is indeed **the Christ, the son of the Blessed**, has been questioned; but we shall see that there are good grounds for accepting both. The question of what they meant, however, cannot be considered apart from the meanings of the term 'son of man', which Jesus used on both occasions.[2]

Now in Mark, the only gospel with any claim to a valid chronology,[3] Jesus' use of the term 'son of man' to refer to himself is inseparable from the prediction of his suffering and resurrection. For, apart from two early instances (Mark 2.10, 28), in both of which the term probably had, originally, the meaning simply of 'a man' or 'a human being' (like 'sons of men' in Mark 3.28), the first use of 'son of man' is here at Caesarea Philippi:

> **Peter, answering, says to him, You are the Anointed. And he ordered them that they should not say (that) about him to anyone. And he began to teach them that the son of man had to suffer many things and be rejected by the elders and the high priests and the scribes and be put to death and after three days rise up. And he was speaking the word very plainly [...]** (8.29b-32).

It appears that Jesus began the discussion of his identity solely in order to introduce this picture of himself as the 'son of man' who would perish in Jerusalem.

Geza Vermes (1983, pp. 160-186) distinguishes three ways in which Jesus used the Aramaic term **bar nash(a)**, (*the*) *son of man*: for the human race in general, for himself in particular, and for the supernatural Son of Man found in Daniel 7.13:

> **I saw in the night visions,**
> **and behold, with the clouds of heaven,**
> **there came one like a son of man,**
> **and he came to the Ancient of Days**
> **and was presented before him** (*RSV*).

To argue, as some have, that all references in the gospels to the Danielic Son of Man are secondary is too easy an escape; Jesus preached the Coming Kingdom, and the evidence of the Synoptics is strong that he often used the Coming of the Son of Man to denote that 'Day of the Lord' which would begin the new era.[4] Vermes' exposition of **bar nash** is taken here as correct; but I suggest that in the particular use of 'son of man' to denote himself, Jesus did not use Aramaic **bar nash** at all, but the Hebrew **ben adam**. Barrett (1967, p.93) argues that to use the Hebrew form would be pointless because there is no difference of meaning; but that overlooks the important fact that they sound completely different.

Ben adam or its plural form are common in the Psalms, and neither is a difficult word; every Aramaic speaking Jew, even if he could only himself read Greek, could be expected to recognise that much Hebrew when he heard it. While most scholars hold that Jesus took for himself the Aramaic **bar nash** in Daniel 7.13, here it will be argued that it is the use of **ben adam** in Ezekiel, denoting the prophet himself, which is relevant.

Following Ezekiel

Ezekiel has usually been rejected as the source for Jesus' use of 'son of man' to mean himself because the apocalyptic content of many Synoptic sayings about the Son of Man *coming* (and notably Mark 14.62) clearly derives from Daniel 7.13.[5] Further, that part of Daniel was in Aramaic, Jesus' mother tongue. Here, however, I suggest that Jesus used Ezekiel's **ben adam** of himself precisely *because* it was different from **bar nasha,** so would not be confused with Daniel's apocalyptic Son of Man; and that the apocalyptic Son of Man references were also spoken by Jesus, but in no case referring to himself.

The second report of Jesus' foretelling of his death runs:

> **For he went on teaching (*edidasken*, imperfect tense) his disciples and telling them that the son of man is surrendered into the hands of men, and they will kill him, and having been killed he will rise up after**

> **three days.** ***But they were not understanding the saying (*****imperfect*****),*** **and they were afraid to ask him** (9.31f).

If proper attention is given to the final sentence, it is clear that, after the Resurrection (whatever the factual nature of that experience) Peter, for one, was convinced that they had not understood Jesus properly before. Yet, is it not more likely that they *had* understood what he meant then, but that this new, unexpected and overwhelming experience made them give his words a new meaning now?

Following the postulate that the humanity of Jesus was sane and normal, he could not possibly have claimed to be himself the mythical Son of Man from Daniel's fantasy; he might as well have announced himself as the archangel Gabriel. That Jesus accepted the reality of that supernatural Son of Man, who would come to judge mankind, is manifest in the Synoptic sayings; but that he ever claimed to *be* that supernatural figure, or that his disciples in his lifetime had ever thought that he did, does not appear to be reasonable, nor is it found in the texts of Mark and Luke. Even in Matt.25.31-46, the parable of the Last Judgement, it is only the church's post-Resurrection thinking which identifies Jesus as that kingly Son of Man, judging the sheep and the goats.[6]

Every saying in which the Son of Man is **coming**, or **seated on a throne** or **at the right hand of God**, or **with the clouds of heaven**, should be reckoned as the word of a genuine prophet, using Daniel's imagery; which, it may reasonably be supposed, gave a commonly understood picture of the Day of the Lord, with emphasis on the Judgement. (The solid evidence of Mark and Q, the two earliest strata of the surviving tradition, should sufficiently establish that the phrase was so understood in Jesus' time. It seems unsafe to reject such a body of evidence merely for lack of corroboration from what other contemporary sources there are.)

Apart from forecasts of his death, Jesus also applies ‘son of man’ to himself in those sayings about inconsistent criticism of the Baptist’s asceticism (**he is mad**) and of his own, normal, lifestyle (**glutton and drinker**) (Matt.11.19; Luke 7.34); and about **the son of man** having **nowhere to lay his head** (Matt.8.20; Luke 9.58). Both of these, by the disillusion in the one and the homelessness stressed in the other, would fit well into this last phase of Jesus' ministry. I suggest that Jesus had deliberately adopted a term without supernatural nuances to use for himself in the very special role to which he now felt called.

Ben adam, human being, would have been appropriate, because it sounded quite different from Daniel’s Son of Man (**bar nash**), and had no superhuman associations. Nor did it overtly make that dangerous claim to be a prophet; but the prophet Ezekiel is always addressed as **ben adam** by heavenly beings, stressing his subordinate, human status. Jesus might have found it a satisfactory term because it could express many aspects of his call to be God's obedient servant, of which a feeling of fellowship with Ezekiel was probably now one.

For Ezekiel is also sent to the house of Israel, **so that, whether they will listen or not dare** (to listen) – **for it is a provoking house** – **yet they shall know that you are a prophet in the midst of them** (Ezek.2.5). Although living in Babylon, so that he had to be **lifted up by the spirit** and **brought** to see the city (Ezek.11.1), Ezekiel focuses on Jerusalem throughout. The same warning which Jesus gives in the Vineyard allegory and in direct prophecy (Mark 12.9; 13.2), is set out in full by Ezekiel: the siege and fall of Jerusalem, the profanation of her holy places, her people's captivity, the ruin of the land. The end has come, the time is here, the day is at hand (Ezek.7.2f).

That Jesus was familiar with Ezekiel shows in two parables, the Lost Sheep and the Last Judgement. While the concept of God as the shepherd of Israel is common to Isaiah, Jeremiah and the Psalms, it is Ezekiel who most definitely has God searching for His lost ones:

> **Behold, I myself will search for my sheep and watch over them. As the shepherd seeks his flock on the day when there is darkness and cloud in the midst of the scattered sheep, so will I seek out my sheep [...] I will seek the lost one and I will guide back the stray** (Ezek.34.11f, 16).

Jesus as usual draws from Galilean life, presenting first the human shepherd recovering his lost sheep; but in declaring, **So it is not the will of my Father who is in heaven that one of these little ones should perish** (Matt.18.12ff), he is almost paraphrasing Ezek.18.23: **'Shall I desire in the slightest the death of the wicked,' says the Lord God, 'seeing that** [I desire] **that he should turn from his wicked path and live?'**, a thought repeated in Ezek.18.32 and 33.11. Jesus has added the ironic contrast between the sinner sought by God and the ninety and nine who need no repentance.

In the parable of the Last Judgement (Matt.25.31-45) Jesus has combined Daniel's Son of Man, of whose coming he spoke so often, with Ezekiel's repeated motif of the glorious throne, simply as the setting for the theme of judgement, in which he again echoes Ezekiel. For the separating of sheep from goats, the sheep to the right and the goats to the left, strongly echoes Ezek.34.17, 20:

> **As for you, my flock, thus says the Lord God: Behold, I will judge between sheep and sheep, rams and he-goats [...] Behold, I myself will judge between the strong sheep and the feeble sheep.**

Furthermore, the point Jesus is making with this judgement theme closely parallels Ezek.18, where the individual is to be judged only for his own deeds:

> **one who shall restore to the debtor his pledge, commit no robbery, *shall give his bread to the hungry and clothe the naked*, shall not lend at interest nor grab a profit, who shall turn back his hand from injustice, shall give a true judgement between a man and his neighbour, and has walked in my commandments and kept my ordinances, to do them – he is righteous** (Ezek.18.5-9)**.**

Jesus expands the concrete example of feeding the hungry and clothing the naked; and, just as Ezekiel had developed the idea of individual responsibility, so Jesus sharpened personal accountability by showing that the way we treat each other is the way we treat God, or more precisely, God's heavenly Judge:

> **Then the king will say […] 'I was hungry and you gave me food, I was thirsty and you gave me drink, I was a stranger and you housed me, I was naked and you clothed me, I was sick and you visited me, I was in prison and you came to see me.'**

Jesus, then, knew and valued Ezekiel, and must surely have had that prophet in mind while pondering his own mission to Jerusalem. His actions (Mark 10.32f; 11.16-18; 13.12) parallel the commands given to Ezekiel:

> **Therefore prophesy, son of man, set your face steadfastly towards Jerusalem, look towards their holy places, and you shall prophesy against the land of Israel** (Ezek.21.2)**; her priests also have cast aside my law and *profaned my sacred places* [...]** (22.26)**; son of man, *prophesy against the shepherds of Israel* [...] Look, you feed yourselves on the milk, you clothe yourselves with the wool [...] but you do not feed my sheep** (34.2f)**.**

Jesus indeed set **his face steadfastly towards Jerusalem** – Luke (9.51) uses Ezekiel's phrase exactly as given in the Septuagint – and began his mission in Jerusalem by clearing from the temple courtyard what he perceived as an abuse sanctioned for profit by chief priests 'feeding themselves on the milk': **'You have turned it into a robber's den'** (Mark 11.17). He took control of the outer courtyard himself (Mark 11.15f); and later he prophesied against the shepherds of Israel, specifically attacking the chief priests, as they well understood, in allegory (12.12), and greedy lawyers in plain speech (12.38ff).

Teaching daily in the temple (14.48), Jesus' fulfilled Ezekiel's own role:

> **Son of man, I have made you a watchman to the house of Israel, and you shall hear a word from my mouth and give them stern warning from Me** (Ezek.3.16f). **And whether they will listen or not dare to listen, for it is a provoking house, yet they shall know that you are a prophet in their midst** (2.5). **But the house of Israel will not be willing to listen to you, for they do not choose to listen to Me** (3.7).

This role, Jesus kept telling his disciples, was doomed to failure. They, no doubt, were thrilled by the enthusiasm with which the master was heard by great crowds: but Ezekiel had been warned not to be deluded by popularity: **They sit in front of you and hear your words [...] And you are to them like a sweet and well-tuned zither, for they will hear your words but they will not do them** (Ezek.33.31f). Jesus had perhaps learned that lesson in Galilee, where so often he contrasted hearing and doing.

A few, says Ezekiel, may respond: **if the ungodly man will restore the pledge, and repay what he has taken by robbery [...] he shall surely live** (33.15). This is the enduring hope of prophet and teacher, for not every seed falls on stony ground; and even failure may not be wholly in vain. Some, too, will escape the coming disaster: **When there are some of you who escape from the sword amongst the Gentiles [...] those of you who escape will remember me among the nations where they are carried captive** (Ezek. 6.8a, 9); and ultimately God will intervene to save the remnant of the nation, and re-establish it in peace and prosperity, under the rule of David (Ezek.34.22-31; 36.24-38; 37.1-28).

Jesus too saw the prophet's mission, though it cost his life, as necessary for the eventual restoration of his people: **For the son of man did not come to be served but to serve and to give his life as a ransom in exchange for many** (Mark 10.45). A ransom (*lutron*) is specifically a payment which secures release from captivity, and fits perfectly the picture of God rescuing his captive people:

> **I will make them *a covenant of peace* [...] and they shall know that I am the Lord when I have broken their yoke. And I shall deliver them from the hand of those who enslaved them,** (Ezek. 34.25, 27), God told

Ezekiel. **This is my blood of the [new] covenant, which is shed for many,** says Jesus.

Ezekiel was told that by faithfully discharging his mission he would, literally or metaphorically, save his own life (Ezek.3.19, 21), but Jesus had seen that literally to save his life was not possible, nor true to his calling, for whoever tries to save his life shall lose it (Mark 8.35). Nonetheless, it was vital that a true warning to the nation should be proclaimed at Jerusalem.

It is difficult to see how Jesus could have overlooked all the close parallels in Ezekiel. They may have helped his thinking, they would surely have reinforced the conclusion to which he was led; most of all by showing that even a mission foredoomed to failure might be part of God's purpose. The conclusion seems inescapable that, when undertaking the same task as Ezekiel, he adopted the same designation: son of Adam.

If Jesus distinguished between himself as **ben adam** and the Danielic figure as **bar nash**, why is there no trace of this in the gospels? Ultimately because, with the Septuagint already using *huios anthropou* for both, no verbal difference would have survived translation into Greek; but the two concepts were probably confused much earlier, in the mental and emotional turmoil in which, after Easter, the disciples had to do some urgent rethinking.

The Servant of God

Jesus, then, saw his role in this mission to Jerusalem as the same as Ezekiel's; but he had to look elsewhere to make sense of the outcome which he foresaw for himself. Understanding that he would not only be rejected, but would die in failure, Jesus may now have come to see his role, as Second Isaiah had seen the nation's, as the servant, son, or child of God, whose obedient suffering was somehow needed before God could remake the world.

It is noticeable that, whereas servant of God in the Old Testament is commonly rendered as ***doulos*** *(*servant, slave*)* ***theou*** by the Septuagint, ***pais theou*** is the usual term in Second Isaiah's four Suffering Servant poems. ***Pais*** also dominates the context surrounding the Songs, with variations on the key theme, ***pais mou ei, exelexamen se*** (You are my servant/son, I have chosen you). ***Pais***, as shown in Chapter One, primarily means young son, and when used of a slave or servant would imply the paternalistic relationship, almost a friendship, enjoyed by a good servant in a good family.

This usage becomes very clear in the second Song (Isa.49.1-6), which, exceptionally, also uses ***doulos***. Here are ***doulos mou su ei***, you are my slave (v.3); ***doulon heauto***, His own slave (v.5); but the payoff is, It is a great thing for you to be called my son (***paida mou***, v.6). ***Pais*** is what the good servant is called, in appreciation of good service. If, as suggested earlier, the Greek version of the scriptures was the text which Jesus is most likely to have been able to read and learn, he would know the Servant, depicted so clearly as an individual sufferer in the Third and Fourth Songs (Isa.50.4-10; 52.13-54.12) as ***ho pais theou***.

It is not suggested that Jesus was unaware that this meant the servant of God, but rather that the use of ***'pais'*** overlapped or even fused the ideas of son and servant, so that the term 'son of God' could equally well mean the prophet, the servant of God. There was no hard and fast distinction in metaphor between the servant and the son, for, as Harvey (pp.159-162) has expounded, a son was obedient to, learned from, and acted for, his father. So too will Isaiah's servant.

Here, then, may be an explanation for Jesus' unambiguous admission later to the high priest that he was the 'son of God'; for in his own deepest experiences, the baptism and the 'transfiguration' vision, the heavenly voice had 'spoken' of him as **son**. Isaiah's Servant Songs show how Jesus could have understood the term in relation to himself and the prophetic role to which he had been called; and, as he followed his call and proclaimed his message in Jerusalem, he could not deny that he was the son, any more than he could deny that he was God's anointed, once the question could no longer be parried or evaded (Chapter.14 below).

Thus the understanding of 'the son of God' as the rejected servant of God in Isaiah's Fourth Servant Song (Isa.52.13-53.12) is the key to the rest of Jesus' revised idea of his mission. By Ezekiel he is guided to go to Jerusalem, and to preach there his word from God, knowing that they will not listen: but it is only in Isaiah that truly, as Jesus said, **'it is written of the son of man** (*ie. myself, the servant of God*) **that he will suffer many things and shall be treated with contempt'** (Mark 9.12); and it is Isaiah who stresses also the positive side, that somehow the servant, through his sufferings, will bring peace and healing to the erring nation (Isa.53.5, 11).

Vindication at the Judgement

Although the Septuagint has been even more definite than the Hebrew about the servant's end (**for his life is taken away from the earth; because of the iniquities of my people he was led to death.** Isa.53.8), yet it is also as clearly written that the servant, in spite of all his sufferings, **shall be exalted and glorified exceedingly** (Isa.52.13), **that he shall divide the spoils with the mighty, because he delivered his soul to death, and he was numbered among the transgressors** (Isa.53.12). Although Resurrection at God's Coming and

Vindication in the Day of Judgment belong to a later period of Jewish thought than that of Isaiah, Jesus believed in both (Mark 13.24-27; Mark 8.38), so they were the obvious way for him to understand Isaiah's promises.

Such later thinking is found, for example, in 2 Maccabees (7.9, 11, 23, 29), and is set out at length in the Wisdom of Solomon:

> **But [godless men] said in their twisted reasoning [...] 'Let us lie in ambush for the upright man [...] for he opposes the things we do [...]. he criticizes us as law-breakers and traitors to our heritage. He has knowledge of God, he claims; he calls himself the child of the Lord. He has arisen as a challenge to all our ideas [...] He says that the end for upright people is happy, and boasts that God is his father'.**
>
> **'Let us see if his words are true [...] For if the upright man is the son of God, God will claim him and save him from the hands of his enemies. Let us condemn him to a shameful death, for by his own words he will be looked after'** (2.1, 12-20).
>
> **But the souls of upright people are in the hand of God [...] In the eyes of the foolish they seemed to die, and their going is reckoned distressing, their leaving us a disaster; but they are at peace. [...] their hope of immortality is complete. And at the time of the Coming [...] They shall be judges and kings over the nations of the world, and their Lord shall be king for ever and ever. Those who have put their trust in Him shall know the truth, and those loyal in love shall dwell with him** (3.1-4, 7-9).
>
> **Then the honest man shall stand, full of confidence, before his oppressors [...] and they shall be horrified to see him miraculously preserved [...] Filled with remorse they will say [...] 'This was the man who used to be our laughing-stock, a byword for our scorn. See how he is counted among the sons of God, and his inheritance is with the saints!'**(5.1-3, 5).

While Maccabees and Wisdom may both tentatively be dated to the first century BC, it is not sure that they were in circulation in Jesus' lifetime, much less that he knew them; but they are good evidence for the way some Jewish thought had been developing.

Also, in the passage above the writer makes no distinction between the ambiguous ***pais theou,*** servant or son of God, in Wis.2.13 and the unmistakable

huios theou, the son of God, five verses later. 'Son of God' would naturally have here the sense of one who faithfully does God's will; the only meaning, when applied to a human, that it could possibly have for any Jew (Vermes, 1983, pp.192-200).

After Three Days

There can therefore be no justification for claiming that Jesus could never have predicted his own death nor his, eventual, resurrection. Nor need we doubt that the whole forecast was repeated again and again. Three repetitions make a story-teller's norm, but Jesus probably told the disciples a dozen times. The detail in Mark's third version (10.34) is indeed too precise to be credible – hindsight has led someone to exaggerate; but that is a common development in oral transmission, and in no way discredits the forecast itself. Common to all three, however, is the phrase **after three days.**

This, almost certainly, was because he supposed that he, with all 'the righteous', would rise from the dead at the Day of the Lord; or more precisely, three days after. Later than Jesus, Rabbinic writings show the belief that the general resurrection of the dead would take place on the third day of the new era. Of the various passages collected by H. K. McArthur, the last he cites is most striking:

> **All its inhabitants shall taste of death for two days, when there shall be no soul of man or beast upon the earth [...]** ***On the third day He will renew them all and revive the dead*****, and he will establish it before Him, as it is said, 'On the third day he will raise us up and we shall live before Him'.**[7]

This seems to have been almost exactly what Jesus himself believed and trusted; but the astonishing events of Eastertide compelled the disciples to change their interpretation to one of immediate, individual, resurrection, with Jesus as precisely **the *first-fruits* of those who have fallen asleep**, in Paul's phrase (1 Cor.15.20).

It is a sign of the authenticity of Mark's wording that the rising again is always (in the best readings) to be **after three days**. Hosea had said **after two days** and **on the third day**:

> **Let us go and return to the Lord our God,**
> **for He has torn us apart and will heal us,**
> **He will wound and He will bandage us.**

After two days he will heal us.
On the third day we shall rise again
and we shall live in His presence
and we shall know Him. (Hos.6.1-3)

The rabbinic dictum cites **on the third day**; and Matthew and Luke do the same. Since the tomb was found empty only thirty-six hours or less *after* the burial (from, say, 5pm on Friday to, say, 5am on Sunday) it probably sounded inappropriate, however one reckoned, to call that 'after *three* days', although Hosea's two would have been appropriate enough. The church sensibly adopted the more suitable phrase to fit the circumstances, Matthew and Luke both using **on the third day**, with many texts of Mark 10.34 apparently modified to conform. Since Mark has nonetheless preserved **after three days**, that is almost certainly what Peter had said. That might be his error; but perhaps Jesus himself had used a looser formulation, like his **today, tomorrow and the third day** in Luke 13.32. If not even the Son, but only God Himself could know the exact day and hour of the Coming (Mark 13.32), perhaps Jesus chose not to presume to exact knowledge of its details, either.

That he would rise at the general resurrection was a consolation which any man could have offered to his friends, without even the benefit of prophetic inspiration or second-sight, but only from religious belief. Jesus' death, once he preached his message of the imminent Coming of God's Kingdom in Roman Judea, was inevitable; and his trust in the mercy of God, who would raise his faithful servants when that Day came, was absolute.

It is most unlikely that any human foresight, however inspired, could have envisaged the startling experiences which the disciples were to have so soon after his death; for even if second-sight, of which well-documented cases do indeed exist, is invoked, the prediction of exact times does not appear to be part of that mode of 'knowing'. **Within the lifetime of this generation** seems to have been the nearest Jesus could give for the date of the impending disasters; **after three days** could be a deliberately imprecise rendering of one minor detail of a theological proposition in which he firmly believed, not psychic foreknowledge.

The Final Task

Jesus, then, has seen his prophetic role as leading him to a certain death, and his death somehow as a part of God's purpose to redeem the nation. Ever since his baptism he had known himself 'anointed' to the service of God as a prophet.

> **The spirit of the Lord is upon me, because He has anointed me; He has sent me to preach glad tidings to the poor, to heal the broken in heart, to proclaim liberty to the captives and recovery of sight to the blind** (Isa.61.1).

It is perhaps unlikely that Jesus used these words of himself at Nazareth, as Luke would have us believe (Luke 4.18), but he must have known them, and understood them to define precisely who he was, and what he was about, in Galilee.

Driven now to take centre-stage on the national scene, it is certainly possible that he understood himself as the Anointed in the special sense of that national leader who would bring in the kingdom; but he would do so at the cost of his own life, which ruled out any prospect of earthly kingship as the Messiah. It was urgent that he should prepare his disciples for that disappointing outcome.

Thinking over the relative failure of his Galilean mission (Matt.11.20-24; Luke 10.13ff), he may have come to see that his aim had always been impossible; that his own call, like Ezekiel's, was not to succeed but to go and fail. Yet, in obedience to that inner voice, he must still proclaim his message as widely as possible and carry the challenge to change one's ways into the heart of the nation, the holy city, where change was badly needed; but with no better hope than to die true to what he taught. Somehow, his obedient failure would advance God's plans; and he must go forward in trust, the doomed prophet of the kingdom to come.

So now, at Caesarea Philippi, **he began to teach them that the son of man must suffer many things and be rejected by the elders and the chief priests and the scribes and be killed and after three days to rise again** (8.31). Peter decided to advise Jesus otherwise, and was very firmly rebuffed; and Jesus went on at once to show how the lesson applied also to his disciples; telling not only them but the ordinary folk who have come to hear him: **If anyone wants to become my follower, he must forget his own interests *and take up his cross* and follow me.** The stakes have been raised: no longer is it enough to abandon home and goods and family and go blithely out to preach the good news. His disciples must understand where this may lead them, and be willing to risk their lives, too; for to treat keeping your life as really important is a sure way to render it worthless (8.34-38).

Notes to Chapter Eight

[1] The substance of this chapter has been set out at length in two articles, published in *Faith and Freedom* nos.163 and 165.

[2] Since our earliest Greek gospels are written entirely in small capitals, all capitals in the English text, or in a modern Greek edition, are the editor's doing. Henceforward I use 'Son of Man' for the heavenly being in Daniel 7.13, 'son of man' for all other uses.
[3] We have argued in the introduction that John is pure fiction, that Matthew's time scheme is based on Mark's, and that Luke's independent time-scheme belongs to a less reliable tradition.
[4] Discounting duplication, there are 3 instances in Mark, 6 in Q, 6 more found only in Matthew or only in Luke.
[5] Hooker rightly disallows Schweizer's attempt to justify derivation from Ezekiel by discounting all apocalyptic references as later additions (Hooker,1991, pp.90ff).
[6] In Acts 7.56 it is again inference by others which claims that the heavenly Son of Man seen by Stephen was Jesus.
[7] See McArthur, 'On the Third Day' in *New Testament Studies 18, '71/'72*, pp.81-86.

CHAPTER 9

The Road to the South

The Vision

The three chosen disciples who accompanied Jesus on his brief visit to the mountain (9.2-13) must have been torn between hope and fear; for while he had not denied that he was God's Anointed, he had foretold to them his own suffering and death. The vision is precisely dated, six days after that day near Caesarea Philippi when Jesus had first begun to tell them of his own death and Peter had objected.

(The place was most probably the same hill-site, almost certainly in Upland Galilee, to which the Twelve had once been summoned and where their training had begun, a site which would have been both familiar and significant. There is possibly a hint that the place is already special when Peter exclaims ***'Master, it is good that we are here'****, and suggests that on that site they should build three shelters to house Jesus, Moses and Elijah.)*

It seems that both aspects of such an experience, the hallucinatory and the psychological or spiritual, can be shared amongst a group;[1] presumably through telepathy with the first visionary. We have Peter's description of what he thought he was seeing and hearing, although he says that it unsettled his wits to the extent that he was babbling nonsense; we may surmise that Jesus too 'saw' Moses and Elijah offering him their support, and 'heard' again the voice from his baptism, claiming him as God's obedient son. If Jesus' understanding of that role is to be inferred from this vision, one reading would be that he saw Elijah, who had already reappeared as John the Baptist, and Moses, who had promised to send the nation a prophet like himself, both confirming him as Moses' prophet and encouraging him to go forward courageously until he, like the reborn Elijah, should meet his death.

The vision's message was something not to be disclosed, until Jesus was not only dead but risen (9.9). This implies that it was therefore a declaration of his being God's Anointed, in one sense or another; since that was the avowal which he would never let the disciples make; which, for as long as he could, he refused to make himself (11.28); and which finally brought, as he knew it would, his instant condemnation (14.62ff). It was certainly a possibility for him now to understand himself as the Anointed in the sense of the last prophet sent to the nation before the Day should Come;[2] and his mind seems to have been running along those lines:

> **And they were asking him, saying, 'How is it that the scribes say that first Elijah must come?' But he was saying to them, 'Elijah indeed comes first and restores everything. And how has it been written of the Son of Man? That he should suffer many things and be treated with contempt.[3] But I tell you that Elijah has indeed come, and they have done to him whatever they chose, as it has been written of him'** (Mark 9.11ff)**.**

At the least, he was seeing his role as 'Son of Man' as complementary to that of the Baptist, and the Baptist's as the return of Elijah; so that, unless Jesus was claiming to be God's apocalyptic superman from Daniel 7.13, it appears that, as they all walked back to rejoin the rest, he was seeing himself as God's last human prophet before the apocalypse which, he was sure, was imminent.

The Last of Galilee

(To reach that hill in Upland Galilee they would have had first to come south and round the Huleh marshes again; so the obvious move would have been to bring the whole group down to Bethsaida. The small party of four could walk the twelve or fifteen miles into the hills during a day, which would not be unduly arduous, and would allow time to rest and escape the noonday heat on their journey. That evening, perhaps, they would gather for prayer on the hill-top, and experience their vision. Next morning they would start straight back, and rejoin the rest before evening.

This would seem now to be the third time that Jesus and the Twelve had recently come to, or passed near, Bethsaida; a largely Jewish town, although not, at this time, included in Galilee. If there is truth in Luke's story of the despatch of some seventy other disciples to Peraea (Luke 10.1ff) – which some indications later in Mark tend to confirm – then, to anyone curious about the logistics of organising such a meeting when travelling about with the Twelve, Bethsaida is the key. Jesus had only to ask one or two disciples from Bethsaida[4] – which is so near to Capernaum that there would surely have been some – to gather others at Bethsaida before he returned from the Decapolis. Meeting them there on his second visit to the town, he could instruct and despatch them, before himself going north towards Caesarea Philippi. (Equally, he might have issued the summons as he passed through Bethsaida the second time, and dispatched them to Peraea when he returned from Caesarea Philippi. That such a piece of organisation should be unknown to Mark implies only that Peter had never found a need to include it in his teaching, nor happened upon it in casual reminiscence.

One reason for believing that the other disciples were indeed sent off to Peraea is the double benefit to Jesus of doing that. Committed now to going up to Jerusalem to confront the authorities there, he would not be able, probably did not wish, to linger long on the way; these disciples, however unskilfully they expressed the great news, could ensure that all who wished to hear Jesus in Peraea were alert for his coming. Secondly, if he was to pass unnoticed through Galilee (9.30), it was imperative that these other disciples, who of all people would have flocked to him at the first rumour of his return, should have been sent on somewhere else.

Later that same evening, as darkness was gathering and few folk were about, Jesus and the Twelve could have walked the few miles from Bethsaida to the house at Capernaum, which, since fishermen tend to live close to the water, might probably have been on the outer fringe of the town. It may have been on this short walk that there was an argument as to which of them was most important; arising perhaps from the singling out, maybe the previous day, of three to accompany Jesus on a trip which they now refused to discuss; with possibly, as suggested earlier, Andrew put in charge of the rest. The dispute would perhaps have concerned only the relative status of these four fishermen, the earliest and probably eldest disciples, whom none of the others could easily rival; but every one could, and would, air an opinion.)

Jesus, having got the disciples safely indoors, was quick to give them a better idea of greatness, with a handy toddler to point the lesson (9.33-37). As Hooker points out, the closing verse, 9.37, **Whoever receives one such child in my name, receives me** would more appropriately end the rebuke to the disciples for trying to stop their master from being bothered with children, found later in Mark 10.13-16; while 10.15, **Truly I tell you, whoever does not receive the Kingdom of God like a child shall not enter it**, could more aptly come here, ending the lesson on humility. As the two sayings are so similar, it would not be very surprising if Mark, or possibly even Peter, had reproduced them in the wrong contexts.

They did not linger at Capernaum:

> **And leaving there they were making their way along through Galilee, and he did not want anyone to know. For he was teaching his disciples and he kept saying to them that, 'the son of man is delivered into the hands of men, and they will kill him, and when killed, after three days**

> **he will rise up.' But they did not understand the saying, and they were afraid to ask him** (9.30-33).

Mark puts this paragraph earlier; either way, the problem is to combine a general paragraph – in which **leaving *there*** probably meant leaving Bethsaida – with a self-contained anecdote which finishes in the (Capernaum) house. The argument might have happened on some earlier occasion, but would fit well at this stage in the story. It is followed by the story of John reporting that they had objected to someone who was not of their fellowship exorcising in the name of Jesus, important because of the positive ruling that **Whoever is not against us is for us** (9.40). Mark then adds in a sequence of sayings, connected only by verbal links.

Peraea

> **And having got up from there (probably still Capernaum) he comes into the land of Judaea and the far side of the Jordan (ie. Peraea], and once more crowds flock to him, and, as he usually did, he was teaching them** (10.1).

Mark Ch.9 and Ch.10 contain various teachings and anecdotes perhaps because this was Mark's last chance to fit in stray items before his Passion story commenced; but the bid by James and John for special status beside the glorified Jesus seems fittingly placed here, with Jesus' repeated foretelling of his resurrection convincing the disciples that the Coming of the Lord was very near, and the vision on the mountain having hinted that Jesus would rank high in the new dispensation. The Bar Zebedees, and their indignant friends, are all again reminded that rank and status are not what Jesus is offering, but rather the opportunity to serve; and it is here that Jesus states clearly that his role is to give his life for the good of the nation – **a ransom for many** must surely be seen in the national context. If he had not thought of his mission thus at the start, the Transfiguration experience should have put it past doubt. It is the national revival of Israel which alone can lead all the world to God (Isa.55.5; 56.3-8: Zech.14.16ff).

There is no indication of how long Jesus was able to spend in Peraea. On the hypothetical time scheme suggested earlier (with Jesus probably intending to spend the worst of the winter in the Gentile town of Cadasa), both his wanderings in Decapolis and Iturea, and the teaching in Peraea, would have to fit into, roughly, February and, say, three weeks of March; with Passover coming near the end of that month or early in April. It is likely enough that February was mostly spent out of the country, and the first two or three weeks of March in Peraea; but we cannot be exact. Eventually, however, Jesus took the road again to reach Jerusalem in time for the feast.

The Seventy

The basic truth of Luke's Mission of the Seventy to Peraea, although most of its detail seems to be taken from the sending out of the Twelve, is confirmed by the unexplained reappearance in Mark of these other followers, on the road to Jerusalem. After a section of teaching (9.38-10.31) the narrative resumes:

> **They were on the road, going up towards Jerusalem, and Jesus was ahead of them and they were very perplexed, while those who followed were afraid** (10.32).

Now if 'they' comes from Peter saying 'we', which here must mean the Twelve; 'those following' make little sense except as Jesus' other disciples, who could at least have gleaned enough about the outcome which he foretold to have reason to be afraid. The identity of the leading group, and their distinction from the rest, are immediately confirmed:

> **And taking the Twelve aside again he began to tell them the things that were about to happen to him, that, look, we are going up to Jerusalem, and the son of man will be handed over to the chief priests and the scribes, and they will condemn him to death and hand him over to the foreigners and they will mock him and spit on him and flog him and kill him, and after three days he will rise up** (10.32ff).

This suspiciously accurate third version suggests that here Peter is recalling the event more clearly than the prophecy; but that Jesus did try to prepare them as fully as he could for the trouble to come is wholly probable. If *anabainontes*, going up, is taken literally, this episode might belong on the 3,500ft climb from Jericho in the Dead Sea Valley to Jerusalem; but the verb is customarily used also of 'going up' to Jerusalem in a more general sense. Rightly or wrongly, Mark sets this third prophecy before they have reached Jericho, having rounded his Peraean section off with the Bar Zebedees' bid for glory.

Jericho

There is no reason to doubt that this was the single occasion during his ministry that Jesus came to Jericho; for only the fourth Gospel's frequent, but probably fictional, visits to Judaea would suggest otherwise. Luke makes room here for his Zacchaeus story by placing the blind man just *before* they reach Jericho.

Mark, however, tersely relates: **And they came to Jericho. And as he was leaving Jericho** (10.46). This odd phrasing lent itself conveniently to interpolation later by the Gnostic author of 'Secret Mark'; and it has led Morton Smith in his book *The Secret Gospel* to insist that something was cut out of the original text of Mark to make this gap. Although that need not be so, the phrasing does raise the question of what Jesus really did do in Jericho which would account for this pause in the flow of Peter's narration, yet not deserve special mention. The obvious answer is that they spent the Sabbath there; probably attending synagogue, where Jesus may even have spoken, but without any incident which called for comment. It seems likely that they arrived at Jericho on a Friday, and departed on the first day of the following week (our Sunday), and it was only as they were leaving that anything memorable happened.

This was the cure of blind Bartimaeus: a Petrine story, shown not merely by the usual **And they** [...] **and he**, but also by the tautology of **the son of Timaeus, Bartimaeus**, which suggests instant translation by the oral narrator; doubly redundant here, since Peter is putting Greek back into Aramaic.

And at once he recovered his sight and followed him down the road. It seems unnecessary to suppose that 'following' or the alternative translation 'along the way' imply discipleship here, literal or metaphorical; rather, it is the final scene in a vividly told story, the healed man following for a while in thankfulness and for the sheer joy of being able to walk freely once more.

Notes to Chapter Nine

[1] Tyrrell 1947, pp.65ff; Ludemann 1994, pp.106f. (I do not accept Tyrrell's ideas about after-life, still less Ludemann's.)

[2] Most subsequent Messianic pretenders have been prophets, not warriors (Rosten 1971, pp.487-93).

[3] Hooker, p.220, suggests this as a possible reading of a difficult passage.

[4] John 1.44 is probably right to say that Philip was from Bethsaida. Philip is reported to have settled in Hierapolis, and his married daughter lived at Ephesus, so family details could have been known in the area where the fourth gospel was most likely written; and Bethsaida seems to be mentioned only as scrap of genuine local knowledge put in to lend verisimilitude (cf. John 5.2, 11.18, 19.13).

PART THREE: JERUSALEM

CHAPTER 10

Sunday: Riding to Jerusalem

Foreword

To follow through the last week of Jesus' earthly life inevitably invites comparison with that fine book, *The Last Week*, by Marcus Borg and J. D. Crossan. The numerous discrepancies which may appear between their account and mine arise from the fact that theirs, like the fourth Gospel, is primarily designed to present a powerful picture of what Jesus should mean to us today. It is a call to action in the modern world, and the authors' reading of history is perhaps distorted slightly by viewing the Roman Empire in terms of those modern oppressive regimes which they rightly oppose; whereas, it cannot be too often stated, during the reigns of Augustus and Tiberius the Roman empire was the best government the world had then seen, and a great deal better than most which have succeeded it. The flaw was that this depended entirely on having a conscientious and able emperor: from 37-70 AD, Caligula, Claudius and Nero let venality and oppression engender all those political evils which are sometimes mistakenly transposed to the earlier period, and which culminated in a hideous five-year war. We should not suppose that there was serious opposition to Roman rule in Palestine during Jesus' lifetime, and his own teaching on tax points towards acquiescence in the *de facto* government. Believing that all earthly government would shortly come to an end, he urged individuals to be more generous and less acquisitive, to ameliorate the actual social and economic evils around them. This too remains as a challenge for today.

More important than any minor distortion of history, however, is the fact that in *The Last Week*, as in the Fourth Gospel, history is subordinate to dramatic effect. The authors state candidly that they are *not* attempting a historical reconstruction, their concern is with the deepest issues involved, the 'passions of Jesus'. Theirs is, in fact, what Clement would call a 'spiritual gospel'; and of great value as such.

We may appropriately illustrate their dramatic use of history by noting that they affirm that Pilate entered Jerusalem with his troops on the same afternoon as

Jesus rode the borrowed donkey. In fact, there no evidence for when Pilate arrived, and common sense suggests that he would have arrived several days earlier, so avoiding confrontation with crowds of excited pilgrims, and obeying the military principle of getting your troops there first. But Borg and Crossan are perfectly right to present their message dramatically, and they do not claim to be writing history. Hence there is no need for concern when this more pedestrian study presents as fact what they have treated otherwise.

A Watchman for the House of Israel

I have maintained that Jesus at his baptism heard himself called to God's service as a prophet, to foretell the imminent Coming of God's kingdom, and that that was how he was seen and saw himself throughout his Galilean Ministry. His new task, to deliver his prophecy at Jerusalem also, if it altered his view of himself at all, would merely have confirmed that he had been 'anointed' as that prophet 'like Moses' who, now that Elijah had returned and been killed (9.13), would be the last forerunner of the Coming. It was as a prophet, and only as a prophet, that he would present himself in Jerusalem; but it would be more than ever important never to claim that status in so many words.

The Approach

It appears that Jesus had spent the Sabbath quietly at Jericho, and left on Sunday morning with his disciples. Although it was only fifteen miles to Jerusalem, and a mile or two less to Bethany, which may have been as far as he intended to go that day, they would have set out early to make the best use of the coolest hours of morning. The healing of Bartimaeus did not delay them long, so that, leaving Jericho between six and seven, and allowing for a slow pace because Jesus and his young men, used to hill country, would know better than to hasten up a climb of some three to four thousand feet, they could still have covered some twelve miles or so before midday.

It is quite late in the day, however, when they reach the temple in Jerusalem (Mark 11.11), not two miles further than Bethany. It was therefore after siesta time when Jesus set out on his ride to Jerusalem; and the natural explanation for the missing hours is that around noon they had found a shady spot where they could stop to eat, perhaps bread, with a handful of olives and a drink of wine, and then take their rest. They would by now be quite near Bethany, where Jesus and the Twelve were to stay; but it would be inconsiderate for so large a party to present themselves just as their hosts were about to eat, nor should guests arrive while their hosts are taking their afternoon rest. It was more thoughtful to wait until siesta time was over before covering the small remaining distance to Bethany. It seems likely that it was during the quiet of the afternoon that the thought or impulse came to Jesus to ride to Jerusalem.

An Inner Voice?

There are various theories as to why Jesus staged what is seen as a symbolic act, while others claim that the tale is too reminiscent of Zechariah 9.9 to be true; but the fact may be that this was an occasion when Jesus was 'driven by the spirit' to perform an unpremeditated action whose purpose was not, at the time, clear even to him: as he had been after his baptism.[1]

George Fox was once driven to abandon his shoes in a wintry field and walk barefoot into Lichfield.

> Then I was commanded of the Lord to pull off my shoes. I stood still, for it was winter. And the word of the Lord was like a fire in me. So I put off my shoes and left them with the shepherds [...] Then I walked on about a mile and as soon as I was within the city, the word of the Lord came to me again saying: "Cry "Woe until the bloody city of Lichfield!' " So I went up and down the streets, crying with a loud voice: 'Woe to the bloody city of Lichfield!' It being market-day, I went to the market-place and to and fro to the several parts of it, and made stands, crying as before [...] and no one laid hands on me. But as I went thus through the streets, there seemed to me to be a channel of blood running down the streets, and the market-place appeared like a pool of blood (Fox, *Journal, 1651)*.

Here is a person who habitually 'waited upon the Lord' receiving, from or through his subconscious mind, an intense compulsion to do something with no apparent sense nor purpose; and he obeyed absolutely, in spite of initial reluctance. William James, indeed, picked this particular incident to back his claim that 'Even more perhaps than other kinds of genius, religious leaders have been subject to abnormal psychical visitations;' choosing Fox because,

> No one can pretend that in point of spiritual sagacity and capacity, Fox's mind was unsound. Everyone who confronted him personally, from Oliver Cromwell down to county magistrates and jailers, seems to have acknowledged his superior power (James 1902, Introduction).

Such an admittedly unusual experience is therefore perfectly compatible with sanity and great ability. It is, however, unlikely to happen except to those who make listening to God their constant, rather than occasional, concern.

Fox's impulse began when he sighted the spires of Lichfield cathedral, 'and they struck at my heart'. Supposing that something of the same nature as what Fox experienced could also have been the experience of a greater religious leader than he, there might have been a visual trigger, like a glimpse of a young donkey, tethered just inside the village street, across from where they were resting – **the village over against us**. Just as Fox's message came in words from Nahum, the compulsive urge might then have presented itself to Jesus in some of Zechariah's words (which only Matthew quotes in this context):

> **Look, the king is coming to you, just and healing,**[2]
> **He is meek and riding on a donkey, even an untried foal** (*Zech.9.9);*

If Jesus had no pretensions to being a king, as that term was generally understood, he could not deny that he was the Lord's Anointed in a different sense, with a mission to lead the nation; and 'just and healing' he certainly was.

The commandeering of the animal is perhaps best explained, not as a conscious claim to a royal prerogative (Harvey, p.123), but as a response to some inner compulsion. Jesus chooses two disciples; probably from amongst 'those who followed', those other disciples who could better be spared to take the animal back later. He tells them to say, if challenged, **The Lord needs him** – meaning, surely, not himself, the prophet, nor the donkey's owner, but the Lord in whose name he spoke and whose instructions he was trying to obey[3] – **and is sending him back here again at once**. Receiving a message from the prophet that God required the donkey and would see to its safe return, it is not surprising that the owner let it go.

Riding to the City

> **So they bring the colt to Jesus and throw their cloaks over it and Jesus got on it. And many spread their cloaks in the road, but others (were) cutting brushwood in the fields.**[4] **And those leading and those following were calling out 'Hosanna! Blessed is the one who comes in the name of the Lord. Blessed is the coming kingdom of our father David. Hosanna in the heights of heaven!'**

Most of their words were the standard welcome to the pilgrim, from Psalm 118.25f; [5] but these enthusiasts seem to have added in a slightly muddled reference to the coming Kingdom of God, crossed with the restoration of the kingdom of David. Jesus had always emphasized that what God's Kingdom required was a new way of living, but that Kingdom could certainly have been expected to restore independence to Israel, and these young disciples would definitely be imagining their Jesus as Israel's new king. The piling of a number of cloaks on the donkey, reminiscent of the throne improvised on the steps for Jehu (2 Ki.9.13), and the strewing of the way with whatever they could find, make clear that they saw this as a royal progress, and it all suggests a lot of youthful emotion, with no clear idea of what they thought would happen. What is significant, however, is that Jesus, who would never let them refer to him as God's Anointed (Messiah) and was quick to ensure that his unexpected anointing later was not taken for royal ceremonial, allowed them to do this; which confirms that he was, like Fox, following no thought or plan of his own, but merely obeying some impulse from an inner voice.

There is no suggestion that anyone but the two groups of disciples were actively engaged; probably with the Twelve leading, grouped closely round the donkey, and 'those who followed' following, except when rushing to the front with a cloak to spread or an armful of brushwood: Mark has no crowds and no palm-branches. Although the event is written up into something much larger in Matthew and in John, Luke confirms that those who took part were ***to plēthos tōn mathētōn***, the full band of the disciples (Luke 19.37). There would probably have been other travellers on the road, a week before Passover, there might even have been those Pharisees whom Luke finds amongst his spectators, but there was no mass demonstration. This accounts for the fact, found puzzling by some, that no action was taken by the authorities: simply, the matter never attracted their attention. Soldiers on the walls of the Antonia fortress, facing the Mount of Olives and overlooking the Kidron valley, would only have seen one more group of excited pilgrims, a little noisier than some. The strewing of the way may well, getting no encouragement from Jesus, have lapsed as they approached the city and the disciples started to sing.

A Moment of Vision?

Luke's account, much of which seems to derive from some source other than Mark, tells of Jesus weeping when, as they rounded the shoulder of the Mount of Olives, the city came in sight (Luke 19.41-44). This should be kept in mind as possibly true, even if Peter was unaware of it. Fox's experience not only demanded of him an obscurely symbolic action, but also led to a vision of a river of blood. If the ride to Jerusalem was indeed an experience of the same nature, it would not be unnatural if something similar had happened to Jesus, and that he should have wept over the city because, perhaps, he had, in a flash of prophetic vision, seen it lying in ruins before him. It is here, if Luke is right, that Jesus first mentions the siege and destruction of Jerusalem rather than speaking generally of the Coming of the Son of Man; and certainly he truly predicted the destruction of the temple a day or two later (Mark 13.2).[6] This Lucan story suggests how Jesus might have come to be so sure and definite.

The ride has been thought of as a 'triumphal entry', ever since the fourth evangelist recast the story for the dramatic effect of showing Jesus welcomed to the city by palm-waving crowds, a worker of incredible miracles at the height of his popularity, with 'the Pharisees' muttering impotently in the background (John 12.13-19). Yet the arrogant gesture of riding into a holy city is inconsistent with Jesus' own teaching of humility (Mark 9.35ff; 10.14ff, 18, 42-45), an attribute also of Zechariah's kingly rider; and when Jesus reached the city gates it was surely time to dismount and let the two disciples who had fetched the donkey make good their promise to take it back at once.

Not even the fourth evangelist states explicitly that Jesus rode into the city itself, although that is certainly where the big dramatic scene he has created is supposed to be taking place. Mark says **And he went into Jerusalem and into the temple** (11.11), and since he certainly did not ride his donkey into the temple, the obvious meaning of the sentence would be that he also entered the city on foot. Mark, if allowed to stand alone, disposes of the idea of Jesus being welcomed into the city as Messiah by cheering crowds who will yell for his crucifixion a few days later: it was not until the following day that Jesus made a real impact, and then quite clearly in the role of Prophet.

Corroboration that this ride was not a deliberate gesture, acted parable, planned political demonstration, nor even Dorothy Sayers' coded message,[7] may be found in the fact that, like Fox's noisier performance in Lichfield, nothing whatsoever resulted. Jesus entered Jerusalem, went to the temple, and having looked round at everything, the hour being late, he went out to Bethany with the Twelve (11.11). This anticlimax makes such a disappointing ending that Matthew and Luke do not accept it; both make the ride to Jerusalem lead directly to the Cleansing of the Temple.[8] In Mark Jesus rides as far as Jerusalem and then goes on to the temple; but there, it seems, the compulsion leaves him. 'When I had declared what was upon me, and felt myself clear, I went out of the town in peace', says Fox. Jesus had not been required to make any verbal statement but, when he had looked round at everything, possibly contrasting present splendour with the ruin he had foreseen, no doubt he too 'felt himself clear' and went out of the city in peace.

The Meaning

This understanding of the episode explains the recorded facts better than does the idea that Jesus deliberately planned such a ride, or that he intended it to demonstrate royal status and claim that he was 'the' Messiah. For if, as seems clear in Mark, it was not a dramatic demonstration but a minor event, of which no one but the disciples took much notice, it could not have established any such claim. More importantly, in Zechariah 9.9 the verse – it begs the question to identify it as a 'prophecy' – could never have furnished even the learned, much less 'the people', with a means of identifying the expected leader. For the crux lies in the improbable combination, **'your king [...] riding on an ass'**, just as in Mark 14.13 it is **'a man [...] carrying a water-pot'**: riding to Jerusalem on a donkey does not show that one must be a king, any more than carrying a water-pot proves that one is a man. Had an acknowledged king – perhaps that crowd-pleaser, Herod Agrippa I – approached Jerusalem riding humbly on a donkey, then Zechariah's words might indeed have been recalled, to the king's credit; but both terms of the equation, king and donkey, must be clearly apparent: one by itself will not suggest the other.

Those words might have come to Jesus' mind, since he believed himself called to a special destiny as a leader of his nation, when he felt impelled to ride to Jerusalem on a donkey; they may certainly have occurred to disciples who wanted to make the ride a royal progress. But it makes no sense to claim that Jesus deliberately staged this event as a proclamation, since to people not already aware of the special role to which Jesus felt himself called, his riding a donkey would mean nothing.

If, however, his experience was, like Fox's, the very direct guidance of the inner spirit, an impulse from or through the subconscious, then it is scarcely profitable to seek a conscious motive. Still, if our further conjecture that Jesus experienced a premonitory vision of the city in ruins were correct, that would show a progression of three unsought mystic experiences: the Baptism vision called Jesus to the service of God and led him, in the wilderness, to the basic conviction that the Day of the Lord was at hand; the Transfiguration confirmed that he must indeed carry God's message to Jerusalem, at the cost of life itself; and the hypothetical vision inferred from Luke's account of the ride would have told Jesus that his prime message of impending doom had indeed been correct, and would mean the total destruction of temple and city. As he walked through the gates of Jerusalem he may have been absolutely sure of the detailed truth of the prediction which, come what might, he must proclaim.

Chapter Ten

[1] Borg (1995, pp.32-36) gives an excellent picture of Jesus' direct experiences of the spirit; although I am not over fond of his term 'spirit person'.
[2] 'Restoring', 'making whole' or 'healing' seem appropriate here, as in Mark 5.23, 28, 34; 6.56; Matt.9.21, 22; Luke 8.36; Acts 14.9 (cf. ***Apollo sōzōn***, Apollo the Healer). The prime meaning of *sōzō* is 'rescue' or 'save' (eg. Matt.8.25, 'Save, Lord, we perish!); but to translate *sōzōn* as 'Saviour', as Brenton does, suggests later Christian thinking.
[3] Since Mark (Peter?) never uses **the Lord** for Jesus anywhere else, it is most unlikely that he does here.
[4] *Stibas* is primarily 'a rough bed of straw, reeds, etc.' Brushwood, which fits this context, was still used for rough beds in rural Crete in the 20th century.
[5] 'Hosanna' is Hebrew, from Ps.118.v.25; v.26 is given as in the Septuagint.
[6] The Synoptics have no earlier reference to this destruction; Luke 13.34, **But now Thy house is forsaken** (from Neh.13.12) alludes rather to the temple's misuse for profit.
[7] Sayers 1943, p.213.
[8] Nineham (1992, pp.293f.) also insists that the Cleansing must immediately follow; but transfers the entire episode to the Feast of Dedication and away from the Passover.

CHAPTER 11

Monday: A Prophet in the Temple

The Fig Tree

As Jesus and the Twelve were walking in from Bethany to Jerusalem next morning there was a curious little incident which, if otherwise of no importance, offers a fine example of a rather sensational story created from very little, through pure misunderstanding: in this case, an error by an eye-witness. Which may serve as a reminder, when we encounter it elsewhere, that the wholly implausible, not to say impossible, can yield a simple solution if taken with a tincture of common sense.

Here we have the case of the Withered Fig Tree (Mark 11.12- 14, 20-23). Assume that Mark is giving Peter's account of the incident: they all saw the fig-tree, but it seems that only Jesus went over to take a closer look, since **And his disciples were hearing what he said** (11.14b) is meaningless unless it implies that he was some little distance away. He is reported as saying after his inspection **'May no one never more eat figs from you'.** When they came past the next morning the tree was **withered from its roots**; Peter commented to Jesus that the tree he had cursed had withered, and Jesus, not apparently disputing that view, replied that anything is possible if you have faith.

Now suppose that Jesus, having more sense than to seek figs out of season as the text claims, in fact went to look at the tree because he had noticed some sign, perhaps a withered branch, that it was not in good health. Inspection confirmed this, and Jesus returned, saying, 'No one will ever get figs off that tree again!' (We have in Greek what Jesus said in Aramaic; but in no language is there much difference between a pessimistic forecast and a malediction.) Nobody thought any more about it until next day, when the leaves were seen to have turned brown overnight; which an informed opinion says is quite possible, given an unhealthy tree and the sharp frosts which can occur in Jerusalem in early spring (Major 1925, pp.60ff).

Peter has interpreted the rest with hindsight. He practically says as much: **And Peter, *remembering*** (what he thinks he heard Jesus say the day before)**, says to him, 'Master, look, the tree you cursed has withered.'** From the tree's obvious change for the worse Peter assumed that Jesus' words foretelling its doom had been a curse which worked a spell. (**Withered *from its roots*** is simply Peter's graphic description, he had not dug up the roots to see.) If Jesus had cursed, then he must have been angry: to be angry with a fruitless tree, he must have been hungry: so hungry, in fact, that he had gone looking for figs even when they could not yet be expected.

The difficulty, both for Peter and for Mark, was that they could not put any limit to Jesus' powers. Against an Old Testament background of arbitrary miracles defying the laws of science, a person in whom God's power manifestly worked for healing might be capable of anything. Consequently, now and again either Peter or Mark draw the wrong inference. It is usually possible, however, as here, to work back to a probable answer.

Deliberate Artistry?

Luke very sensibly refuses to repeat such a tale at all; but Matthew, always eager for a miracle, makes the tree wither at a word, instead of overnight (Matt.21.19). Possibly because of that, commentators speak of Mark deliberately splitting the story into two parts, on Monday and on Tuesday morning, and the 'inclusion' of the Cleansing of the Temple within the two parts of the Fig Tree is claimed as theologically significant; a possible conclusion if one joins the scholars in abandoning any idea that such a story might be fact and make sense. Other examples of supposed 'inclusion' are The Healing of the Woman's Haemorrhage, set within the story of Jairus' Daughter (Mark 5.21-43), and the Death of The Baptist, placed between the sending out of the apostles and their return from their mission (Mark 6.7-30).

These alleged examples of Marcan artistry are better understood as mere narration of what actually took place. There is indeed a touch of ingenuity in Mark's use of the Herod story to fill the gap while the disciples carry out their teaching mission, but even there it seems mistaken to look for any deeper significance than Mark's constant preoccupation with fitting together separate fragments of material to make a coherent whole.[1] Other cases may result only from Peter telling it as it really was: the woman did touch Jesus' robe and get her healing as he was making his way to Jairus' house; and now, it is most likely that Peter did indeed see the fig-tree inspected by Jesus one day and find it withered on the next. How much stranger and less credible if he, like Matthew, had claimed that the tree withered instantly when Jesus spoke! The split suggests that Mark is holding to the time-scheme as told to him, rather than inventing one of his own. The critics' mistake is to assume that because the incident could not in all respects have happened as described, it never happened at all; therefore the story must be symbolic fiction and its division into two sections Mark's doing.

Really, all Mark has done is to tack on two extra sayings, linked in his usual way by the verbs 'to trust' and 'to pray' as theme-words (11.22-25).

The Sacrilege of Greed

On Monday morning, however, the fig tree was not of great interest. Jesus led the Twelve into the city and there made his definitive challenge to the temple authorities. It is John's dramatic version which has supplied most of the visual images of the Clearing of the Temple; in Mark there are no cattle, no whip, no violent action beyond the upsetting of tables and stools. No doubt, once the prophet took the lead, all his disciples – the whole number, in Luke's phrase – would follow his lead, and other zealous pilgrims might join zestfully in this harmless mayhem, with money-changers and traders too busy scrambling to rescue their cash or save their stock to be able to withstand eviction.

The temple-authorities may not at this time have been as flagrantly greedy in their pursuit of wealth as they are said to have become a little later, but some of the notorious 'sons of Annas' must already have been part of the temple's executive body, known to us as the 'chief priests'; for Annas' son-in-law was already high priest, and five of his sons and a grandson rose later to hold that office. It has been suggested that a prime cause of the later poverty of Judaea was the power of capital wielded ruthlessly by the temple authorities, who had in their control the immense wealth of the temple.[2] For the temple itself was a unique commercial phenomenon: apart from one dissident temple in Egypt, this was the *only* temple, of the *only* god, of an entire people. It was no wonder that it prospered.

Only coincidentally does this action have a political dimension. High priests were appointed by Rome, but there is no suggestion that Jesus objected to their cooperation with the governor; his concern was with their exploitation of the pilgrim crowds. It would be anachronistic and exaggerated to call Jesus 'anti-capitalist', but undeniably he saw wealth as a formidable barrier to a true concern for the welfare of others; and who shall say that he was wrong? He may or may not have been sufficiently sophisticated to grasp the economic factors fully, but he knew blatant commercialism when he saw it; and his protest probably aimed less at the traders themselves than at the high priests who for profit leased out pitches on temple premises. Not even the outer court, the court of the Gentiles, should be so misused: for,

> **Is it not written that**
> **'My house shall be called a house of prayer** ***for all the Gentiles*****?'**
> **But you have made it a den of robbers**[3] (Mark 11.17).

Nor, having made his protest, would Jesus go away. His action, unlike the donkey-ride on the previous day, won him much attention and strong support from the crowd, to whom he now appeared in the light of a commanding, national, religious leader. He built further on this, staying in the temple and expounding his message to a growing audience. **And he was not allowing any man to carry any container through the temple. And he was teaching and saying to them [...]** (11.16f): these imperfect tenses suggest action over a period. He had established his rule over the temple's outer court, and clearly intended to maintain it.

Hooker (1997, p.265) holds that Jesus was preventing 'would-be worshippers buying sacrifices or offering the half-shekel tax' and that the status quo would necessarily, therefore, quickly have been restored. But the traders and money-men would immediately have set up again in the streets around the temple, to which the buyers had, willy-nilly, followed them out (11.15b).[4] Loss of a privileged pitch was irritating and inconvenient, but trade, and worship, would go on.

The Prophet has his Way

This bold move by Jesus had won him such popular support that the real losers, the temple authorities, were temporarily paralysed. So there was a triple challenge to the chief priests: their greed was condemned, their control over temple premises defied, and their ability to act effectively in response put in doubt. Their piety, their authority and their credibility were all under attack, their loss of face was massive. The prophet, on the other hand, had tacitly asserted his claim to the full solemnity of that role; by the people he was now clearly seen as a man sent by God to speak His will, even to the ordering of the temple itself (cf.1 Macc.14.41).

It appears, too, that he maintained his position in the days that followed, arriving early each morning to dominate the outer court, allowing no sale or exchange there, and backed by growing numbers of the ordinary folk, who found that his teaching spoke to something in them: **And all the people came to him early in the morning to hear him** (Luke 21.38). He would stay there, teaching, right through the busy part of the working day until the post-noon break; then the crowds would disperse and he, like everyone else, would seek a shady place, there to have a little food and something to drink, and to take a siesta. **And when**

it got late (like the Spanish *tarde*, the Greek *opsia* effectively runs from siesta-time to nightfall) **they used to go away out of the city** (Mark 11.19).

When the supportive crowd started, like everyone else, to disperse, it would have been very foolish for Jesus to linger in the city. Commonly Jesus and the disciples would probably have gone first to the Mount of Olives; and remained there, no doubt, through the heat of the afternoon. That certainly is where they went on the day that Jesus, as he left the temple, had told a disciple who was admiring Herod's magnificent buildings that the whole would be destroyed, not one of those vast stone blocks left standing on another. **And when he is sitting on the Mount of Olives opposite the temple on his own Peter was asking him, and James and John and Andrew [...]** (13.3).[5]

Luke's claim, in apparent contradiction to Mark, that that was where they spent their nights (Luke 21.37), seems likely to be a confusion by Luke's independent source of the fact that they spent every afternoon there, with the fact that they also went there on Thursday night.

Since Judas, on that night, knew whereabouts on the Mount of Olives to look for them, it is likely that the grove called Gethsemane was where they had always rested. Luke's confusion of the times, too, arises most easily if there is but one place involved. After the day's siesta there would be a leisurely return to Bethany, there to eat and talk and sleep.

This appears to have been their daily routine until Thursday afternoon.

Notes to Chapter Eleven

[1] The two references to Jesus' family which bracket the 'Beelzebub' argument, (3.21-35) simply show Mark trying to make coherent narrative from thematically linked material.

[2] M. Goodman, 'The First Jewish Revolt: Social Conflict and the Problem of Debt', *Journal of Jewish Studies, 33*, p.421. The wealth of the temple is unquestionable: Crassus looted 2,000 talents (say 50 tons) of gold in BC 54; Sabinus took 400 talents in 4 BC; after the sack in 70 AD, so much gold flooded the market that the price dropped 50% (Josephus, *Bellum Judaicum* 6.317), yet Titus had kept enough for the most lavish triumph Rome had ever seen.

[3] *Lēstēs* need not imply, as some claim, a rebel; most outlaws in any age are against the law, not the government.

[4] Harvey 1982, pp.129-135, perhaps overlooks the numerous followers accompanying Jesus, who made violence unnecessary and the traders' expulsion

---

swift. The Roman garrison would more likely have enjoyed the spectacle than wished to intervene.

[5] A classic example of Mark having difficulty in transposing Peter's first personal account into the third person.

CHAPTER 12

Tuesday to Thursday: Moves And Countermoves

Tuesday, Wednesday and much of Thursday are taken here together, because although certain events clearly belong to Tuesday morning, and the dinner at the house of Simon the Leper probably to Wednesday evening, many of the controversies, and as much of Chapter Thirteen as belongs to this last week at all, might be assigned to any of these days. Mark has done his best, but only a few episodes have any kind of dating, and even that dating does not always seem to be properly understood.

The Crucial Question

The second part of the Fig-tree story, however, as they went by in the morning (11.20), must be Tuesday; and so too the first countermove by the chief priests. For Mark has told us that **the chief priests and the scribes heard it** (ie., Jesus' remark about **a den of robbers**) **and sought a way to destroy him; for they feared him, because the crowd was spellbound by his teaching** (11.18). There is no need naively to suppose that Peter or any other disciple had knowledge of the chief priests' councils: rather, this is inference from what actually took place; which was the obvious countermove of challenging Jesus to say what right he had to interfere with the arrangements in the temple.

For this was a double-pronged question. If he said he acted on the authority of God, they could charge him with being a false prophet; yet, if he disclaimed divine authority, he would disappoint and disillusion his supporters, the captain of the temple would then be able to arrest him, and he could be charged with a variety of misdemeanours, possibly amounting to sacrilege. He would at best stand wholly discredited.

> **And they come into Jerusalem again, and in the temple as he is walking along the chief priests and the lawyers and the elders come up to him and they were saying to him, 'By what sort of authority do you do these things? Or who gave you this authority so that you should do these things?'** (11.27f).

Jesus countered with his question about the Baptist's authority, leaving his interrogators looking foolish, and followed that with his Vineyard allegory, which cast them as the villains who were going to murder God's son, His special prophet, so that their exploitation of His people might continue undisturbed. To this he added a quotation from Psalm 118 which implied the final vindication of the good, following rejection by those who should have known better. Not surprisingly, **they wanted to arrest him, and they were afraid of the crowd, for they knew that he had spoken this parable against them. And leaving him, they went away** (12.12).

Controversy

Until this point there is a single narrative containing, not mind-reading, but legitimate inference from the actions, words and demeanour of the hostile priests. That the chief priests then sent to Jesus certain of the Pharisees and the Herodians might be observation, but is probably inference; the question, about paying tribute to Caesar (Judaea, unlike Galilee, being directly taxed by Rome) was also double-pronged, clearly meant to get Jesus into trouble with either the crowd or the governor, so might well have been planted by the temple authorities. 'Herodians', unless Herod's officials wore some kind of badge, or one of them was well known, may also be mere inference, possibly no more than the upcountry peasant's view of smooth city types in expensive, but not overtly religious, clothing.

The question about the marriage after the resurrection hardly sounds like an orchestrated political gambit, although its intention is obviously to score off Jesus by setting him a question with no good answer; it may have been a malicious piece of individual enterprise. With the question about the most important commandment, however, Jesus himself recognises its sincerity and compliments the enquirer.

The introduction to the poser set by Jesus himself – how could the Anointed be David's son, as the scribes taught, when in the Psalms the author, assumed to be David, refers to him as Lord? – signals a break in the sequence. For, **And answering he said, as he was teaching in the temple** (12.35), when in the previous verse we already know that he is in the temple and has himself been the last speaker, must be the context of a separate anecdote, and a sequence on the theme of scribes, moving on to widows; just as the previous sequence was themed by particular groups – chief priests, Pharisees and Herodians, Sadducees, a lone scribe – putting questions. The first sequence concludes with the statement that **after that no one would dare to ask him anything** (12.34), and it seems unlikely that even Mark would start the next sentence **And answering**, unless he had to piece together different scraps which he heard from Peter. Any particular story, therefore, might equally belong to Monday, Tuesday, Wednesday or Thursday.

The same is perhaps true of the setting for the 'little apocalypse' in Chapter Thirteen. Much of the chapter consists of varied items compiled in Mark's usual way, but the opening incident, when the four disciples question Jesus, belongs to these few days. It might possibly fit more easily to Wednesday than to Tuesday, when, with arrest recently threatened, the disciples might not have stood there gazing at the buildings, but there can be no certainty.

The Signs to Come

During one afternoon's siesta, Peter (and James and John and Andrew) asked Jesus privately when the total destruction of the temple, to which he had alluded just as they were leaving it, would take place, and what sign would there be when these things were just about to come true?

> **And Jesus began to say to them, 'Look out that no one misleads you. Many will come in my name saying 'I am the one' and they will mislead many. But when you hear of wars and rumours of wars, do not be alarmed; it has to happen, but it is not yet the end. For nation will rise against nation, and kingdom against kingdom; there will be earthquakes in some places; there will be famines; these things are the beginning of labour-pains** (13.4-8).
>
> **But in those days, after that affliction, the sun will be darkened and the moon will not give her light, and the stars will be falling from the sky; and the powers in the heavens shall be shaken, and then they will see the Son of man coming on the clouds with great power and glory. And then he will send his angels and gather his chosen from the four winds, from the ends of the earth to the limits of the sky.**
>
> **Learn a lesson from the fig tree. When already its branch becomes tender and puts out leaves, you know that summer is almost here. So also you, when you see these things beginning, know that He is near, at the gates. Truly I tell you, that this generation shall not depart until all these things have happened. But about that day and that hour nobody knows, not the angels in heaven, not the Son, but only the Father. Keep your eyes open, stay awake; for you do not know when the hour will come** (13.4-8, 24-33).

So much may fairly be taken as words of Jesus spoken on this occasion, unless one chooses to deny that Jesus ever preached the coming apocalypse or understood it in the language of the prophets. Except that they are more explicit, these passages simply repeat what Jesus had been saying ever since he first came into Galilee **preaching God's great news and saying that the time is fulfilled and the Kingdom of God is very near** (1.14f). They combine to make a single coherent statement, and the pronouncement that not even the Son knows the day nor the hour (13.32) must come from the mouth of Jesus himself, since the church, hailing him as the Son in every meaning, would hardly have set limits to his knowledge.

Indeed, conventional believers may still expect Jesus to have had better than human foreknowledge of the Coming; but if he had, how could he ever have predicted that **this generation will not depart before all these things have happened** (13.30; cf.9.1)? 'It is of the glory of the Incarnation that Christ accepted those limitations of knowledge which are inseparable from a true humanity' said Vincent Taylor.

A number of scholars, starting with Victor of Antioch in the fifth century, have claimed that the disciples ask one question and Jesus answers another; but in fact they ask two, and the second, **What will be the sign when all these things are just about to come true?** suggests, as Hooker points out, a great deal more than simply the destruction of the temple. There is no need to suppose with Hooker that Mark put this clause in himself, for the assumption that the coming disasters would herald the Kingdom seems to have been in line with Jesus' own thinking; but Jesus corrects the crude idea that as soon as the trouble starts the kingdom will necessarily arrive quickly. The end is not yet, and the timing men cannot know, nor supernatural beings either, only God himself. From the start, his teaching of sharing and caring had anticipated a troubled world ahead; he would not want the disciples obsessed now by a grim nor by a glorious future, for life must be lived today, not tomorrow.

Although it is possible that Jesus also added in the little parable of the Servants of the Absent Master (13.4) to underline the warning to stay alert, it is clear that Mark has found here an appropriate place for a group of sayings, none of them connected to the discourse other than by the common theme of **'Watch!'** Some, at least, of the warnings about specific troubles for disciples (13.9-13) may also be from Jesus himself; but while there is nothing here that requires preternatural foresight, it is very likely that Peter has over the years rounded them out from his own experience. The passage reads more like an assembly of separate sayings – 13.9f, 13.11, and 13.12f, perhaps – and it does not fit well here. If we credit Jesus with the ability to stick to the point and answer the question, this digression very likely comes from words spoken at other times.

The notorious **abomination of desolation** passage (13.14-20), in which the phrase **let the reader understand** suggests a document incorporated into Mark's narrative, is so unmistakably an intrusion that it is really irrelevant here; we may just note in passing that all the details of the passage fit the circumstances of Caligula's attempt to have his statue erected in the temple at Jerusalem in 40 AD, but are inconsistent with the destruction of the temple in 70 AD.

The Anointing

What truly belong to either Tuesday or Wednesday are the plotting of the chief priests and the Anointing at Bethany.

> **It was then the Passover and the feast of Unleavened Bread in two days time. And the chief priests and the scribes were seeking how, taking him by stealth, they might kill him. For they were saying, 'Not during the feast,**[1] **lest there be a riot of the people'** (14.1). **And Judas Iscariot, he who was one of the Twelve (*ho eis tōn dōdeka*) went off to the chief priests in order to betray him to them. Hearing this, they were glad and promised to give him money. And he was seeking a good moment to betray him** (14.10f).

These two passages, which in Taylor's reconstruction begin the earlier, better written, Passion narrative, certainly read as though they were originally one passage, into which Mark has inserted his Anointing story. It is quite possible that its authors, if they were affluent Diaspora Jews from Rome, at Jerusalem for Passover that year, had better sources for what had happened behind the scenes than did the peasants from Galilee; but this may still all be hindsight. It is much what they, and Peter, could have inferred from what actually happened; and their guesswork was probably right. The temple executive would not have published their plans, yet their hostility had been plain to see (11.28; 12.12) and could hardly be doubted. Since the prophet was gaining great support by defying the ruling clique, his potential for damaging its interests was enormous, and it is no wonder if they wished him dead.

The high priest's motives need not have been entirely commercial nor wholly egotistic. As the ruler, under Rome, of the nation, he saw an eloquent, charismatic prophet with great popular support, well able to lead people into riot or armed rebellion – as Judas of Gamala had done in 6 AD, and as later Theudas and 'the Egyptian', and later still Bar Kochba, would also do – and so, by defying Rome, lead many ordinary people to a futile death. Normal political expediency, as put into the mouth of Caiaphas in John 11.50, urged that they should follow the example of Herod Antipas, and eliminate such a prophet before he started serious trouble. Many governments have, and most would, do the same.

The phrasing does suggest the disciples' horror that it should have been one of the Twelve, the most trusted friends, who betrayed that trust. Mark knows nothing of motivation; that the priests promised money may have been inferred, or learnt afterwards from common gossip, but it is not put forward as a motive. Nor today is it possible to go beyond the obvious: that Judas must once have believed wholeheartedly in Jesus and in his mission to fit the nation for the coming of God's kingdom; else he would never have been a disciple, much less one of the elite Twelve. Now, however, he has decided that Jesus must be handed over to the authorities; presumably because he either believes that Jesus is about to plunge the nation into war or, more probably perhaps, that he is not. His intention seems to be to force Jesus' hand – or God's.

Whatever the motive, the betrayal is perhaps most intelligible as the act of a clever youngster, convinced that he knows better than anyone else. The ingenious ploy, emotionally driven, ill thought out, and blind to any possible outcome except the one intended, would be typical of the sometimes horrifying follies of the adolescent. If Judas was of the age-group we suggested earlier for the majority of the disciples, eighteen or nineteen perhaps, such an act becomes easier to understand. To withstand or part company with a friend may be needful, but nothing justifies betrayal: an adolescent lack of judgement and experience might, however, best explain how a friend could do such a terrible thing. As to Mark's motive for inserting the Anointing here, the one least considered, although quite possible, is that he thought, or even knew, that it took place then, two days before the feast. Possibly Peter believed that Judas' treachery had somehow resulted from it; as indeed it may have done. The Anointing could certainly make sense as a first attempt to force Jesus' to declare himself Messiah, in open revolt against the power of Rome, with the Betrayal as the second.

The incident is not quite as bizarre as it may seem today, since the use of oil as a cosmetic, for hair and face, was common amongst the better off, especially for a dinner party; although it must have been unusual for an unknown woman, as she appears to be, to gate-crash a party, nor was the breaking of the container and pouring the entire content over one man's head normal practice. It would have made the disciples, already dreaming of Jesus as the Anointed, the Messiah, and maybe others too, think of a royal coronation, of which the oil poured lavishly over the head was the vital act; and recall the improvised anointing which forced

Jehu into immediate rebellion (2 Ki.9.1-13). Yet if there was here any intention of forcing Jesus to do the same, it failed. Jesus commends the reckless generosity of the action, but deftly relates it rather to his burial, refusing what might have seemed a perfect opportunity to declare himself God's Anointed. Whether that was a final act of evasion which led Judas to try to force his hand through treachery cannot be known; merely, Mark's placing of the story might possibly suggest that Peter thought so.

A Single Witness

At this point, before launching into the Passion story proper, it is time to restate that here we take the position that Mark's account, with Petrine reminiscences inserted into the pre-existent Passion narrative possessed by the Roman church (and therefore known to Peter) is the *only* valid account we have. For Matthew's narrative is Mark's, with a handful of doubtful episodes added; Luke is marching to a different drummer, but seems the less probable whenever he disagrees with Mark, although when he does not he occasionally offers details worth considering; and the fourth Gospel is creative historical fiction, as witness the carefully inserted earlier hints at the evil and venality of Judas (John 6.71; 12.6), which prepare the reader for later treachery, or the gripping but implausible 'secret signal' episode at the Last Supper, where the traitor is cryptically challenged by Jesus, and his identity signalled to the 'favourite disciple' (John 13.23-26).

So here, with the Anointing, Matthew's corroboration of Mark adds nothing to, nor does Luke's quite different story take anything away from, Mark's credibility; while John's version, placed six days before the Passover, set in the home of a family apparently concocted by himself with names culled from Luke, and garnished with extra detail (it is now Mary who anoints Jesus, and the house is filled with the scent of the myrrh) has no bearing at all on the facts. All through the Passion we must beware of letting Mark's original account be distorted or overlaid by the later improvements which are known so well and trusted too much.

Notes to Chapter Twelve

[1] Jeremias' conjecture that *heortē* means here 'festival-crowd' rather than 'festival' would make sense; but evidence for this usage seems thin.

CHAPTER 13

Thursday Evening: The Last Supper

The Date

The first question, vitally important to the credibility of Mark's account of what followed, is whether Thursday evening was Passover night, the beginning of Nisan 15, and the Last Supper therefore the Passover meal; or whether it was Nisan 14 instead. The question is confused – as Mark too may have been – by the fact that the Hebrew calendar reckoned the days from sunset to sunset,[1] while the Romans reckoned their days as we do, from midnight to midnight; and it is further complicated by the apparent desire of some scholars that the Last Supper *should* be the Passover, perhaps so that the Christian Eucharist may be considered as deliberately superseding the more ancient feast. Although the Passover lamb was killed in the afternoon and eaten that same evening, yet by Hebrew reckoning it was killed on Nisan 14, but eaten, after sunset, in the first hours of Nisan 15; therefore, in saying, **And on the first day of Unleavened Bread, *when they kill the Passover*** *(lamb)*, **his disciples ask him, "Where do you want us to go to prepare for you to eat the Passover?"** (14.12), Mark unmistakably gives the date that afternoon as Nisan 14, the day the Passover lambs were killed. John's Gospel, however, holds that Nisan 14 only started that Thursday evening, and on this one point it must be correct: not because it comes from the apostle John, nor the Unknown Disciple, nor Lazarus, nor even John the Elder, all of whom have been claimed as sources for the Fourth Gospel, nor because its unknown author ever shows the slightest concern for historical fact; but because the authority for dating the crucifixion to Friday Nisan 14 is not the evangelist, but the entire Asian church, who had from the beginning commemorated the correct Hebrew day, as taught to them by the apostles. They fasted during Nisan 14, remembering the Crucifixion, and then celebrated Christ's triumph that evening, with a feast which, for the original apostles and their many Jewish converts, would have been the Passover. When this, the Quarto-Deciman (ie. Fourteenthers) practice, was decried by Rome, the issue was whether to celebrate Good Friday and Easter on the correct Hebrew dates or on the correct days of the week; the accuracy of that Hebrew dating was not questioned then, and should be accepted now.

The Compiler's Error

V. Taylor (1953, p.660) credibly conjectures that Mark has inserted Peter's story of the disciples and the man with the water-pot at the wrong place into the written Passion narrative, which might originally have run **And on the first day of unleavened bread, when they kill the Passover lamb** (14.1)**, when evening was come he comes with the Twelve** (14.17)**.** This would, like John, give the first, evening, hours of Nisan 14 for the Last Supper. Peter would naturally speak of a festival in terms of Hebrew days, changing at sunset; while Mark would be thinking of Roman days, ending at midnight. But if 14 Nisan was the date of the crucifixion by the Hebrew calendar, then it was equally the date of the Last Supper, which had been eaten after sunset the previous evening, with Arrest, Trial, Crucifixion and Burial all following during that single Jewish day; until, when the sun went down, after the burial, it became Nisan 15, when the Passover lamb was eaten, after sunset; in this case, on the Friday night, when the Sabbath also had begun.

Paradoxically, however, convicting Mark of misdating Thursday night makes his account of the following day much more credible; for it is in the highest degree unlikely that the high priest and the chief priests, the most august figures of their religion, would have spent a most important feast day in midnight interrogation and public trial, or managed to convene the whole Sanhedrin at daybreak; much less that some of those chief priests found time later to jeer at the victim (Mark 16.31). The speed with which proceedings were conducted also points to the need to have the man dead and buried before the great day started. Mark's account of events, therefore, becomes much more credible using John's dating.

Making Ready

Mark's, probably ill-placed, insertion, following **And on the first day of Unleavened Bread, when they kill the Passover lamb**, runs:

> **his disciples ask him, 'Where do you want us to go and prepare so that you may eat the Passover?' And he sends two of his disciples and he says to them, 'Go off into the city, and a man carrying a pitcher of water will meet you. Follow him, and where he enters, say to the householder that the Teacher says, 'Where is my guest-room, where I may eat the Passover with my disciples?' And he will show you a big**

> **upstair room (*with couches*) made up ready.**[2] **And there make ready for us.'** (14.13-15).

Such a recognition signal and message are not only prearranged, but require a degree of timing; no matter what psychic abilities one may have, such detailed and precise knowledge lies beyond the scope of telepathic or mystic experience. Jesus must have arranged at what time of day and by which gate to send his men; but not the day, since the man with the pitcher could follow his routine every afternoon until the need was past.

Bethany, nearly two miles off and on the wrong side of the mountain, would be too far away for control of timing; nor is there any indication that any disciples but the Twelve were lodged there. The convenient, if not the only, time for the whole band to be alone with their master was the afternoon siesta-period amongst the olive trees; and from Gethsemane Jesus could despatch two of them across the Kidron valley to the visible gate in the eastern wall, knowing accurately enough when they would reach it.

After siesta it would be, by Greek reckoning, the first hour of 'evening', a natural time for anyone to be fetching more water. Mark, believing this to be the day when the Passover lamb is killed in the afternoon, naturally supposes that the Passover meal, about which he may not have known very much, will be eaten that night. **And the disciples went away and entered the city and found all as he told them and they prepared for the Passover** (14.16); but such preparation included making sure the day before that the room was ritually clean of every form of yeast; and these disciples would also need to know where to find the kitchen, where to draw wine or water, or sharpen a knife for carving.

Mark is not helped by the fact that *etoimasan to pascha*, very likely Peter's own phrase, could equally well have meant that they were to prepare the Passover itself; Taylor (1953 p.538n) renders it 'prepare for', pointing out that more was needed than the mere furnishing of couches. Probably Peter meant prepared (*things*) for the Passover, which would have made sense, while Mark understands him as meaning by 'Passover' the supper on Thursday night. Like donkey-minding, this was not work for which Jesus would have wished to spare any of the Twelve just then, and it is clear, since he comes **with the Twelve** (14.17) that he had not.

Ever since his decision to go to Jerusalem, foreseeing clearly that he would there be killed, the training of the Twelve, on whom the continuance of his mission would depend, had become most important. Moreover, by keeping all of them with him, Jesus could for the present keep Judas under his eye without having to single him out.

The Meal

> **And when evening had fallen he comes, with the Twelve.[3] And when they were reclining and eating, Jesus said to them 'Truly I tell you, one of you who is eating with me will betray me.' They began to be grieved, and to say to him one by one, 'Surely not me?' But he said to them, 'One of the Twelve, one who dips into the same dish as me. Because the son of man departs indeed, as it is written about him, but, oh, I am sorry for that man through whom the son of man is betrayed. Better for that man if he had never been born'** (14.17-21).

The next Jewish day has begun, it is now the Day of Preparation. The need to specify **one of the Twelve** here suggests the presence of other disciples; probably the two who had prepared the room, now fetching and removing dishes and pouring wine as needed, but not reclining to eat with the main party. The saying may be taken as historical; Jesus may even have known exactly what Judas was doing, for secrets leaked as easily then as now (cf. Acts 23.16), and a sympathiser may have given a warning. This seems a last attempt to get through to Judas and save him from himself.

Most translations of *Ouai* (woe) make it sound like a curse, but this is the *Oy!* or *Ay!* which echoes from one end of the Mediterranean to the other, and primarily expresses grief, rather than anger. Jesus, accepting his own fate as somehow the will of God, is distressed that his friend can so have lost himself as to be ready to commit an act which he will find very hard to live with afterwards: and Jesus would not, therefore, help Judas to commit it. So although, in John, Judas is now sent off to do his worst (John 13.27-30), in fact it seems that there was no such release, that Judas had to stay to the end and share the bread and wine of the new ritual; finally slipping away in the dark, perhaps as they left the house. This might also explain why it took so long for the high priest's men to reach Gethsemane.

Now, even accepting that this meal takes place, after sunset, on Nisan 14, and so cannot be the Passover, yet such resemblance as the Last Supper has to the Passover meal is surely significant. Certainly Jesus deliberately arranged to hold a meal in Jerusalem, at night, which concluded with a hymn (probably the *hallel*), during which he made a parabolic or allegorical interpretation of the bread and wine. There is no nothing mentioned to identify this as the Passover, no lamb, no bitter herbs, no question from the youngest; yet since everything that is mentioned is consistent with Passover, we must accept that it was at least a formal meal using some or all of those elements of the Passover rite which it was also permissible to use on other occasions.

Jeremias (1966, pp.50ff) argued that the drinking of wine would be improbable at any other meal than Passover; but a preference for water instead of wine seems, from the specific examples he cites, to be required only by asceticism or great poverty. Passover pilgrims were commanded to do themselves well, and Jeremias himself elsewhere quotes both Philo and Josephus on this, and says 'it was part of this full enjoyment of life to have an abundance of good food and drink' (1969, pp.102f). He shows how the money of the 'second tithe' was intended to be spent, at Jerusalem, **on oxen or sheep, on wine or on strong drink, or on whatever your soul desires** (Deut.14.26). There is nothing improbable in the drinking of wine at the Last Supper.

Variant Custom ?

In the Diaspora, that is, the Jewish communities existing in so many Gentile cities, 'Synagogues supplied the setting for communal dining, particularly for the celebration of festivals, the commemoration of key events in Jewish tradition that helped to define the community' (Gruen 2002, pp.117ff); Julius Caesar had granted them the exceptional right **to gather and feast according to their ancestral customs and laws** (Josephus, *Ant.*14.216). Diaspora Jews, recorded as celebrating Sukkoth and Yom Kippur, cannot have ignored the Passover. Probably, I suggest, Jews who were unable to go to Jerusalem would have met together to mark the night of Passover with a communal meal using some elements of the Passover ritual; for it would have been important then, as now, that children should grow up knowing about Passover and how to keep it properly when they had the chance. It is at least possible that some similar custom – Gruen stresses a lack of uniformity about Diaspora ways – obtained also in Galilee; and that Jesus, foreseeing that he would not now be able to share the Passover meal itself with his disciples, as he had hoped (Luke 22.15), used or adapted such custom to come as near to a proper Passover as he might. Into such a substitute ritual, which would not have the inviolable tradition of the actual Passover, there was no reason why Jesus should not introduce new words and concepts; and Jeremias (1966, p.61) himself cites a rabbinic story to show how 'the annual interpretation of the special elements of the Passover meal became a model for other such occasions'.

The Eucharist

The narrative gives no special significance to the meal itself, although it seems to have been a formal meal of a special group of friends, reclining in a proper dining-room; but,

> **as they were eating, having taken bread, after giving praise, he broke it and gave it to them and said, 'Take, this is my body.' And having taken a drinking vessel, after giving thanks he gave it to them, and they all drank from it. And he said, 'This is my blood of the [new] covenant which is poured out for many. Truly I tell you that I shall never drink of the fruit of the vine until that day when I drink it new in the kingdom of God'** (14.22-25).

The giving of praise or thanks for the food about to be eaten was normal Jewish practice, using the customary 'blessings', just as for centuries it was the custom of all Christian families to say a grace before meals. The words that followed, however, were charged with meaning. Their significance as a rite may be left to theologians; but, as already suggested, this may also be seen as Jesus' last parable, teaching a final lesson.

The Costly Covenant

When, near Caesarea Philippi, Jesus had begun telling his disciples that he was called to challenge the authorities in Jerusalem as 'son of man', and to suffer there and die, he had challenged them too: **If anyone wants to follow after me, he must forget about himself and take up his cross and follow me**. Now, passing round the broken halves of a circular, unleavened loaf, he says, **Take a piece. This is my body**. And later, as the cup goes round, **This is my blood of the covenant, which is poured out for many**. Could it be clearer that, as his disciples, they must now share in his suffering? When he is gone, they are heirs to his mission, to liberate many; and also to its cost.

As history, this may have been the inspiration of the moment, Jesus having planned in advance only a surrogate 'Passover feast' of a kind perhaps well known; or these words, and the structure of the meal itself, may have been specially thought out beforehand. However it came about, this was, accepting the reading '*new* covenant' as most probably what Jesus said, although probably not what Mark originally wrote,[4] a crucial statement of Jesus' final understanding of his mission.

The son of man goes, he had said, **as it is written of him**, and it has been suggested already that Jesus now saw himself as God's chosen servant, who would suffer and be treated with contempt and die, as it is written of him in the Suffering Servant Songs of Isaiah. It is precisely in the context of those passages that the word 'covenant' starts to be used positively in Isaiah,[5] and although (which might be thought to support Mark's version here) Isaiah never specifies a *new* covenant, this covenant is the key or essence of that new order for God's people which the servant's sufferings will help to bring about.

In the great passage which Luke believes that Jesus openly took to himself, **The spirit of the Lord is upon me, because he has anointed me; he has sent me to preach glad tidings to the poor** (Isa.61.1), the commissioning of God's prophetic servant, his anointed, leads directly into a picture of the new order:

> **They shall build dwellings on the ancient wastes [...] and strangers shall come and feed thy flocks [...] But you shall be called priests of the Lord [...] For I am the Lord who loves righteousness [...] and I will make an everlasting covenant with them** (Isa.61.4- 8).

In Isa.59.21 the nature of that covenant is clear: **And this shall be my covenant with them, said the Lord; My spirit which is upon thee [...] shall never fail**; which is the same as Jeremiah's explicitly *new* covenant:

> **I will put my laws firmly into their minds and write them on their hearts [...] And they shall no way teach each one his fellow-citizen, and each one his brother, saying, 'Know the Lord'; for all shall know Me, from the little to the great** (Lxx Jer.38.31-34: which is AV Jer.31.31-34).

This seems precisely Jesus' own view of the kingdom of God, for which he had tried to prepare the nation by spreading the good news that all, from the humble to the rich – if the rich could escape their possessions – could carry the law of God in their hearts, forgiving and loving their fellows. The old covenant, now explicitly replaced by the new one (Lxx Jer.38.32), had been sealed by Moses in the blood of cattle, poured upon the altar and sprinkled on the people (Ex.24.5-8); Jesus could see that the blood which sealed the new covenant would be his own. The son of man, he had told the Bar Zebedees, did not come to be served but to serve, and to give his life as a ransom for many (Mark 10.45).[6]

Yet if Jesus now saw the meaning of being 'given as the covenant of a nation' in Isaiah's terms: **for a light to the Gentiles; to open the eyes of the blind, *to bring the bound and them that sit in darkness out of bonds and out of the***

prison house (Isa.42.6f), neither Pilate nor Antipas seem to have been great imprisoners, provided law and order were not threatened. The troubles of Palestine were economic, and the commonest cause of imprisonment was debt. There were also slaves and bond-men and women, and many poor folk oppressed as the rich made themselves richer, buying up land and running their big estates more profitably, to undercut peasant-farmers and force yet more of them to sell their land; often bringing them to destitution, imprisonment for debt, or even slavery. **And I saw and the people had become looted and robbed [...] They became plunder, and there was none who rescued the victim, and no one who said 'Give back!'** (Isa.42.22).

The chief priests, the temple executive, were probably leading this economic oppression through their investment of the enormous sums which they held in trust or had deposited with them: the Clearing of the Temple had been made by one who surely was saying, '**Give back!**', a protest against the greed of those who were exploiting even holy premises for gain. An earlier allusion to Nehemiah's Cleansing of the Temple, **Behold, your house is forsaken** (Luke 13.35; Neh.13.4-14), suggests that this had been in his mind before ever he reached Judaea. He had demonstrated against the priests' most blatant display of greed, and knew that he could not now evade their hostility.

The giving of the bread and wine can therefore be seen as the epitome of the whole of Jesus' ministry; and whether or not he told them in so many words to do this 'in remembrance of him', there is little doubt that he so intended, and none that this became their practice. They were now to carry on his work, sharing the great news with all, and they had to understand what it might cost them.

And having sung a hymn they went out to the Mount of Olives (8.27).

Notes to Chapter Thirteen

[1] J. Finegan, *Handbook of Biblical Chronology*, Princetown U.P. 1964, pp.8ff, argues for an older Hebrew method 'maintained in parts of Galilee', of reckoning from sunrise to sunrise, but his evidence is weak, better accounted for by the elder Pliny's verdict that **all common folk reckon from daybreak to darkness** (*Naturalis Historia* 2.29.188), as their daily living demanded. Feast days, however, like Sabbaths, went by the official calendar.

[2] *Estrōmenon*, ' made up', is from *strōnnuō*, to spread, used most often for the making up of beds or couches.

[3] Mark's unqualified use of **the Twelve** here disposes of Luke's claim that Peter and John were sent to prepare the room; especially if Peter is Mark's source.

[4] Found in Codex Alexandrinus and some later versions of Mark only; probably borrowed from 1.Cor.11.25.
[5] Earlier instances in Isaiah refer to invalid or broken covenants.
[6] Cf. Barrett, 1972, p.24, on **a ransom for many**: 'the phrase in which Jesus expressed his devotion – a devotion that would shrink from no sacrifice – to the true welfare of his people, the 'many' (*polloi, rabbim*)'.

CHAPTER 14

Thursday Night: Arrest and Interrogation

Forecast of Flight

Until the interrogation before Caiaphas, the narrative should still be Peter's eye-witness, and so it reads; full of irrelevant extra details which he happened to remember, and of loose ends that it did not occur to him to explain. So, for example, it can only be conjectured that Judas found an opportunity to slip away in the darkness; his disappearance possibly went unnoticed because at least one other young man, as we are told later (14.51), and maybe more,[1] accompanied them to Gethsemane.

On the way, Jesus is reported to have foretold the disciples' flight, his own reappearance to lead them again, and Peter's repeated denial. All these have been doubted, but all will stand unprejudiced scrutiny. Mark 14.27 reads:

> **You will all desert me, as it is written,**
> **'I shall strike the shepherd,**
> **and the sheep will be scattered'.**
> **But after I am raised, I shall lead you to Galilee.**

To tell the disciples that they would run when he was arrested might be no more than Jesus' understanding of human nature, and of these untried youngsters in particular; a probability which he simply found confirmed in these words from Zechariah. Matthew's eagerness to use Zechariah, on every occasion,[2] makes scholars query the authenticity of any such quotation; but with Zechariah's concern centred on the judgement and redemption of Jerusalem, Jesus could hardly have failed to recall Zechariah 9.9 after his ride to the city, even if not before; nor Zech.14.21b when he excluded traders from the temple. There are also echoes of Zechariah (2.6, 10) in his prophecy of the Coming of the Son of Man (Mark 13.27). It is very likely therefore that he might quote that prophet appositely, even if not exactly; Mark 14.27 does not entirely follow the Hebrew, and is yet further from the Septuagint, but a later addition would probably have quoted exactly.

The prediction that Jesus would, when he had been raised up, precede them or lead them to Galilee, is confirmed by the later narrative, although passing almost unnoticed here. Peter then objects that he, at least, would die rather than desert, whatever the rest may do, and is told that, worse, he will deny Jesus. This also he vehemently rejects. **And they all kept saying the same**.

To take this as historical is not to say that details may not have been improved. Peter had been telling the story over some thirty years, and the precise and neat prediction that he will deny three times before the cock crows twice may well have adapted itself to the facts, or *vice versa*. 'Cockcrow' was the third (Greek) or fourth (Roman) watch of the night, but the 'second crowing' of the cock, whose use by both Juvenal and Aristophanes implies some fairly specific meaning, probably meant the end of the last watch of the night, when all the cocks crow as dawn breaks. If so, it adds little to the typically Petrine **today, this same night** (14.30), but may well have been the phrase which Jesus used. That he could actually tell exactly how many times Peter might need to lie about their association that night may perhaps be doubted, for whether it comes from premonition or from knowledge of his man, so precise a prediction is implausible. 'Three times' may be a later improvement which has crept in – like the second crowing of that cock in some texts of Mark – or it may be metaphorical, not arithmetical, a colloquialism for 'several times' or 'again and again'.

Gethsemane

Peter does not depict either himself or Jesus as supermen, admitting his own folly and his master's distress. At Gethsemane, the choice of the three closest friends to share Jesus' vigil, the fact that Jesus goes only a little further, not out of earshot, the description of him as bewildered and distressed, corroborated by his own words, the repeated failure of the trusted three to stay awake, all suggest a factual account. There are problems with some of Jesus' words – does 14.41 start with a question, **'Are you still sleeping and resting?'** – but such difficulties would be *less* likely if the passage had been invented, and not merely recalled. One has only to consider how Matthew and Luke have tidied the language, cutting out, for example, the Aramaic '*Abba*' and the duplication of Jesus' prayer. Where Mark records that Jesus spent three sessions in prayer, Matthew writes in a second prayer for variety, while Luke simply reduces three sessions to one.

Some things in Mark's account are inference, or simply stereotyped phrasing, like the arrest-party being sent by **the chief priests and the scribes and the elders**; which, also found in 8.31 and 11.27, may be taken as a stock phrase of Peter's, linking the three groups whom he holds responsible for Jesus' death. A direct order from the high priest to his own household seems more likely, and a mob with knives and sticks sounds like Caiaphas' servants, mobilised at short notice; certainly it is a servant of the high priest who loses an ear (Mark 14.47).

His assailant is only described as **one of those standing near**, perhaps because Peter did not wish to embarrass a friend, more probably because this was one of the 'other' disciples. Had it been himself, as the fourth evangelist alleges, Peter would surely have said so, since he seems determined to make a clean breast of every error; had it been one of the Twelve, he could have said that, withholding only the name.

It should be noted that all the so-called swords at Gethsemane, including those of the *ochlos* and Luke's much quoted pair which the disciples seem to be told to bring with them from the dining-room (Luke 22.36ff), are the all-purpose sheath-knives or daggers which most men would always carry. That is the primary meaning of *machaira*;[3] and had Jesus wanted a sword, Luke could have specified *rhomphaia* (Cf. Luke 2.35). Somebody had a knife, and used it, rather amateurishly, on one of the high priest's servants.

That Judas had told the party that he would identify their man with a kiss is justifiable inference, that being what he did; although perhaps Peter heard it later, in the high priest's courtyard. Matthew and Luke both improve the occasion with responses by Jesus to Judas' greeting, and to the wounding of the slave. In Mark, Jesus remains silent; no word is recorded until he challenges the men who have seized hold of him, asking if they think him a bandit, that they have come with knives and sticks? **Every day I was there in the temple, teaching in front of you, and you did not arrest me** (14.19).

> **And leaving him they all fled. And a youngster was standing close behind him (*synēkoluthei autō*), with a linen cloth thrown about his naked body, and they grabbed him. But he, leaving the cloth, fled naked** (14.48-52).

Having discarded romantic identifications of the young man with John Mark, and of either or both with the evangelist, what remains? Whoever he was, he had either been washing or in bed, and rushed out in a great hurry with, it seems, only a large towel or a sheet against the cold of the night. Dressed thus he would probably be noticeable when he joined the main party, so presumably he was thought to have some right to do so; being one of the lesser disciples, or someone from their Jerusalem host's family; the latter is perhaps implied in his being allowed so close to the Master. It is not implied, nor likely, that he stayed by Jesus when all the rest had fled, only that he was standing so close as to be within easy reach, and only escaped the arrest party by abandoning his wrap and joining the general panic.

Peter's Venture

Discarding again the novelistic inventions in John, Peter's entry to the high priest's premises was basically a heroic solo attempt to find out at least what became of Jesus, perhaps even with some naive hope for a possible rescue. Few people would have done as much, and no one else did. He managed to get as far as the high priest's courtyard; presumably slipping in at the tail of the arrest-party, since in Mark there is no helpful friend who knows the household. There, however, whatever hopes he had came to grief. To be revealed as one of Jesus' followers would at once destroy his chance of taking any opportunity that might arise; so when the maid came and peered at him (*emblepsasa*) and told him she recognised him as one of Jesus' men, he sought, in the best cloak-and-dagger tradition, to conceal his identity by denying his connection with Jesus; and his answer amounts to little more than 'I don't know what you're talking about.' Yet in the end, as he was challenged again and again, he, who had said he would be loyal when all others deserted, ended by denying his master furiously with oaths; fear for himself perhaps having crept in, his heroic attempt having become a total fiasco, and the denials which had started as a legitimate ruse-de-guerre now making him bitterly ashamed of himself as he realised how juvenile had been his dream of heroic intervention and how pointless from the very beginning his denial. **And he wept uncontrollably** (14.72). Those who are sure that they would have done better may pass judgement.

One should not, however, think of Peter himself as forever haunted by that denial, the gaunt apostle with the palsied hand depicted by Kipling.[4] Peter can tell this story now to Mark because he has long since accepted that he is a fallible human being; who can nonetheless act bravely enough through God's strength, not his own. Mark has placed the beginning of this story before the 'trial' of Jesus, and the rest later, which probably follows naturally from the way Peter told it, his entry setting the scene and accounting, to some degree, for his knowledge of what happened to Jesus, but his own humiliation told afterwards.

Caiaphas and his Advisers

The accounts of proceedings conducted *in camera* in the high priest's house face the valid objection that none of the disciples can possibly have witnessed what took place. Since the device of an unknown disciple with privileged access to the high priest's house, as produced by the fourth evangelist, or the later notion of Joseph of Arimathea as a source of information to the disciples, may both be dismissed as fanciful, no reliable source of information is immediately obvious.

Peter is an eye-witness as far as the courtyard and no farther; he remained **below in the courtyard** (Mark 14.66), implying that the interrogation was taking place in some conveniently large room indoors. After the servant girl had first spoken to him, Peter moved to the *proaulion*, the gateway or porch, leaving the light, warmth and gossip around the courtyard fire. He had no chance to hear or see anything of the interrogation, nor does it seem that he lingered to pick up the gossip after it was over.

This need not mean, as Taylor supposes from the lack of vivid detail in the interrogation, that Peter may not here be Mark's source; only that he is not here recalling what he saw and heard himself, but perhaps giving, as he has done before, his inferred understanding, based on such facts as he had, of what really took place.

The first statement presents no problem. **And they took Jesus before the high priests, and all the chief priests and the elders and the scribes assembled** (14.53). There can be little doubt that Caiaphas would have summoned his ten-man temple executive (the chief priests), some senior members of the Sanhedrin (elders) and his lawyers (scribes). Peter would have been able to glean this general picture from gossip round the courtyard fire, or may have seen such people passing through the courtyard as they arrived. 'All' might have been meant to refer only to the ten chief priests, with the scribes and elders being only those whom Caiaphas thought would be most useful. But when we are told next that the chief priests and the whole council (*sunedrion*) were seeking witness against Jesus to put him to death, and they found none, the natural meaning of **the whole council** must be, as in Mark 15.1, the full Sanhedrin, and it is almost certainly wrong; possibly loose phrasing by Peter, but as likely a misunderstanding by Mark, who probably knew little of Jewish legal bodies or procedures. It seems improbable that even the high priest's house had a room which would accommodate the whole council sitting in judgement, or that Caiaphas could have mustered them at short notice in the middle of the night; further, it was probably illegal under Jewish law then, as certainly later, for a capital case to be tried at night; but crucially, Caiaphas would not have wanted the whole council involved until he had a watertight case to bring before them.

Political Factors

There could never have been any difficulty in persuading Pilate to execute a prophet who proclaimed the end of the earthly empire of Rome and the destruction of Jerusalem; who had set himself up to challenge the temple authorities, and, worst of all, had now the backing of a large proportion of the fervid and volatile mass of pilgrims assembled for Passover. Such men are dangerous. Further, in flouting the authority of the Roman-appointed High Priest he had attacked the prerogative of Rome herself, attracting the backing of a potentially rebellious mob; and his preaching could be seen as little less than incitement to overthrow the rule of Rome. No conscientious colonial governor could tolerate such a threat, risking riot, or even rebellion, with huge and unnecessary loss of life. So once Jesus could be delivered to Pilate he was a dead man, as Caiaphas and Pilate had probably already agreed in private; his trial would be merely a correct formality.

Pilate would seem to have had recent experience of a festal crowd turning to riot; for if Josephus has listed every unfortunate incident he can find for which to blame Pilate, then the Galileans **whose blood Pilate had mingled with their sacrifices** (Luke 13.1),[5] must have died in the riot when the feast-time crowd were stirred up by the malicious rumour that Pilate had used the sacred Corban money to finance his new aqueduct. He had dispersed that mob by using, as riot-police, soldiers armed only with clubs; but his men were over-enthusiastic and many Jews were clubbed too hard, or trodden to death in panic flight. This was still news when Jesus was making his way towards Jerusalem, so had probably happened at the previous feast. The governor was now only prudent if, by the elimination of its potential leader, he sought to stop the next riot before it could begin.

The real problem was how Jesus could be got into Pilate's hands. If the governor sent troops to arrest a popular prophet at feast-time, he would immediately spark off the very violence he was trying to prevent; even by night, soldiers enough to withstand any counterattack could never have reached Bethany, where the prophet slept, without attracting attention; least of all at Passover, when many slept out on the hills because the city was overcrowded and overpriced (Jeremias 1969, p.61). Even for Caiaphas, whose servants would be less conspicuous than soldiers, arrest did not seem possible until Jesus himself was spending a night in the open, close to the city, and a traitor was ready to guide the arrest-party to the place and to the man.

Yet before the high priest could hand over a Jewish prisoner to the foreign power, the consent of the Sanhedrin was needed; and only exceptionally would the surrender of a fellow-Jew to the Romans be approved. So the prisoner must first be interrogated by the High Priest and his supporters, in order to find charges sufficiently serious in Jewish law to convince the Sanhedrin next morning. Any Jewish trial would have been too long and too uncertain; as Harvey shows, the plan was to convene the full council only on Friday morning, then to take a prompt executive decision to hand Jesus over to the governor.[6]

Blasphemy

To obtain a quick assent, however, Caiaphas needed evidence of a serious breach of the Torah, and this was hard to find. It sounds as though he had had informers trying to overhear Jesus' talk with his disciples, and that these agents produced garbled versions of the forecast that the temple would be destroyed, mixed with Jesus' other prophecy that he would rise again on the third day (14.57f);[7] but their witness did not agree, and Caiaphas resorted to asking Jesus the direct question: **'Are you the Anointed, the son of the Blessed?'** Matthew and Luke tone down Jesus' response, but according to Mark he replied unequivocally, **'I am'** (14.61f).

The Anointed (*Messiach* in Hebrew) at this time covered a variety of more or less vague expectations of a future leader; so that when the term was used it was often qualified, as 'the Anointed of Aaron', 'the Anointed of Israel', or 'the Lord's Anointed' (Harvey 1982, p.79). Jesus was known to be adept at turning awkward questions: had he been asked only 'Are you the Messiah' he might, taking that in its popular meaning of a future warrior-king, have answered 'No, I am not.' It is therefore highly likely that Caiaphas extended his question in something like the form reported, in which 'son of the Blessed' would mean God's chosen servant, His trusted agent, one who speaks in His name; the same usage that Jesus had employed in his vineyard allegory, and which defined his own prophetic role.

This was essentially the same question which Jesus had side-stepped at the beginning of the week: **'By what authority do you do these things, or who gave you the authority to do them?'** (11.28). As Harvey (1982, p.134) has said, once Jesus claimed to act with God's authority, he had either to be obeyed or to be eliminated: 'no middle position was possible.' On oath, Jesus could neither keep silent, nor deny his own understanding of his role; he was a man acting directly as God instructed him, and the admission which he had been evading all week must now be made. He had strongly denounced those who said that it was not the Spirit of God that worked through him (Mark 3.29f), he could not now deny that Spirit himself; his answer was simple and unequivocal. Then, knowing that he had already sealed his own fate, Jesus foretold that of his judges. With prophetic fervour he told them that they would see **the Son of Man, seated at the right hand of the Power, and coming with the clouds of heaven** (14.62); which is clearly Daniel's heavenly Son if Man, coming in judgement. Since whatever Jesus said now could make no difference, there was no point in caution any more.

Then the high priest dramatically ripped his robes and asked those present for their judgement, and inevitably they agreed that Jesus deserved to die. Caiaphas had at last a case which he could lay before the Sanhedrin with confidence: 'he has claimed to be God's special servant, His Anointed One'. Unless the councillors were willing to accept Jesus' claim as true and his authority therefore as overruling theirs, they must reject him as a false prophet and a blasphemer: which they did.

Reliable Reporting

Now, in his report to the Sanhedrin, Caiaphas must have been scrupulously accurate, for unless he repeated the exact words, Jesus could deny them; that would mean a protracted argument, leading possibly to a full trial before the Sanhedrin, who might never have agree a verdict (Harvey 1982, p.28), since the Sadducee ruling clique did not have control of the Sanhedrin, where the Pharisees took their own line and often got their own way (Jeremias 1969, 262-6). Any delay, with the prisoner still on his hands, was what Caiaphas wanted least. He would therefore have been careful to repeat question and answer word for word to the council; Jesus could not then deny his answer, and that answer was sufficiently damning.

On Friday morning, it follows, a exact version of the crucial words was given to some seventy councillors;[8] and known also to all the clerks, servants and guards who had heard them, either when first said or now when they were repeated. At a conservative estimate, at least a hundred people, not all of high social position, must have heard them; which might well mean that, even before the day was over, a fairly accurate version was known all over Jerusalem. There is also, however, another factor in the political calculus, one which Harvey scarcely takes into his reckoning: the danger of what the crowd might still do.

The Importance of the Crowd

Harvey, like other modern scholars, has taken both the 'entry to Jerusalem' and the 'cleansing of the temple' as prophetic gestures, of which the latter would have offended religious sentiment in many, and annoyed the pilgrim purchasers; and nowhere does he seem to give weight to the very strong popular support for Jesus attested in Mark.[9] But once Jesus had tacitly declared himself a prophet by clearing the traders from the temple, any small inconvenience was surely balanced by the excitement: people would be glad to have such a tale to take home. No one was going to weep for inconvenience to the moneychangers and dove-sellers, whose charges they probably resented: for Jerusalem traders, however legally, made a very good thing out of the pilgrim traffic. Next day, Jesus had flouted the authority of the chief priests, and in his answer to them had publicly ranged himself against them by siding with the people's hero, John the Baptist. He had continued daily in the temple (14.49a), presumably maintaining his ban on trading and trafficking, and thereby also upholding his claim to be the moral arbiter of the nation. People thronged to hear him, and had great hopes, no doubt, that this might lead to something more. According to Mark, from Monday morning to Thursday night the crowd are the sole but insuperable factor hindering the arrest of Jesus, and the reason why he must be arrested by stealth.

Tonight, the high priest has Jesus in custody; but in the city outside, there are still those thousands of sleeping pilgrims who will reappear tomorrow, with time on their hands, full of religious zeal and possibly of wine, and much too ready for trouble. The risk of action by the crowd is high. Unless the wide support for Jesus amongst some hundred thousand pilgrims can be neutralised,[10] it may be impossible even to deliver him to Pilate's Residency; any Roman trial might be submerged in riot and rescue, and his public execution would require more troops than Pilate has at Jerusalem. It is essential that not only the Sanhedrin, but tens of thousands of pilgrims, shall be convinced without delay that Jesus deserves to die and can fittingly be handed over to Pilate.

It follows that Caiaphas would take appropriate action. His shrewd political competence is evidenced by nineteen years tenure of a post held at the discretion of the Romans, who frequently demoted high priests. He would hardly overlook the obvious need; and it is plain, from the fact that on Friday there was not a blow struck for Jesus, scarcely a voice raised in his support and many in derision, that the crowd's attitude has been altered. They have been turned against their hero, which could have been achieved through a clever piece of character-assassination: 'Discredit, then eliminate' is only a twentieth century formulation of a much older practice.

The unsubstantiated story that Jesus had claimed that he would destroy the temple and rebuild it in three days, although useless before a Sanhedrin demanding proper evidence, was ideal for scandal: a good story, with the would-be prophet guilty either of sorcery (Deut.18 9-13), or of empty boasting. With that would go the damning report of the crucial question and answer: probably still accurate, since what was good enough to sway the Sanhedrin could hardly be improved. Jesus had claimed to be God's Anointed, leader of the nation, and had ranted that his accusers would face the Son of Man, seated at the right hand of the

Power, and coming on the clouds of Heaven; the High Priest, appalled at this demonstration of a blasphemous false claim to be prophet and Messiah, had ritually torn his robes; all the weighty lawyers and councillors who witnessed the scene had been unanimous that Jesus deserved to die.

Nineham (1963, p.417) shrewdly comments later, when Mark states that the high priests stirred up the crowd to ask for Barabbas (15.11), that 'it is not clear how the priests would have had time to influence the crowd's attitude towards Jesus between the suggestion of Pilate (15.9) and their reply'. True enough; so the crowd's changed attitude must have been contrived earlier. It seems likely that Caiaphas might, at the same time as he summoned the Sanhedrin to an emergency session at dawn, also have sent people out to spread these damaging stories, in which the hard facts were that the prophet had been arrested, had proclaimed himself as God's Anointed, had been condemned for blasphemy by the high priest and would appear before the Sanhedrin in the morning. This, garnished with more highly coloured gossip, would then have made the sole topic of conversation that morning, and would have spread very quickly. The allegiance of all but Jesus' closest supporters would be shaken by such tidings; pilgrims who had remained indifferent before would now be actively against him; and when he was next seen, no longer a man in command of the situation but exhausted, battered, bound and wholly helpless, disillusion would have been complete. Such a defeated man could not be God's Messiah, to set the nation free; and after the way of crowds whose hopes have been disappointed, hero-worship would have turned into hatred and derision proportionate to the expectations previously entertained.[11] Those who saw Jesus on the way to Pilate would have felt little zeal to interfere; later, when Pilate's troops had finished with him, he looked a great deal worse; and the placard which then hung round his neck showed that Pilate too could use ridicule as a political weapon.

Although the early spreading to the general public of a derogatory statement by Caiaphas is surmise alone, it accounts, as nothing else does, for the attitude of the crowd, and for the definite statement that the chief priests stirred them up against Jesus. In Mark's narrative Jesus is taunted on the cross both with the claim that he could rebuild the temple in three days and with the claim to be the Messiah (Mark 15.29-32): if this is Peter's reporting, it corroborates the surmise offered; from any other source it is at least consistent with it. Consistent too, although late and partly legendary, is the account in the Talmud that Yeshu was condemned **because he practised *sorcery* and enticed *and led Israel astray*** (my italics).[12]

There can be little doubt that a version of what had passed between Jesus and Caiaphas was soon widely known; in which case, since those words, if possibly improved a little, could hardly have been forgotten by Jesus' followers, Mark's account of the interrogation is likely to be passably accurate. The description of Jesus' maltreatment after he was condemned is not, however, covered by any disclosure for legal or political motives. It might be inference and imagination on the part of one who saw him on his way to Pilate that morning; but it was most likely gossip spreading from the high priest's servants, who would have been eagerly questioned throughout the remainder of the feast as witnesses to this unprecedented sensation.[13] In neither case is it necessary to believe that it was truly the assembled priests and elders who began to slap and punch him, although, by distinguishing some other people (*tines*) from the 'officers' who take Jesus in charge (and who also knock him about), this seems to be implied; but gossip is only gossip, and peculiarly liable to exaggeration.

Notes to Chapter Fourteen

[1] The two who prepared, and probably served, the meal, are unlikely to have stayed behind; but hardly to have worn so little as the youngster in the linen towel.
[2] Eg., Matt.23.5ff, the ass *and* the foal, from Zech.9.9; Matt.24.31 where he has added a trumpet-call (Zech.9.14) to Zech.2.6, which Mark had already used; Matt.26.15, 27.3ff, the thirty pieces of silver, given and thrown back, from Zech.11.12f.
[3] The confusion arises from the use of *machaira* for the short Roman *gladius*, shaped like a large dagger; and its use also in phrases for slaughter, where English prefers 'sword' but Greek more realistically says 'put to the knife'; cf. Spanish 'guerra al ***cuchillo***', 'taking no prisoners'. 'Knife' would again be better in Matt.10.34, **not peace but a knife**, for Jesus is emphasizing division (**a man against his father**), the prime function of a knife; not a sword made for violence and death.
[4] 'The Church that was at Antioch' in *Limits and Renewals,* 1932.
[5] The phrase must be metaphorical. Pilate cannot possibly have slaughtered Jews actually sacrificing in the temple, or both Josephus and Philo would certainly have set that damning sacrilege down against him, and Tiberius would have recalled him. For a full study of this protest see Morison 1939, pp.132-147.
[6] For this whole paragraph, see Harvey, 1982, pp.11-35.

[7] The public challenge to destroy the temple for Jesus to rebuild in three days (John 2.18-22) should be taken as fiction, extrapolated from Mark 14.58, not as independent witness.
[8] So the proceedings of the Sanhedrin in Luke 22.66-71 seem substantially correct, although this version of the words of Jesus is later, and probably less accurate, than Mark's.
[9] See Mark 11.18, 32; 12.12; 14.2; supported, perhaps independently, by Luke 21.38.
[10] A figure cautiously derived from the revised estimates of Jeremias, 1969, pp.100-4. Borg and Crossan (2008) suggest twice as many.
[11] Cf. Paula Radcliffe, whose web-site was flooded with hate-mail following her failure in the Athens Olympic marathon.
[12] Babylonian Talmud, *Sanhedrin 43a*. A parallel statement in the uncensored version confirms: **and a Master has said that 'Jesus the Nazarene practised magic and led Israel astray'**.
[13] A well-wisher in the High Priest's household is, after all, the most likely source for Jesus' knowledge of Judas' treachery.

CHAPTER 15

Friday, Dawn To Sunset: Trial And Crucifixion

A Roman Trial

> **And as soon as it was morning the chief priests and the elders and the scribes and the whole Sanhedrin made their decision, and binding Jesus they took him away and handed him over to Pilate** (Mark 15.1).

There was no Jewish trial, because the high priest was able to present a convincing case that Jesus deserved to die, and that the Roman governor, who alone in Judaea had the right to execute anyone[1] would also see Jesus as guilty of a capital offence. It was only necessary for the council to agree that it was therefore right in this case that Jesus should be handed over to the governor.[2] That was in effect to sentence him to death, and it is in that sense that Acts makes Peter lay the blame on his own nation: **'by the hands of men without the Law** (ie., non-Jews) **you crucified and killed him'** (Acts 2.23).

> **And having bound Jesus they led him off and handed him over to Pilate. And Pilate asked him, 'Are you the king of the Jews?' But he answering said to him 'So you say'** (*ie. 'That's not how I'd put it myself'; modern American 'If you say so'*). **And the chief priests charged him with many things. So Pilate asked him again, saying 'Do you not make any answer? See how many charges they are making against you.' But Jesus did not answer anything further at all, so that Pilate was very surprised** (15.1-5).

This describes a brief but correct Roman trial *pro tribunali*, held in public (Sherwin-White 1969, pp.17-24). Pilate's first question to Jesus may be taken as introductory, possibly jocular, probably part of the proper confirmation of the accused's identity: in effect, 'Are you the person they say you are, the one who prophesies the coming of a new kingdom?' Here, although the Christian church, claiming that Jesus was the Messiah and would come back to rule as king, might have been expected to prefer a very positive answer, Jesus, who had so clearly affirmed his role as defined by Caiaphas, gives Pilate, to whom 'Messiah' probably always implied 'king', a much less definite reply.

He was, perhaps, unwilling to endorse such a crudely political view of his role; but his whole attitude suggests a lack of interest in such pointless proceedings. To the Roman governor, however, proper trials were a vital part of good government and essential to the Roman way of life. The outcome might be a foregone conclusion, but the correct procedures must be observed.

So now the accusers, here members of the temple executive, must put their evidence. The prisoner, if he offers no defence, must be found guilty, but the governor, before giving his verdict, correctly gives him the chance to change his plea: 'Are you going to make no answer to all these charges they lay against you?' The prisoner is silent: having as good a grasp of the political realities as anyone, Jesus had probably recognised that this trial, however correct, was mere formality: why should he prolong it?

Where were the Disciples?

How well informed would our sources be here? Various scholars have assumed that the disciples stayed in hiding, or even ran all the way back to Galilee, but that can hardly be so. They had not been pursued from Gethsemane, nor was there any likelihood that anyone wanted them or indeed that anything of weight could have been charged against them; they were not facing the Inquisition, the Gestapo, the KGB nor even Senator McCarthy. It would be natural to want to remain inconspicuous, but the best place for that was in Jerusalem, mingling with thousands of other pilgrims; a party leaving Jerusalem during the feast would have attracted far more attention. We may suppose that those who ran from Gethsemane regrouped at Bethany overnight and, desperate to know what would happen to Jesus, mingled with others coming in that early morning. There were also other disciples, who had not even had to run for it, and a good many women.

That the account of the trial seems sound need not, however, mean that it is eye-witness by Peter. Everything which happened in public that Friday is likely to have been known to someone among the disciples, but probably no one was always in the right place at the right time. Nor, since it is unlikely that Pilate conducted his trials at the top of his voice, can we be sure that any disciple was sufficiently near the front to be able to hear exactly the words from the raised tribunal, rather than having to rely on what was passed backward from one member of the crowd to another. There was very little room for error, however, in so short a trial, and what is reported will stand scrutiny: the charge, not denied by the prisoner; the evidence, which he does not attempt to refute; condemnation and sentence.

The Passover Prisoner

The story about Barabbas, placed here, before sentence is carried out, raises such questions that many scholars have judged it to be invention. No record of any such practice as the annual release of a prisoner chosen by his countrymen is known; although it is clear from the later actions of Albinus, procurator in 62 AD, that a governor might release prisoners not guilty of capital offences on payment of a fine (Josephus *Ant.*215); and Philo's statement that in order to celebrate the emperor's birthday it was proper for executions to be postponed, or at least mitigated by allowing the dead to be buried by their kin (*Against Flaccus*, 81-84), shows that some leniency to mark a great annual occasion might be expected. Taylor (1953, p.580) cites an instance of the governor of Egypt releasing a minor offender to please the crowd, instead of scourging him. There is no *a priori* reason to doubt that Pilate might, perhaps on advice from Caiaphas, have formed the custom of releasing without punishment some prisoner chosen by the people, to garner a little goodwill at the particularly trouble-prone feast of Passover.

Where, however, the story passes belief is in suggesting that a Roman governor could ever have considered releasing any prisoner convicted of sedition. The choice must have been limited to minor felons, due for a fine or a whipping. Barabbas was only a man **put into prison with the rioters who had killed in the riot**. (*Stasis* covers any major disorder from riot to civil war, but the only serious outbreak at Jerusalem which Josephus finds in Pilate's record was the Corban riot, which he too terms a *stasis*.) When Pilate's riot-squad had moved in, Josephus tells us, the rioters showed no lack of courage and many were killed on the spot; which means that some stood their ground and, although unarmed, probably pulled out the knives which most men carried. (*Ant.*18.62). Mark's oddly phrased sentence, which does not say that Barabbas himself had killed anyone, suggests that he had simply been rounded up with others who had. If he had done no more than defend himself, without killing anyone, he should have been eligible for release in due course; for even when armed Samaritans got into a real skirmish with Pilate's troops, it was only the ringleaders whom Pilate executed (*Ant.*18.87).

The other gospels heighten the contrast with Jesus by painting Barabbas blacker. He becomes a ***notorious*** prisoner (Matt.27.16); thrown into prison **for riot *[...] and for murder*** (Luke 23.19); and finally ***an outlaw*** *(lēstēs)* (John 18.40b): someone whom even a venal governor like Albinus would have executed without hesitation. Since, however, there are no historical grounds for preferring their statements to Mark's, and every reason to suspect exaggeration, Barabbas remains a reasonable candidate for release.

It seems impossible, however, that Pilate ever considered releasing Jesus; but the governor's dialogue with the crowd makes sense if in fact **the one called Barabbas**, in Mark's elliptical phrase, also had the extremely common name of Jesus (Aramaic *Yeshua*, Joshua). The name is given as **Jesus Barabbas** in a number of texts of Matthew (27.16, 17) and accepted now by scholars and translators, for it seems incredible that Christian copyists would have added in the name Jesus for Barabbas, rather than preferred to leave it out. Pilate had probably found Jesus guilty before turning to the business of the Passover prisoner. But when the crowd began to call for 'Jesus Barabbas', probably with counter-shouts of 'Jesus Christos' from disciples or other supporters in the throng, Pilate would have needed to know 'For whom are you asking? Is it Jesus the king of the Jews you want me to release to you?' Such a question would have encouraged any disciples to hope that their Jesus might indeed be set free; but the crowd roars for Jesus Barabbas, drowning out opposing voices, and Pilate, relieved, is happy to agree.

The statement that Pilate realised that the chief priests' motive was jealousy can only be editorial, a conjecture, probably by Peter, about both parties; and the statement that the chief priests stirred up the crowd in favour of Barabbas has largely been accounted for; although, even if the trial of the prophet was over, some of his accusers may have stayed to see the Passover prisoner released, and would certainly have encouraged the choice of Barabbas. Pilate, too, shrewdly judging the mood of the crowd, may have decided to exploit their antagonism to Jesus, and asked them, 'So what do you suggest I should do with this "king of the Jews", then?', and elicited the answer which confirmed popular support for the sentence he gave, or had already given.

That the governor next asked them 'What has he done wrong, then?' seems at first sight so incredible that the story of Pilate's Wife's Dream, which Matthew inserts here, may well have sprung up to explain it. It makes sense, however, as another step in Pilate's manipulation of the crowd, aiming to work them up a little further, which certainly it did. 'Is he really as bad as all that?' he asks, in effect, when they call for their fallen hero to be crucified; **but they shouted at the tops of their voices, 'Crucify him!'** (Mark 15.14). Pilate would not now need to worry about opposition from the crowd when he sent Jesus to Golgotha.

Harvey examined the Barabbas episode in support of his contention that Jesus of Nazareth was already known in his lifetime by the nickname 'Jesus Christ'; which, although not essential to the interpretation given above, would make it more likely that Pilate had genuine difficulty in knowing for which of the two the crowd were shouting. 'King of the Jews' seems throughout to have been Pilate's equivalent for 'Messiah' or 'Christos', which by itself conveyed little to non-Jews;[3] but Matthew elucidates Mark for us: **Which [is it] you want me to release for you, Jesus Barabbas or Jesus called Christos?** (Matt.27.17).

Although it is only in a minority of ancient texts of Matthew that the name Jesus Barabbas is found, it may have come from Mark originally, for Mark 15.7 would read more naturally if a name stood before **the one called (*ho legomenos*),** which usually introduces a nickname, essential to identify men of the same first name; and since the name 'Jesus' for Barabbas seems to have been censored from all but a few copies of Matthew, it may simply have been removed from *every* copy of Mark. It is possible, but unlikely that Matthew draws here on a superior tradition, since there is no sign of one anywhere else; throughout the Passion he appears to be following Mark's account step by step and often word for word, merely explicating in his usual way and inserting into Mark dubious dramatic tales, such as the message from Pilate's wife (Matt.27.19) and the even more suspect ritual washing by Pilate of his hands to make the crowd morally responsible for Jesus' death (Matt.27.24f).

The whole trial is seen through the eyes of Jesus' followers, led by their last hope to take Pilate's question as a genuine offer to release their master, and promptly disappointed. Whatever they had hoped or we may now conjecture, the one sure fact is that no Roman governor would ever have released a prisoner with a serious potential for rebellion. Jesus, who offered no defence against charges which would have included defying the local government of the high priest, predicting the imminent end of all earthly government, and claiming to be God's Anointed – which to Pilate meant 'king of the Jews', but in any case meant one who would, if so guided, defy all earthly authority – would never have been pardoned, as he himself knew. Contrariwise Barabbas, who *was* released, must have been arrested for some lesser offence, such as assaulting or obstructing Pilate's riot police in the execution of their duty; and Mark does not allege anything worse against him.

Flogging and Mockery

For sedition, the sentence was always flogging before crucifixion; and as soon as he was finished with the choice of Passover prisoner, Pilate would have had the sentence carried out as soon as possible, for he understood the propriety of completing the execution before the feast began.[4] The same hostility to the Jews which had led Pilate's club-wielding soldiers to hit out more savagely as riot-police than he had intended, may now have made them flog Jesus even more severely than was normal; for there must be some reason why he died after only some six hours on the cross, whereas survival for three days was not unusual.

Pilate's label for the victim, 'The King of the Jews', may have encouraged extra brutality in the flogging, as certainly it stimulated the whole squad to have their fun with Jesus afterwards.[5] The sequence in Mark accords perfectly with Roman practice and with common sense. The fourth evangelist, however, by putting the flogging before the verdict, and then having the soldiers bring the prisoner back to their commanding officer still ridiculously arrayed from their own tomfoolery, defies both sense and custom; although he thus creates a visually striking and deeply moving scene.

According to Mark, the flogging and mockery of Jesus took place, like his trial, at the Praetorium, the Governor's Residency, which was probably the old Hasmonean palace, close to the temple and not far from the Antonia fortress housing his troops. (Herod the Great's new one, further away, presumably belonged to Herod's heirs.) The trial would have been in full view on the raised tribunal at the front of the building and, Mark seems to say, the flogging was also public, which again is likely: as Wellington said, 'All punishment is for the sake of example'.

And when he had scourged him he handed Jesus over to be crucified. The soldiers led him off inside the palace which is the Praetorium, and they called together the whole detachment (15.15f). It seems unlikely that any disciple was in a position to watch the mockery of Jesus, although not impossible: there would have been people going in and out of the courtyard of the governor's residency all day, lawyers, petitioners, messengers, tradespeople and slaves, for a large household, with Pilate's guards to feed as well, would have much business. There would at any rate have been no lack of witnesses to carry the story out onto the streets.

And when they had mocked him, they took the purple cloak off him and put his own clothes back on him. And they took him out in order to crucify him (15.20). The clothes were the perquisite of the execution squad (Sherwin-White, p.46), who would therefore see that they were not left behind for their comrades to steal; reclothing the prisoner meant that he took his clothes to the place of execution, where the soldiers could later while away the time by dicing for them.

Jesus would presumably have been led out with the *titulus*, a wooden board saying 'The King of the Jews', hung round his neck; since in three recorded cases which have made the histories (suggesting a quite common practice) the point of this additional humiliation was for the man to be paraded wearing his label for all to see – **taking him through the middle of the market-square with a label setting out the charge for which he was condemned to death and, after that, crucifying him**, to quote one example.[6]

Crucifixion

There are no such accounts to tell us exactly how the 'cross' (better, 'cross-piece', *patibulum*) was carried. Religious pictures always show, if not the whole cross, then a crossbeam of much the same dimensions as the upright post;[7] but there is no likelihood that the 'crosses' were as thick as the uprights – a stout pole would do, say six or seven feet long and perhaps four or five inches in diameter; or it might have been squared timber, or a branch from a tree. Such a pole might not have lasted long if big nails were hammered into it every time, but Mark does not mention nails; indeed, in the whole New Testament, only the fourth gospel does, and even so not in describing the crucifixion but later, in a single verse of the story of Thomas (John 20.25). Nails were often used to secure the feet to a replaceable block fastened to the upright, but the wrists were commonly tied to the crosspiece.

It seems likely that ties were used here; and normally the felon would be bound to his 'cross' before he was led out. It would be stupid to hand a desperate man a six-foot beam without making sure it could not be used as a weapon; but tying his outstretched arms to it first would make violence and flight equally impractical. At the place of execution it remained only to heave the beam up into its socket and nail the prisoner's feet.

Probably, therefore, Jesus would have been brought out, stripped to the waist, with the placard hung across his chest for all to see. That the label was later fastened to the cross might be inferred from the point at which it is first mentioned in Mark (15.26), and although this is inference, (later stated by Matthew and Luke as fact) it seems probable, as a continuation of the soldiers' mockery or the fulfilling of their orders. We may suppose that it was written in Greek, the language which could be read by almost everyone who could read at all. The fourth evangelist's claim that it was written out in three languages (John 19.20) is not practical for large letters on a small board; **HO BASILEUS TON IUDAIAON** is quite long enough.[8]

In the case of Jesus, it is not clear whether he was at the start carrying his cross-beam, or whether the soldiers realised before they set out that he was by now physically incapable of doing so. Even at the size suggested, a cross-pole able to bear a man's weight would have been heavy enough for men who had just had a Roman flogging; and Jesus, it appears, had been flogged till he could hardly stand. At all events, Simon the Cyrenian was impressed to carry it, and **coming in from the country** (15.21) may be his own account, since the reference to his named sons shows that he was, then or later, known to Peter or to other Christians.

At Golgotha, Jesus was stripped by the squad, and he was fastened onto the cross-beam, which would then be heaved up and probably dropped into a bracketed socket on the upright. His feet would be secured to the post, probably with nails, agonisingly, through the ankles. (It is possible that they did also put unnecessary nails through his hands, as one of those additional cruelties which were sometimes practised.)[9] Then, the prisoner could simply be left there to suffer until at last he died, while the guard's job became no more than vigilant crowd control.

Midmorning

It was now about 9am by our reckoning, the third hour of the day. The fourth evangelist says noon, probably to make the crucifixion coincide more nearly with the sacrifice of the Passover lamb, which took place in the afternoon of Nisan 14; and the three-hour Good Friday services of the church have reinforced the impression that Jesus was crucified at noon, just as the Stations of the Cross sanctify legends, unknown to the gospels, of Jesus falling as he carries the cross. Luke's unlikely story of Jesus sent to Herod by a Roman governor unwilling to take responsibility for his execution is sometimes invoked to explain the equally implausible time-lag in John; for noon was the time to consider ending the business of the day rather than starting it.

The time given by Mark is surprising only in that it was no earlier. With the Sanhedrin meeting at day break, and coming to a quick decision, Jesus might have reached Pilate's residence by 7am, by which time the governor could certainly have been ready to proceed, for Roman law-courts normally opened at dawn, or at least during 'the first hour' (Carcopino 1956, 155f; 188f). The trial, even if the business of the Passover prisoner was, improbably, settled before Pilate sentenced Jesus, would surely have ended by 8am at the very latest; and even preparing three prisoners for execution should not have taken very long. However, the 'hours' of the ancient world were by most people reckoned only by the sun or from the phases of daily activity, so Mark's 'third hour' might be almost any time between 8 and 9 am. Certainly it was well before *agora plēthousa*, 'full market place', the bustling forenoon.

Derision

Jesus was not, however, allowed to die even in what peace might be achieved in such pain. The purpose of Pilate's label was to encourage ridicule, and the temple executive had, personal malice apart, an interest in discouraging any revival of support for Jesus. There were thousands of folk in Jerusalem on holiday, seeking entertainment; there would be many spectators walking by to see the spectacle of a crucified prophet.

> **And the passers-by were reviling him, wagging their heads and saying, 'Hah! He's the one who is going to destroy the temple and build it in three days! Save yourself by coming down off the cross!' In the same way, even the chief priests, mocking him to each other with the scribes, were saying 'He saved others, he can't save himself.' And those who were being crucified with him insulted him** (15.29- 32)**.**

Note that the ordinary folk jeered and yelled; the priests, as befitted their standing, merely commented audibly to each other; the two felons could be seen shouting at Jesus, but probably what they said could not be distinguished in the general hubbub.

Holding on to Faith

So the day dragged on till noon. By then the last of the mere spectators would be thinking of returning to lodgings, or finding a shady place, for their siesta. Jesus' supporters are soon almost the only spectators. The disciples could not turn away from their tortured master while he lived; but for every one not kept there by love or by duty, this was *agorēs dialusis*, 'market's closing', when everyone goes home. Later that afternoon, many men would have been due to take their Passover lamb to be sacrificed at the temple; the women would then have to roast it, and all would want to furbish themselves for the feast. But there was no rest for the men on the crosses.

> **And when the sixth hour (noon) had come, it became dark over all the land until the ninth hour [roughly, 3 pm]. And at the ninth hour Jesus cried out in a loud voice, 'Eloi, eloi, lama sabachthani?' which in translation means 'My God, My God, why did you forsake me?** [10]

Often claimed to be a cry of despair, these are the opening words of the very affirmative Psalm 22. The psalmist is indeed in the depths of misery;

> **I am a worm and not a man [...]All who saw me mocked at me, [...] (saying) 'He hoped in the Lord; let Him rescue him, let Him save him, since He wants him.'**

and suffering terribly;

> **I am poured out like water; and my bones are all dislocated; my heart is [as weak] as melted wax, sunk to my belly; My strength is dried up like broken earthenware, and my tongue is glued to my throat; and You have brought me down into the dust of death.**

Yet still he trusts his God;

> **But You, Lord, do not set my rescue far away; be ready to help me. Save my soul from the sword and my precious one from the power of the dog**

and looks to be vindicated;

> **I will declare Your name to my brethren; in the midst of the assembly I will sing Your praise [...] for He has not scorned [...] the plea of the destitute, nor turned His face away from me, but when I cried to Him He heard me [...] All those who descend into the earth shall bow down before him; my soul also lives for Him, and my seed shall serve Him.**

What the psalmist originally meant as a promise of rescue in this life, Jesus could, in his suffering, perhaps still hold onto as confirming that vindication after death of which he had spoken so often to his disciples.

Death

The fourth evangelist's tender scene with Jesus' mother and friend standing at the foot of the cross, a theme for so many artists, is completely unrealistic in terms of military practice in any army or in any age; but certainly now the disciples could, with the crowd gone home, have pressed forward within earshot and caught any words that were said. They would also have heard when **some of those standing by** (which, from what follows, must mean some of the guard, probably Syrian levies), having heard Jesus cry out, said, **'See, he calls upon Elias'**.

> **But one, having run and soaked a sponge with sour wine, stuck it on a cane and gave him a drink, saying, 'Let's see if Elias will come and take him down'** (15.35f)**.**

With his words this man is joining in the joke the others were making; but what he did was a simple act of kindness, for a drink was universally recognised as a grace to those dying in pain. Suggestions that the giver was not one of the soldiers ignore the fact that no one else would be allowed near enough, let alone allowed to interfere.[11]

> **But Jesus, having let forth a loud cry, ceased to breathe. And the curtain of the temple was torn in two from top to bottom. But the centurion who was standing facing him, seeing that he died like that, said 'Truly this man was a son of god.'** (15.37ff).

The darkness **over the whole land** – which in common speech means 'as far as the eye could see' – cannot have been an eclipse of the sun, which is impossible when, as at Passover, the moon is full. It may have been simply a large-scale, somewhat unseasonal, gathering of thundercloud: the story of the rending of the temple veil suggests that lightning struck, or appeared to strike,[12] what was by far the tallest building for miles around, standing some 150-180ft high on top of its hill; for the veil of the temple hung outdoors, on the east face of that towering structure.[13] The doorway opening into the sanctuary building had gilded doors, approximately 70 feet high and 16 feet broad. In front of these **hung a veil of the same length, a Babylonian tapestry embroidered with blue and with fine** (so, near-white) **linen, with scarlet and also deep purple, marvellously worked** (Josephus, JW.5.210- 212).

The key to the rent veil story is the ancient world's deep belief in omens or 'signs'. The whole story might therefore have been invention; for from Golgotha no one could see the east face of that towering temple. On the other hand, if there was a lightning-strike, startling enough in itself, the rending of the veil may merely have been an embellishment, perhaps on the basis of some small damage sustained. Or the veil may truly have been badly damaged, even cut in two, by a bolt of lightning, but then taken down and replaced or hastily repaired in the few hours left before sundown, when the Sabbath, and this year the Passover, would begin; either way, while there would have been much talk, hearsay is all that Peter could have gathered.

The same interest in signs and omens would also explain why, even if there was a flash and a great thunderclap, Peter does not mention them; for to him, once he had heard the story, it is clearly the rending of the veil which was truly significant. To the Gentile centurion, however, the darkness, with thunder and lightning coinciding with the death of his unusual prisoner would certainly seem ominous; and his instant verdict, **'Truly, this man was a son of god'**, seems to demand more than mere observation of the prisoner's demeanour.

If this is the witness of Peter – and the death-scene is surely one which Mark would have heard related by the apostle himself – the lightning theory is almost demanded. For it is consistent with the great darkness which Peter does mention; it explains what gave rise to the story, true or false, of the torn veil; it explains why a hard-bitten centurion should suddenly make such an unusual judgement on a man he has just executed; and it offers a starting point for Matthew's earthquake story.

Matthew 27.51-53 shows how exaggerated the story had become; yet in verse 54, this account of the centurion and his men, deeply awed on seeing **the earthquake and the things that happened**, saying **'Truly this man was a son of god'**, makes the same connection, that the centurion's reaction was prompted by a natural phenomenon; and Matthew's earthquake would be an easy step of exaggeration from our suggested lightning.

The whole conjecture is, of course, unproven; yet it shows that Mark's account, which we attribute to Peter, is not impossible nonsense.

That the disciples did indeed witness the crucifixion, however, does not rely on mere probabilities; for in the statement **But there were also women** (*ēsan de **kai** gynaikes*) **watching from a distance** (15.40) 'also' must surely imply 'as well as those of us standing closer'. Amongst the women are named Mary Magdalene, Mary the mother of Little James and Joseph, and Salome. **These, when he was in Galilee had followed him and looked after him, and many other women [were also watching], who had come up with him to Jerusalem'** (15.41).

Burial

When Jesus was dead, there was nothing more that his disciples could do; and the men and most of the women will have returned to wherever they were due to spend the night. For at sundown it would be the Sabbath, and the night of the Passover too; and they must go and eat their ritual meal, in the proper way. Despondent but dutiful, the male disciples would have gone back to prepare themselves for that. But Mary Magdalene stayed, and with her the other Mary; although Salome went back (probably to see to the cooking, for families must be fed, though the heavens fall). The two who stayed were able, as perhaps they had hoped, to see what became of the body.

> **And now that it was getting late, because it was the Preparation, that is, the day before the Sabbath, Joseph of Arimathea, a well respected**

councillor, who himself was also looking forward to the kingdom of God, having gone, screwed up his courage, went in before Pilate and asked if he could have the body of Jesus (15.42f).

Philo's indictment of Flaccus, mentioned above, makes clear that families were sometimes, as a special favour, perhaps on the eve of an important holiday, allowed to bury those who had been executed; and there was no reason why Pilate should refuse such a request made by a responsible citizen in good standing. It is quite possible that Joseph had agreed, if reluctantly, that morning, that the young prophet must, for the sake of law and order, be handed over to Pilate; he might already have been feeling that Jesus had gone too far in defying the authority of the chief priests; but whatever had been his position, he had still a regard for Jesus the teacher, and did not care to think of his body being shovelled into a common felons' grave or left to rot on a cross. The time-scheme seems to require that he was sufficiently concerned to have stayed watching until Jesus died, so that he was then able to go promptly to Pilate; which explains Mark's *elthōn*, **having gone**, meaning 'from Golgotha'. Pilate, having, in some surprise, sent for the centurion to confirm that the man was really dead so soon, then made a gift of the corpse to Joseph.

And having bought a length of linen cloth, having brought the body down, he wrapped it in the linen and laid it in a tomb carved out of rock and rolled a stone against the door of the tomb (15.45f).

We need not suppose that Joseph did all this single-handed, for 'well respected' usually implies 'well off'. He may have had a servant or two with him, and a few coins would purchase the willing help of some soldiers to take the body off the cross. (The fourth gospel's story in John 19.39 of Nicodemus coming to help and bringing a vast quantity of spices appears to be pure invention.) The Marcan account suggests a man not practised in the laying out of corpses, struggling to achieve a decent disposal of the body in the short time available; who wrapped (*eneilēsen*) the body in a piece of linen because he had not the time, or it may be the skill, nor the materials, to swathe it with bands in the customary fashion.

And Mary Magdalene and Mary the mother of Joses saw where he was laid. (15.47)

Notes to Chapter Fifteen

[1] See Sherwin-White 1969, p.15 (governor himself must hear any capital case); pp.41ff (governor alone empowered to sentence to death). The lynching of Jesus'

brother James later cost the high priest his job; it took place precisely because at the time there was no governor of Judaea in post (Josephus, *Antiquitates Judaici* 20.200).

[2] Sherwin-White disagrees with this conclusion, but his facts support it; perhaps he does not give Mark sufficient priority, nor allow sufficiently for simple error in retelling the story. Much material in this chapter was first published in my article 'King of the Jews?' in *Faith and Freedom*, Autumn 2008.

[3] So ***Christos***, 'smeared with oil', has in Suetonius (*Claudius, 25*) become, more intelligibly, ***Chrēstos***, 'The Good'.

[4] Neither Luke's suggestion that this was a lighter, cautionary whipping, nor John's that the flogged Jesus was displayed in a vain attempt to evoke pity (both evangelists depicting Pilate as hoping to release Jesus) is consistent with the damning charge, made and never denied, 'Are you the King of the Jews?'

[5] Crossan 1994, p.382, is not the first to suggest that the scene is invented, deriving from the faintly similar later incident of the mocking of Herod Agrippa at Alexandria by dressing the local idiot up as a 'king'; but similarity goes no further than the use of 'crown', 'robe' and 'sceptre' to show a mock king. Once Pilate had labelled Jesus as 'King of the Jews', his troops naturally made fun of their prisoner: it would be more remarkable if they had refrained. Its invention by Christians as fulfilment of the sufferings of Isaiah's Servant might be credible if this story were first found in Matthew; but hardly in Mark.

[6] Dio Cassius 54.3.7. Cf. Suetonius, *Caligula* 32; *Domitian* 10.

[7] Similarly, art and theology demand a victim/saviour raised high; but efficiency requires that the cross-beam, with the victim hung upon it, should not have to be lifted far: arms-reach for a standing soldier would suffice.

[8] In the only case with the words cited (Suetonius, *Dom.10.1*), they are of almost identical length: **IMPIE LOCUTUS PARMULARIUS**.

[9] Josephus, *Bellum Judaicum.* 5.45. Grotesque positions shown in graffiti are reproduced in I. Wilson *Jesus the Evidence* (London: Weidenfeld & Nicolson 1996), pp.129, 131.

[10] Nineham 1992, p.429 claims that Jesus must have used Hebrew 'Eli, Eli', for anyone to mistake this as a reference to Elijah; but even if the soldiers (Syrian levies?) knew Aramaic, and had heard of Elijah, these words, spoken by a man in agony, near death, were probably recognisable only to someone familiar with the psalm (Ps.21, Lxx; our Ps.22). The narrator obviously has the whole psalm in mind, for echoes of its other verses are found in Mark 15.24 & 29.

[11] The offering of drugged wine before the execution by respectable Jewish ladies (***Talmud**, Sanh.43a*) was a recognised act of charity, quite different from allowing unknown spectators to approach too close during the actual execution.
[12] *The Guardian*, 01/09/11, printed a dramatic photograph in which a bolt of lightning *appeared* to strike the Eiffel Tower.
[13] Symbolically-minded Christians have preferred the inner curtain which divided the Holy of Holies from its outer sanctuary; but if the story is fact, it must be the exterior curtain, as the unknown early Christian who doctored the text of Josephus understood. (See *Bellum Judaicum*, Loeb edition 1960, vol.3, p.460).

PART FOUR: ENDING IN TRIUMPH

CHAPTER 16

An Unfinished Gospel

Current Theory

Towards the end of the nineteenth century it was established that the genuine text of Mark ended at Mark 16.8, verses 9-20 being a later addition by a different hand; subsequently it became widely accepted that, since the story is unfinished and appears to stop in mid verse, the evangelist had been prevented, by arrest or sudden death, from completing his work, or else the original scroll had lost its final page. However, in 1950 R. H. Lightfoot propounded that Mark intended his gospel to finish at 16.8, and this is now the received wisdom; for, it is argued, had the original manuscript been left unfinished by the author, it would have been completed by some friend or disciple; while, after publication, the loss of any page could soon have been made good from another copy. To suppose that, at some later date, *all* the copies simultaneously lost their final pages seems quite unrealistic. The deliberate removal of all their endings is thought equally impossible, on the grounds that the copies of Mark used by Matthew and Luke, in 80 or 90 AD, plainly stopped at 16.8, yet no one had so early the authority which wholesale censorship of Mark would have required. This last argument, it will be shown, is not as secure as it seems; but most scholars today hold that there can be no adequate explanation for the total loss of an original ending, and that therefore to finish at the words **For they were afraid** (Mark.16.8), with the resurrection announced by **a youth in a white robe** but with no appearance by Jesus himself, must have been what the author intended,[1] a deliberately inconclusive ending. Yet this theory raises a number of other difficulties.

Loose Ends.

Such an ending would flout the practice of all ancient, and probably all modern, authors; leaving a hotchpotch of mysterious events unexplained, and concluding in total anticlimax. If Mark really composed this scene himself, he did it very badly. Ancient authors do not leave difficulties unexplained: they ingeniously expound, for example, how a heroine whom we have seen stabbed and disemboweled, or beheaded by pirates (*Leucippe*, 3.19-22; 5.7), can still be alive; how the daughter of Ethiopian monarchs is born fair-skinned and raised abroad (*Ethiopian Story*, 10.13-17); or how a crowd left on the far side of the Sea of Galilee can reach Capernaum in time to hear Jesus preaching on the following day (John 6.22-36). Ancient novelists also liked to explain their story's transmission: in *The Wonders beyond Thule* the tale is written on tablets of cypress, kept safe in a temple, and discovered centuries later by Alexander the Great; in *Daphnis and Chloe* the story is pictured on the walls of their cave;[2] and Bowie has shown that this 'authentication' of a fictitious source, by various means, was a common practice of ancient authors;[3] not least, we may add, of our Fourth Evangelist (John 18.15; 19.35; 21.24). Mark 16.1-8 baldly presents an unknown stripling, formally dressed, sitting in an open tomb from which the body has vanished, delivering an amazing message for the disciples, but frightening the women into total speechlessness, thus making it uncertain whether their message was ever delivered. Would anyone ever deliberately have ended a story so?

The claim that Mark had no need to explain what the church already knew is idle; the church knew that Jesus had been crucified, yet Mark describes the Passion at length. Since no mention of empty tomb, young man or even angel is associated with Jesus' resurrection before the appearance of Mark's gospel,[4] it seems probable that what most Christians had been taught was,

> **that Christ died for our sins, according to the scriptures, and that he was raised on the third day according to the scriptures, and that he was seen by Cephas, etc** (1 Cor.15.3-5).

The events at the tomb, if too unusual to forget, were too odd to be helpful in preaching the message.

Unfinished Narrative.

Modern criticism has made a virtue of necessity, arguing that the inconclusiveness of Mark's abrupt ending makes it 'an open story, designed to draw us on further' (Best p.74). As outlined by Rhoads, Dewey and Michie (1999, p.59):

> The fulfilment of prophecies within the plotted events enables Mark's narrator to end the Gospel in a powerful and enigmatic way. Throughout the narrative by means of prophecies in oracles, riddles and warnings, Jesus foreshadows for the reader the future of the story world [ie., that

> created by the author] after the plotted events will end. Because the reader has good reason to believe that Jesus' words about the future will come true – as his word has come true so frequently within the narrative – the narrator is able to end the story abruptly and without closure, with the women saying nothing to anyone about the risen Jesus. And the reader expects the not-yet-fulfilled prophecies to come true.

Momentarily, when put so lucidly, it may sound plausible; but N. F. Petersen, propounding this theory in 1980, admitted that it implied a writer deliberately composing his final sentence to be disbelieved.[5] Whether it be claimed, as he does, as 'irony', or described as 'a deliteralizing of the women's behaviour which cancels its terminal finality', real authors do not do that.[6] Petersen (p.165) claims that leading the reader to believe in the prophesied resurrection, which had not been related, would assist belief in the Parousia, which had not yet happened; but one cannot convey one point merely by omitting another, and no author, having introduced prophecy, can forbear describing how it comes true. The first argument against Mark's gospel being intended to finish at 16.8 springs from the demands of narrative.

Oral or written, new or familiar, narrative must offer a proper ending – as anyone knows who has ever told a story to a child. In classical plays, the audience knew that Clytaemnestra would be killed by Orestes, Antigone sent to her death by Creon, or Alcestis brought back from the dead by Hercules, *but the plays cannot end without these events being enacted*; even though Alcestis in the final scene has to be played by an extra, and so cannot utter a word.[7] In the romances, too, endings are properly finished: lovers reunited, friends rewarded, the gods thanked.[8] Among Graeco-Jewish 'novellas',[9] *Judith* similarly recapitulates her triumph, in song, with worship and feasting, before living to a grand old age. *Esther* and *Tobit* also have detailed finales.[10]

Mark is closest in form, as both Burridge and Wills have pointed out, to the *bios*, the ancient form of life-story of a dead hero or teacher;[11] and if that genre of somewhat novelistic biography is relevant to Mark, so too is its type of ending. For example, *The Alexander Romance* has the proper ending for its kind: the dying king considering the succession, then writing to his mother; heavenly omens at the moment of death; Ptolemy taking the body to enshrine at Alexandria; and finally a summary of Alexander's achievements. Another semi-biography, *The Life of Aesop,* little more than anecdotes and fables cobbled into narrative, is probably the closest parallel to Mark; and ends, after the execution of Aesop for blasphemy, by telling in two short sentences, how he was vindicated by

Zeus and how Delphi was penalized for killing him (Wills 1997, pp.181-215). A more polished biographer like Suetonius closes each emperor's *Life* with several paragraphs, much the same length as the endings of the shorter stories in the Apocrypha. Thus the later additions of the Longer Ending, now Mark 16.9-20, and the Shorter Endings of only a verse or two, followed established patterns; and both demonstrate that to end at Mark 16.8 was not found acceptable. No ancient writer would have left it so; and the more the scene is claimed to be the author's own composition, the less it satisfies either literary precedent or narrative instinct.

Too Many Opinions

A major difficulty with this 'inconclusive ending' is the subtle interpretation it requires. Lightfoot believed that the reader was meant to infer from the failure of all disciples, including now the women, that only the Risen Lord can be a source of real strength.[12] Perrin (1977, pp.35-8) sees the youth's mention of seeing Jesus in Galilee as foretelling the Parousia, while Best (1983, pp.74-8) takes 'he is going ahead of you', or 'leading you', as referring to the presence of the living Christ in the young church. Hooker (1997, p.393) suggests that since an angel's message must be true, it is certain that the disciples will find the courage to go to Galilee and see Jesus again; G.Stanton (2002, p.53) refers ambiguously to 'the messenger', and sees the truth of his message guaranteed by the earlier prophecies in Mark. W. H. Kelber (1997, p.129) says that the disciples 'never learn that the signal has been given for reunion with the resurrected one', and consequently have no claim to apostleship! Yet all this subtlety was lost on the early church, which preferred the finished gospels,[13] and soon added a 'proper' ending onto Mark.

A Parable?

Kelber (p.62) further explains the gospel's structure as due to the 'parabolic style' of the gospel. Parables, he claims,

> insofar as they are hermeneutically unfinished stories, stimulate a process of interpretation which is never fully brought to completion or under control.

Asserting that the whole of Mark is told as a parable, he cites in support R. W. Funk's statement that 'the parable does not have a conclusion' (Funk 1996, p.196). Now certainly, in a parable, the story often closes abruptly, as in a joke – the two forms are very similar. A parable makes a single point and should finish on its punch-line: so we never hear whether the elder brother joined the feast, nor where the foolish virgins spent the night. Jonah, being indeed a book-length parable, also closes on a fine line:

> **And should not I pity Nineveh, that huge city, in which there are more than a hundred and twenty thousand people who cannot tell their right from their left, and many animals too?**

How Jonah responded, and whether he got safely home, are not revealed, because the point has been made.

The open-ended, unfinished parable is a chimera. It may indeed end with a question, like **Which of these three, do you think, was neighbour to him that fell among thieves?** But what answer can there be, except **The one who had pity on him** ? (Luke 10.36f). Mark's gospel is not parabolic, for its inconclusive ending does not make any clear point, as the varied interpretations above demonstrate, and it ends in bathos.[14] The Synoptics show Jesus as a teacher, using parables as a type of graphic metaphor to get his teaching across to crowds of ordinary people (eg. Mark 4.33, 34);[15] which rules out intellectual subtleties in meaning or in structure. He was a peasant-artisan, teaching orally, mostly to others of his own sort: not a rabbi, nor a professor writing to impress scholars.

A Feeble Sentence

The use of language here is also unsatisfactory. *Ephobounto gar*, **for they feared**, makes a limp final sentence: but worse, it conveys nothing not already known. Mark often has clauses, seemingly redundant, which actually make his meaning stronger or clearer;[16] but this does neither.

In 16.8a the women flee in shock, shaking with fear; 8b adds that they said nothing to anyone; 8c says **For they feared**. Sentences with *gar* give, or request, explanations of what has been said previously, and out of 55 instances in Mark, this one alone adds nothing; for we already know that the women are terrified. That they are speechless, from panic, needs no explanation; certainly not a pale reiteration of what has just been stated so emphatically: **they fled from the tomb, for shuddering and terror possessed them**. The new sentence with *gar* ought to introduce a new factor. As Lightfoot showed, *Ephobounto gar* can, in the right context, be a complete sentence; but here, logically, it cannot.[17]

In 54 previous cases, the words which Mark puts *before* **gar** are the least important, like 'what', 'no one', 'whoever', or colourless verbs like 'he was', 'they were' 'he knew'. When a stronger verb, like 'shall arise', comes before *gar,* it is because even stronger words, like 'nation against nation', will follow. Every instance is meaningless without the words which *follow* ***gar,*** and if **they were afraid** comes before ***gar***, as it does, something of greater importance should have come after.

Mark's story, too, requires a reason for the women's terror. Panic flight is never, anywhere in the bible, a possible reaction to seeing an angel: people prostrate, freeze motionless, or faint, but never run.[18] Yet flight is not a usual reaction, either, for three adult women, two of them mothers of grown sons, meeting a beardless adolescent, a *neaniskos*.

Ephobounto gar, usually taken as referring to **And they said nothing to anybody,** immediately before, need not do so, in Mark. Thus, in 12.12, **And they wanted to arrest him, but they were afraid of the crowd, for they knew** (*egnōsan gar*) **that he had spoken this parable against them**, what they knew explains why they wanted to arrest Jesus, not why they dared not do it. Again, 16.4b **For it was** (*ēn gar*) **really huge** relates not to the preceding clause, **and looking ahead they perceived that the stone had been rolled away** (16.4a) but back to 16.3, **'Who will roll away for us the stone from the doorway?'** It is the huge stone which explains their worry, not the fact that the tomb is open. Thus 16.8c may have been the beginning of the explanation of 16.8a, the women's panic: but the explanation itself has been lost.

A Spurious Angel

Worse still, the 'inconclusive ending' theories depend on assuming that the youth at the empty tomb in Mark 16.5-8 is meant for an angel. Vincent Taylor stated (1953, pp.606f) that the terms 'young man' and 'dressed in a white robe' suggest an angel, that 'the presence and words of the angel more naturally account for the quaking and amazement of the women', and that, 'without questioning the existence of supernatural beings, it is probable that Mark's description is imaginative'. Most subsequent treatments of Mark seem to rely on Taylor's verdict, which is, indeed, a prerequisite for all 'inconclusive ending' theories;[19] for without the angel there is no authoritative attestation of the resurrection. Unfortunately, therefore, Mark's youth has none of the attributes by which the ancient world might have recognised a heavenly being: not the splendid physique, not the bright shining appearance, nor even the spell-binding presence which induces reverent awe: instead, there is panic-stricken flight.

Immature

Bless the Lord, all you his angels, mighty in strength, says Lxx Ps.102.20 (AV Ps.103); and the same example which Taylor gave to show that *aner,* man, and (*neanias*) young man, are often used to describe angels also reveals that these must be young men fully grown: **outstanding in their strength, most beautiful in their glory and magnificently dressed** (2 Macc.3.26). But Mark writes not of *neanias,* the young male adult, but of *neaniskos*, the beardless youth:

> Not yet old enough for a man, nor young enough for a boy; as a squash is before 'tis a peascod, or a codling when 'tis almost an apple; 'tis with him standing water, between boy and man (*Twelfth Night* 1.5).

The diminutive ending of *neaniskos* implies someone too immature to be taken seriously; when applied to someone older it is contemptuous, 'that stripling', or pitying, as in 'that poor boy'. *Neanias* and *neaniskos* correspond exactly to the Spanish *joven* and *jovencito*:[20] when used outside their literal age-range, they bring positive or negative nuances.

Neanias has his full strength, as athlete or warrior: Orestes, winning every event at the Delphic games, or Cleobis and Biton, who in place of oxen, haul their mother's ceremonial carriage themselves; as a child, Cyrus the Great is urged to eat meat, so as to grow up to be a *neanias.*[21] But the youngest, so least alarming, men, selected by the Scythians to seduce marauding Amazons into peaceful ways, are *neaniskoi* (Herodotus 4.110); Joshua similarly chooses *neaniskoi* as his spies (Josh.2.1), which might also explain Rahab's protectiveness. *Neaniskos* is the adolescent, who should hold his tongue before his elders (Ecclus.35.7-9). In legend, *neaniskoi* may be precociously predatory (Sychem, Gen.34.19), or prodigiously wise (Joseph, Daniel), or valiant (David); but the word is used to emphasize how sensationally young they were.

In real life, *neaniskoi* often have charm, but never authority. No more fit for war than the elderly, they may be seen showing off:

> **Judea was quiet all the days of Simon [...] The old men sat in the streets, and the *neaniskoi* dressed themselves up in the glamorous array of war** (1 Macc.14.4, 9).

Ridicule is one nuance; the pathos of dying young is another, as in **chosen youths who have gone down in slaughter** (Lxx Jer.31.15 = AV Jer.48.15). Soldiers alive and hostile, like those manning the walls at Ephron, are *neaniai* (2 Macc.12.27), but *neaniskoi* can emphasize the youthful daring of two brave young soldiers (4 Macc.3.12), or ridicule the youthful overconfidence of Rehoboam's army (2 Chron.11.1).

Throughout the Bible, as in classical texts, the uses of *neaniskos* all stress adolescence, as opposed to adulthood,[22] or pity for the slain, or servitude;[23] and these are not compatible with appearing as an angel. The proof is that *neaniskos,* the beardless stripling, never is recognised as a supernatural being; whenever angels do appear as *neaniskoi* they are taken for mortals: by sinners in Sodom (Josephus, *Ant.*1.200), by the virtuous in Media (Tobit 5.5,7,10).[24] The god Hermes as a lovely stripling passes unrecognised at Troy (*Iliad* 24.331ff). How then could this *neaniskos* at Jerusalem be recognised as God's angel?

Although *neaniskos* is more used than *neanias* in post-classical Greek,[25] (for in a world of professional armies and athletes, *neanias*, formerly the city's hero and defence, has lost his special importance), yet in New Testament usage the meanings remain distinct. Saul, abetting the stoning of Stephen, is *neanias* (Acts 7.58); the young nephew who later saves his life is a *neaniskos*, and if Paul is tactful enough to call him *neanias*, the centurion is not (Acts 23.17-22). The *neaniskoi* who bury Ananias and Sapphira are specifically the youngest men (*neōteroi*) (Acts 5.6,10).

In the Gospels, since Mark described the rich would-be disciple as running up and falling to his knees, Matthew rightly calls him *neaniskos* (Mark 10.17; Matt.19.20, 22). When Jesus' addresses the widow's 'dead' son (Luke 7.14) as *neaniske,* this is probably literal, but might be friendly encouragement (like *teknon,* child, to the paralytic in Mark 2.5). Mark himself only uses *neaniskos* elsewhere for the youth who ran naked from Gethsemane; so there is no instance in the whole New Testament to suggest that *neaniskos* means other than a beardless stripling.

Lacklustre

God makes his angels spirits, *and his servants a flaming fire* says the Septuagint version of our Psalm 104.4: the twist given to the original by the Septuagint,[26] and endorsed in Hebrews 1.7, shows that both these Hellenised writers saw angels as radiant. The clothes, and often the persons, of avowedly celestial beings always glitter. A plain white garment is no good; hence Luke's two 'men' have **brightly shining robes** (Luke 24.4) and Matthew's angel has a **dazzling appearance** and **his clothing as white as snow** (Matt.28.3). Mark understood this, for, at the Transfiguration, Jesus' clothes became **glittering, very white indeed, the way no fuller on earth could whiten them** (Mark 9.3): not at all like the plain white worn by this youth.[27]

Although Taylor (1953, p.606) claims that *peribeblēmenos stolēn leukēn*, **wearing a white robe**, is 'the conventional language in which such (angelic) beings are described', white *(leukos)* is never, in the Old Testament, used to describe the dress of angels: it was inadequate to suggest supernatural beings. It is indeed found of angels in Matthew, John and Acts,[28] who have probably all taken 'white' from the Marcan story; but we may note that these white apparitions are either specifically named as angels or, in Acts 1.10, introduced into an already supernatural context.

A white robe was, in fact, proper best wear for men: to enjoy life properly, **Let your clothes always be white, and do not fail to put oil on your head** (Eccles.9.8). *Stolē*, a robe down to the ankles, is correct for men feasting (Luke 15.22) or at leisure, like the scribes criticised in Mark 12.38, who stroll about in long robes;[29] and Marcus Aurelius employs the same phrase as Jesus, *en stolē peripatein*, when criticising the ostentatious folly of going about all dressed up in one's own home (*Thoughts*, 1.7). A white robe suggests a human in his Sabbath best; which anyone who possessed such clothes would have been wearing the previous day, for Sabbath and Passover.

Taylor cited *peribeblēmenoi stolas leukas*, of the martyred dead who have washed their robes in the blood of the Lamb (Rev.7.9, 13), and *peribeblēmenon nephelēn* of the angel who is wrapped in a cloud (Rev.10.1); but the faithful dead are human yet, however blissful. White here symbolises their purification, as promised in Dan.12.10 – **tested and well whitened and tried in the fire and sanctified** – and recommended to Sardis and Laodicea (Rev.3.4f, 18).[30] The true relevance of that cloud-robed angel is the rest of his description:

> **A powerful angel [...] and the rainbow was on his head and his face was like the sun and his legs like pillars of flame** (Rev.10.1).

That, now, is a proper angel.

Herod Agrippa's death confirms that supernatural beings dazzle. Acts 12.21-23 tells only how an audience he addressed called out that a god was speaking, not a man, and considers the king's subsequent collapse his punishment for blasphemy; but Josephus explains how this happened. The king,

> **wearing a robe woven entirely of silver, so that its texture was quite marvellous, entered the theatre as day was breaking. There the silver, glittering as it was caught by the first rays of the sun, was marvellously dazzling, shining as an object of awe and inspiring reverence in the fascinated spectators. Immediately his flatterers**

> **lifted their voices on every side [...] proclaiming him a god** (Josephus, *Ant.*19.344f).

Fiction offers corroboration. In one ancient novel, fierce brigands are daunted when the heroine stands up against the light of the rising sun, which makes her appear **bigger and more godlike [...] the gold thread of her robe glittering in the sun;** later, that robe makes her seem **more like the statue of some goddess than a human being** (Aethiopica 1.2; 10.9). The priestess at Ephesus, in jewels and a purple robe, shone with such glittering loveliness that they believed her to be the goddess Artemis herself (Apollonius, 39).[31] The common perception of immortal beings was that their clothing radiated light.

Angels and deities wishing to pass *incognito,* like Raphael serving Tobias, the god Dionysus visiting Thebes in the *Bacchae*, Hermes escorting Priam to Achilles (*Iliad* 24), must therefore use ordinary dress and appearance.[32] It is possible to entertain angels unknowingly (Heb.13.2); and such angels, to be known, must proclaim themselves by deed (Judg.13.20) or word (Tob.12.15).[33] Neither in Old Testament nor Apocrypha does plain white serve to identify an angel: how could Mark suppose that it would do so here? Even as late as the Apocalypse, white is specified only for human figures, like elders and martyrs in white cloaks or robes (*himatia leuka, stolai leukai*) (Rev.3.4, 5; 4.4; 6.11; 7.9, 13).[34] Mark could never have intended a youth in a plain white robe to be recognised as an angel. And if unrecognised, where was his authority?

Unimpressive

But if the youth's appearance rules out equating him with an angel, it is the women's flight which clinches the argument, for flight is irreconcilable with angelic visitation. It is the ghosts of the dead which induce panic:

> **when they saw him walking on the sea, they thought it was a ghost, and cried out; for they all saw him and were aghast (*etarachthēsan*)'** (Mark 6.9f; cf. Luke 24.37).

That might, had they not been in a boat, have precipitated flight; but, as Matt.28.9, 17; Luke 24.5 and Acts 9.4 make clear, the awe induced by a heavenly apparition leads one to prostrate oneself in a trembling reverence which precludes flight.

Those visited by gods and angels do indeed fear and tremble: Hagar, Gideon, and Manoah expect death.[35] So does Isaiah, seeing the Lord in vision (Isa.6.5); and Daniel is so fearful of Gabriel that he falls unconscious (Dan.8.17). The

Baptist's father was **shaken and frightened**, Mary was **deeply perturbed**, the shepherds **feared a great fear**, the disciples at the Transfiguration were *ekphoboi*, **frightened out of their wits** (Luke 1.12; 1.29f; 2.9; Mark 9.6), but no one runs away; least of all when an angel has commanded them not to fear.[36]

The Greek convention is similar. It is fatal to see God as God really is, as Semele discovered; gods therefore appear in human form, but splendid and radiant, while mortals, like Apollonius and his daughter mistaking a priestess for Artemis, prostrate themselves, but never run away. Even Pheidippides, the great runner, does not run when confronted by Pan; it is that god's *unseen* presence which creates panic (Herodotus 6.134).

What the women would have done on seeing an angel was to prostrate themselves on the ground; as they do in Luke (24.5); as, in Matthew, they do immediately afterwards, on meeting Jesus, and as the disciples do when they see him in Galilee (Matt.28.9, 17).[37] Cornelius was too petrified by his vision even to move, but later prostrated himself to Peter: **But Peter raised him, saying 'Get up. I am a human, too'** (Acts 10.4, 25f). Since in this case the women, far from being immobilised by awe, run away while the youth is still trying to deliver his message, he cannot have been an angel.

To sum up, Mark 16.1-8 is full of loose ends, and lacks the closure required by all forms of ancient narrative. Thirdly, although parables do indeed finish abruptly, they make their point; whereas Mark's final clause notably fails as a climactic finishing line, let alone as a clear message. Linguistically, it seems incredible that Mark should, for his final sentence, use *gar* as he has never done before (and as few writers ever did), yet fail to offer the new information which is the purpose of any *gar* clause.

Mark's youth is too young and too plainly dressed to be recognisable as an angel, and the women's flight would not have been possible had he been one. Thus the 'inconclusive ending', now lacking even an authoritative angelic statement of the resurrection, is hardly a valid ending to any gospel, since the prime element of the early church's belief has never been properly set out. Who would believe something so astounding as resurrection on the word of an adolescent boy, reported by three terrified women? The disciples themselves did not (Luke 24.21).

Finally, the early church *never* accepted 16.8 as an ending: Matthew and Luke not only 'improve' Mark, but complete their gospels suitably; as later the Longer and Shorter endings also did for Mark.

Notes to Chapter Sixteen

[1] Eg. R. H. Lightfoot 1950, pp.80-97; A. Farrer 1951, p.179ff; R. H. Fuller, pp.53-70; N. Perrin 1977, pp.23-38; J. D. Crossan 1991, p.396.
[2] All novels cited are found in Reardon, 1989.
[3] E. Bowie, in 'Philostratus: Writer of Fiction' in Morgan and Stoneman 1994.
[4] Disregarding the chronology proposed in Crossan 1991, pp.427-434.
[5] N. F. Petersen, 'When is the End not the End?' *Interpretation 34*, 1980, pp. 151-166.
[6] *Villette* is enigmatic, its ending interpretable as tragic or happy; but either way, Charlotte Bronte has concluded her story, and certainly without bathos.
[7] In Greek drama, written for competitive performance, the rules allowed three actors only, to cover all speaking parts.
[8] The ending of *Chareas and Callirhoe* takes all of Book Eight; most, eg., *An Ephesian Tale, Leucippe and Clitophon, An Ethiopian Story* and *Apollonius, King of Tyre*, are shorter. Lucian's self-styled *True Story* is the exception, the final lie being that the tale will be continued.
[9] I owe the term to L. Wills, 'The Jewish Novellas', in Morgan & Stoneham 1994.
[10] Even Plato's dialogues have appropriate, if brief, finales: Socrates strolling home after the *Drinking Party*, or a noble epitaph to Socrates to close *Phaedo*. (*Timaeus* has only the briefest summary, because it continues in *Critias; Critias* was never finished).
[11] R. A. Burridge 1992. He presents a strong case, but classes the Synoptics together and does not discuss the ending of Mark. L. M. Wills 1997, pp.15ff; 23-50: strictly, Wills classes Mark as aretalogy, the *bios* required for a cult-figure. He suggests (p.153ff) Mark 16.1-8 as a truncated version of the earliest gospel, and the Longer Ending as possibly earlier.
[12] Lightfoot 1951, p.92: 'in the last verse (Mark) is only concerned to emphasize human inadequacy, lack of understanding, and weakness in the presence of supreme divine action and its meaning.'
[13] V. Taylor 1953, p.9.
[14] D.E.Nineham 1992, pp.447f, claims *oudeni ouden eipan* as so strong that it implies that the women *never* said anything to anyone, thus making a good conclusion; but 'never' is precisely what it does not say; and the conclusion is the weak 'for they feared'.

---

[15] The explanation of parables as intended to *conceal* reality (Mark 4.10f), like the clumsy allegorizing (4.14-20), are probably from Peter, not Jesus.
[16] Eg. **very early, while it was still dark; there was no room, no, not even round the door; those around him, sitting around him in a circle** (Mark 1.35; 2.2; 3.34).
[17] In the closest parallels (Lxx Gen.18.15b; 45.3b) the brief *gar* clauses are meaningful, because fear has *not* previously been mentioned.
[18] The same seems true in Classical Greek. See '*How Unlike an Angel*', and '*The Wrong Conclusion*', ***Theology***, Sept/Oct 2008 and March/April 2010, for a fuller version of much of the argument of this chapter.
[19] Eg., Kummel 1970, p.72, 'the command of the angel'; Fuller 1980, p.204 n.2, 'there can be no doubt that this is an angel'; Anderson 1981, p.355, 'a young man who is nonetheless clearly an angel'; Nineham 1992, p.444, 'undoubtedly an angelic being is meant'; Best 1994, p.74, refers ambiguously to 'the young man who may represent Jesus himself'; Hooker 1997, p.384: 'The young man [...] is recognizably an angel'. None cite any evidence except that used by Taylor.
[20] The Spanish suffix *-ito*, like Greek *-iskos*, is diminutive, affectionate, sympathetic or contemptuous.
[21] Herodotus, *History*, 1.31; Sophocles, *Electra* 750; Xenophon, *Cyropaedaeia* 1.3.
[22] Young's *Concordance* and Mounce's *Analytical Lexicon* both give 'one in the prime of life' for *neaniskos*: an excellent definition if 'in the prime' is properly understood as 'at the beginning', not in its modern sense of 'at the peak'.
[23] *Neaniskos* is also used for 'servant' (parallel to *paidiske* in, eg., John 18.17), as in Herodotus 4.17. In Lxx Judg.19 the young man is *neanias* to the narrator (vv.3, 9, 11) but *neaniskos* to his master (v.19). Possibly in Lxx Judg.18.3 *neaniskou* implies that the Levite *neanias* has now become a servant, as domestic chaplain to Michaiah.
[24] I owe both references to D. Catchpole 2000, p.7; regarding Tobit 5.5,7,10 (Lxx, Sinaiticus only) where young Tobias addresses the man-for-hire as '*Neaniske*', see also n. 24 above.
[25] Liddell & Scott, ninth ed. 1968, p.1164.
[26] The Hebrew is given by *NEB* as **Thou makest the winds thy messengers, flames of fire thy servants**.
[27] John's' **angels in white** are minor figures, not further described; but the risen Jesus dressed like a gardener is a breach of convention, for which **'I have not yet ascended to the Father'** seems to be John's excuse (John 20.12,15).

---

[28] In Acts 10.3, 30, Cornelius' vision is defined as **an angel**, described as **a man in shining clothing**.
[29] Or for men whose work is ceremonial, like the Levites (2 Chron.5.12).
[30] Maccabees has one angelic horseman in white clothes, but marked as supernatural by his **golden armour and weapons** and the plain statement that he **appeared before them [...] as a helper from heaven** (2.Macc.11.8, 10).
[31] See Reardon 1989.
[32] The appearance of Jesus to the disciples on the road to Emmaus resembles the way in which Hermes the Wayfarer appears to help travellers, unrecognised until he has brought them to their destination. See W. K. C. Guthrie 1968, p.90f.
[33] In Gen.18, Sarah never apparently recognises the visitor as the Lord; it is unclear when or how Abraham does. (Gen.32.20-30 is similarly ambiguous). Jesus is recognised only at Emmaus; perhaps through his breaking of bread?
[34] The only possible exceptions are the followers of the Man on the White Horse, who also ride white horses and wear white.
[35] Gen.16.13; Judg.6.22f; 13.22.
[36] Apparent exceptions prove the point: Manoah's wife runs to fetch her husband, for the angel has not yet revealed his identity (Judg.13.10); Daniel's companions can run only because they have *not* seen the vision which paralyses Daniel (Dan.10.7f).
[37] Likewise Moses (Exod.34.8), Manoah and his wife (Judg.13.20), Balaam (Num.27.31), David and the elders (1 Chron.21.16), Ezekiel (Ezek.1.28; 43.3; 44.4), Daniel (Dan.8.17) and Saul of Tarsus (Acts 9.4).

CHAPTER 17

Losing The Ending

Improving on Mark

It is indeed true that Matthew and Luke reinterpret Mark's youth as an angel, but what choice did they have? Only thus could they bring coherence to the very perplexing data which Mark had left them; and improving Mark's stories was their habit. We, conditioned by them to accept Mark's version as a sketchy representation of an angel, easily overlook how odd his brief narrative really is, and how impossible it was for Matthew and Luke to accept it as they found it. Changing Mark's unknown white-robed young lad into a heavenly visitation was their only way to convert that inexplicable farrago of mysteriously open tomb, enigmatic messenger, astonishing message and panic reaction, into a consistent episode with a satisfying supernatural dimension.

Matthew, characteristically concerned for apologetic, miracle and decorum, keeps his tomb guarded until it is opened by a most impressive angel, whose reassurance to the women explains why they do not then prostrate, while his command to **go quickly** sanctions their running (Matt.28.8); thus deftly converting a prosaic hotchpotch into an agreeably marvellous episode. Luke, for his more sophisticated Hellenistic reader, barely mentions the empty tomb – seventeen words only – and his heavenly pair, before whom the women prostrate, although possibly inspired by Mark's two men at the Transfiguration, might rather recall the Dioscuri, the Heavenly Twins of Greek myth. Luke, adapting from Mark to suit the Mount of Olives setting which he himself prefers, omitted earlier the words spoken on the way to Gethsemane about *meeting* again in Galilee, so now his messengers cite similar words as *uttered* in Galilee, without commanding a return thither (cf. Luke 24.49-53; Acts 1.4-12). The women's sedate departure contrasts favourably with Mark's original frenzied flight.

The Missing Clause

If, however, we now accept that Mark could not have meant his youth to be an angel, since the stripling shows no characteristic which would allow anyone to think so, Taylor may then also have been wrong to rate this account as 'imaginative': for we are left with a set of data so odd as probably to be true. If

Mark 16.1-8 were a fragment of fact, it would admit of rational explanation; outlining one possible scenario will show that it does.

The general belief in 'shadowy phantoms' of the dead, accepted by the philosopher Plato (*Phaedo* 81c,d), was, we have seen, shared by Jesus' disciples who, seeing him apparently walking on water, **imagined he was a ghost** (*phantasma*)**, and cried out; for they all saw him and were terrified** (Mark 6.49, 50a). On Easter evening, when Jesus appeared, **startled and terrified, they imagined they were seeing a spirit** (Luke 24.37; cf. Acts 12.15). Since apparitions, Plato says, notoriously appeared at tombs and monuments, might not these women, surprised by a white-clad form *in the shadows of a tomb*, have reacted similarly?

Mark's usage with *gar* was shown (Chap.16 above) to require that an explanation should follow **they were afraid** in 16.8c. The women's panic, it was also shown, is neither a possible reaction to seeing an angel nor a normal one to meeting a beardless youth, so requires a better explanation. Yet if Mark originally wrote, *Ephobounto gar,* ***dokusai hoti phantasma estin:*** For they were afraid, **imagining him to be a ghost,**[1] such a statement would both agree with his invariable previous use of *gar* and explain the women's panic; it might even suggest a motive for its later deletion. Yet even with this conjecture to complete the sentence, there is still no proper closure to the story. What then became of the rest of the original ending?

The Dating Fallacy

Quite apart from the difficulties which, as seen above, the 'inconclusive ending' theory creates for itself, its basis also reveals a serious flaw. The seemingly solid foundation laid down by Lightfoot was the lack of any acceptable explanation as to how Mark's ending could ever have been completely lost; but Norman Perrin's lucid summary of what is now the conventional position (Perrin 1977, pp.20ff) reveals also its weakness. Rightly ignoring romantic scenarios like the author's arrest, and arguing that to end with *gar* is not inconceivable in Mark's workaday Greek, he first claims that the evidence of the ancient manuscripts is

> that the only text of the gospel that ever began to circulate in the ancient world ended [...] at what is now Mark 16.8.

However, since no existing manuscripts of Mark are earlier than fourth century, they prove only that, some three hundred years after publication, the genuine Marcan text always ended at Mark 16.8.[2] Therefore the claim that this was the only text which ever *began* to circulate relies, not on manuscript evidence, but on

Perrin's next proposition, that 'Matthew and Luke [...] both worked from a text (*of Mark*) which ended at 16.8'. This would have allowed only ten or twenty years for a Marcan ending to have disappeared, in which case Perrin's arguments might be unassailable; but it is on that completely unproven assumption that this theory rests.

Lightfoot had stated firmly that 'it is agreed that the copies of Mark used by the two other synoptists ended at 16.8'; which ignored both the dissent of H. D. A. Major (1925, pp.100-3) for one, and a total absence of evidence. How, without knowing what Mark might have written to conclude his story, can one tell whether the others knew it or not? What if Luke knew a lengthier ending of Mark but, having other material of his own, chose not to use it? Luke 24.1-3 corresponds recognisably to Mark 16.1-4, but his next verses alter Mark 16.4-7 almost beyond recognition, and of Mark 16.8 no trace remains; must we then suppose that Luke's copy lacked that verse also? In fact, given Luke's established pattern of omitting some Marcan episodes, such as Walking on the Lake or Cursing the Fig-Tree, preferring more wonderful versions of others, and using also material unknown to either Mark or Matthew, his final chapter is exactly what he might have been expected to produce, whatever Mark had written: it says nothing about where Luke's text of Mark ended.

Then consider the contrary case for Matthew, whose gospel includes almost all of Mark, and who follows Mark's narrative closely throughout the Passion, although interpolating such episodes as Pilate Washing his Hands or The Death of Judas. Suppose that he continued in the same way, incorporating into his text a complete Marcan ending, with only his normal embellishments: how, without possession of that Marcan original, could we know that he had done so?

Dating any loss to 'shortly after AD 70', Perrin argues that mutilation, accidental or deliberate, could only have been that of the autograph copy, or another very early copy from which all subsequent copies were made;[3] and that it is very hard to imagine 'any circumstances in which the author, or one of his followers, would not have repaired an accidental mutilation'. True enough, if his dating were secure; but it appears not to be, since Matthew and Luke could well have known a Marcan ending now lost.

Opportunity

Nevertheless, no revised time-scheme will allow *accidental* loss as the answer. Pages of a scroll could be lost, easily enough, and D. B. Taylor (1992, p.20) has listed classical texts now missing their last, or first, pages, but these are necessarily cases where only a single copy survived the Dark Ages, so that a lost page could never be replaced. That offers no solution for Mark; for a substitute ending had been added to Mark before 150 AD,[4] when there would have been plenty of copies: the use of Mark by both Matthew and Luke suggests its wide early dissemination – natural enough if Mark was the first narrative account. Accidental loss during the second century could therefore easily have been made good, and cannot explain numerous copies all losing endings without replacement. The only possibility for complete loss is deliberate censorship.

As Lightfoot had stated, no special sanctity attached to the gospels at first – witness, he said, the freedom with which Matthew and Luke have altered the text of Mark. From this Lightfoot argued that, had an ending been lost, someone would promptly have restored it; but it is equally possible that those early Christians, if convinced that Mark's ending was wrong, might have felt free to remove it.

Means

The total loss of an ending presuposes an authoritative consensus, which could easily have eliminated some verses of Mark over a decade or two; or a year or two, considering the ease of communication within the Roman Empire. No such consensus to truncate or censor Mark would have arisen until the more impressive Gospel of Matthew had become established, say around the end of the first century, as superior to Mark. However, the appended Longer Ending is already accepted as Mark's own by Irenaeus, c.180 AD, and probably known to Justin as early as 150 AD. Thus a likely era for the suggested truncation would be the forty years of Trajan and Hadrian (98-138 AD), which saw much Christian writing, relatively little persecution, and strong-minded bishops; yet is early enough for the Longer Ending to be well accepted by 180 AD.

It is also claimed that:

> In the circumstances of the Christian communities shortly after AD 70 it is equally difficult to think of anyone with the authority to carry out a deliberate mutilation and successful suppression of an original ending (Perrin p.22).

True again; but that does not mean that ecclesiastical censorship had to wait until a single supreme authority had been established. The second century knew the authoritarian bishop, as the *Letters* of Ignatius (d. 115 AD) make clear. Writing on his way to martyrdom at Rome, he constantly reiterates the theme of obedience to one's bishop: it is wicked to disobey him, one should do nothing independently of him: **look upon the bishop even as we would look upon the Lord himself** (*Ep.Eph.6*).

This possibly extreme point of view must yet arise from the general, if less well defined, practice of his time; and the next century betrays positive evidence of ecclesiastical censorship. The 'Secret Mark' letter establishes, not indeed Morton Smith's claim that canonical Mark is abbreviated from a 'Secret Mark', but certainly that passages were interpolated, possibly on more than one occasion, into an original text of Mark (Smith 1974, pp.14-17). The writer (possibly Clement of Alexandria, c.210 AD), although he asserts that 'Secret Mark' is authentic truth, specifically instructs one Theodore to exclude or deny specific passages, because **Not all true things are to be said to all men**. Here, it appears, is a third century churchman writing a private letter to instruct another to excise from Mark's gospel what is seen as an unfortunate truth. Might not second century bishops have done the same? The case of heretical Marcion, c.140, cutting out of the gospels whatever he disliked, suggests that the orthodox might sometimes have done the same.

Motive

We may agree with R. H. Fuller that motives suggested hitherto for censoring the close of Mark's gospel are unconvincing (Fuller 1980, p.65 and n.42); but, looking at the second century church, a really strong motive can easily be perceived, for Ignatius' other preoccupation is false Christology. Pagans argued that the Jesus seen after death was an unreal illusion (Origen, *Contra Celsum*, 2.55), the Docetics that Jesus' living body had been illusory (Ignatius, *Ep.Trall.*10.1). Jesus, Ignatius contends,

> **was truly born and did eat and drink. He was truly persecuted under Pontius Pilate, he was truly crucified and died [...]. He was also truly raised from the dead** (*Ep.Trall.*9).

So Ignatius might well have seen danger in the inclusion among the resurrection narratives of the phrase suggested to complete Mark 16.8c properly: *dokusai hoti phantasma estin,* **imagining that it was a ghost**.[5] Although referring not to the risen Jesus but to the unknown youth at the tomb, yet these same startled women are, almost immediately, Matthew's first witnesses to the resurrection; and if they were mistaken at the tomb, are they not still mistaken when they think they see the risen Jesus? And if some disciples had imagined ghosts, were not all the appearances similar imaginings, as Celsus argued?[6]

Ignatius strongly attacks the idea that Jesus only suffered in appearance (*to dokein*, from which Docetic); neither *dokusai* nor *phantasma* would be words which Ignatius cared to see in the resurrection story. It is certainly possible that he, or some like-minded bishop, may have urged, in private letters to fellow bishops, the quiet suppression of an ending which now seemed unfortunately worded; for it was important that Mark's narrative, with the prestige of Peter behind it, should not mislead the faithful nor encourage unbelievers.

The church had early realised the need to emphasise the physical reality of Jesus' resurrected body. When Matthew has ghostly apparitions (27.52f), these are emphatically **the *bodies*** (*somata*) **of the saints who had fallen asleep**; his women show, by grasping his feet, that Jesus, too, is substantial (28.9b). Luke (24.36-43) and John (21.19-29) explicitly portray incidents in which the physical reality of the resurrected Jesus overcomes doubt. *The Acts of Pilate*, written, following Julian the Apostate's campaign against Christian belief, 'to afford overwhelming proof of our Lord's resurrection',[7] reworked this theme, with Joseph of Arimathea mistaking the risen Jesus for a phantom (*phantasma*). To exorcise it Joseph recites the commandments; but Jesus says them too, and then proves his identity by transporting Joseph to the tomb and showing where he himself was laid!

However bizarre the invention, the church was probably correct to insist on distinguishing the resurrection experience from a mere apparition; for it was a deep, transforming experience, as the lives of the apostles prove. Therefore, for the later evangelists, Mark's account would not do; and once Matthew had transformed it into an intelligible, decorous and triumphant ending, Mark's original became dispensable. If, as suggested, Mark had here repeated his word *phantasma*, that would have been particularly unwelcome: Plato so describes his shadowy ghosts, Tertullian uses it to define an illusory appearance.[8] Any mention of a *phantasma* – unreal by definition – in connection with that particular tomb on Easter morning was surely most undesirable.

Mark's Original Ending?

If Mark's gospel originally did, as clearly it should, go on to relate the fulfilment of its repeated prophecies of resurrection, Matthew would almost certainly have used that; for, although he inserts dramatic episodes of his own, like the Death of Judas, Matthew's narrative of the passion seems to depend entirely on Mark's; and Matt.28.5-8 follows Mark 16.6-8 very closely. It is highly unlikely that, having so far omitted only some 50 verses of Mark, Matthew would now fail to incorporate the rest of any original Marcan gospel.

Here, then, is put forward a possible reconstruction of the original ending of Mark, such as might well lie behind Matthew 28.8-10, 16-20 if Mark had, as I argue, concluded his story properly. There cannot be certainty; but the draft below would offer a proper foundation for Matthew's text, yet would have been so out of tune with second century church views as to warrant its own suppression.

In Marcan Greek (italics show words added to, or altered from, the existing texts of Mark or Matthew):

> [Mark 16.8.c] **ephobounto gar, *dokousai hoti phantasma estin.***
>
> [From Matt.28.8-10] **Kai *euthus* ho Iesus hupēntēsen autais legōn, Chairete. Hai de *prosepesan pros* tous podas autou. Legei *de* autais ho Iesous, Mē phobeisthe. Hupagete apaggeilate tois adelphois mou hina apelthōsin eis tēn Galilaian, kakei me opsontai.**
>
> [From Matt.28.16-20] **Hoi de hendeka *apēlthan* eis tēn Galilaian, eis to oros hou etaxato *autous* ho Iesous. Kai idontes auton *gonupetēsan*, oi de edistasan. Kai proselthōn ho Iesous elalēsen autois legōn, Edothe moi exousia en ouranō kai epi tēs gēs. *Exelthontes kēruxate to euaggelion eis tas synagōgas eis* panta ta ethnē, didaskontes autous panta hosa *edidaxa* humin. Kai idou, ego meth' humōn eimi pasas tas hēmeras eos tēs sunteleias tou aiōnos.**

In English:

> [Mark 16.8bc] **[...] they said nothing to anyone; for they were afraid, *imagining that it was a ghost.***
>
> [From Matt.28.9-10] **And *straightway* Jesus met them, saying 'Rejoice'. So they *fell down before* his feet. *But* Jesus says to them, 'Don't be afraid. Go and tell my brethren that they are to go away to Galilee, and there they shall see me'.**
>
> [From Matt.28.16-20] **So the Eleven *went away* into Galilee, to the mountain where Jesus had appointed *them*. And seeing him they *fell on their knees*, but some hesitated. And coming forward Jesus spoke to them, saying, 'Power has been given to me in heaven and on earth. *Go out and preach the good news in the synagogues in* all the nations, teaching them everything which I have *taught* you. And lo, I am with you always, even to the ending of this age'.**

Positive Indications

Although *euthus*, 'straightway', and *de*, 'but', are merely the vocabulary which Mark would have used where Matthew has *idou*, 'behold' and *tote*, 'then', other changes are more important. The first oddity in this passage of Matthew can best be explained by the Marcan vocabulary of an original version. D. B. Taylor (1992, p.354f) noted the difference between the male disciples' experience, 'unmistakably a visionary appearance', and the women's, which their grasping of Jesus' feet leads him to define as a 'solid' appearance. From this he infers that the women's experience was not part of the original Marcan narrative which he too believes to lie behind Matthew 28; but *proskuneō,* 'worship', is Matthew's standard expression for people prostrating themselves before Jesus;[9] Mark would more probably have put 'they fell down at his feet' (*prosepesan pros tous podas autou);* and that mention of *tous podas autou*, ' his feet', could easily have given Matthew his cue to write **they grasped his feet and worshipped him** (*ekratēsan autou tous podas kai prosekunēsan autō*), a small, but a significant, change. But Mark can also use *gonupeteō*, to kneel, so if in his Galilee story he put *gonupetēsan*, 'they knelt', with no mention of 'feet' to cue the same change again, that would explain why, as Taylor asks, Matthew made the first appearance 'solid', but not the second.

Then comes the doubt or hesitation of some disciples when they saw Jesus in Galilee (Matt.28.17). It would be more typical of Mark than of Matthew to show disciples as ordinary, uncertain humans, and much more like Mark to offer no explanation of this emotion – compare Jesus' anger in Mark 1.41.

The loose grammar in v.16, where *eis to oros hou etaxato autois o Iēsous*, defies easy translation, makes a third anomaly. *Tassō,* to marshal for battle, to post as sentry, hence appoint to a task, later became also to decree, fix or settle; as, **having fixed a date for him** (Acts 28.23): it is not elsewhere applied to mountains. The use of *hou* (where, whither), instead of *ho* (which), is awkward; literally the clause reads, **to the mountain where Jesus had appointed for them**, forcing paraphrases like 'to the mountain where Jesus *had told them to meet him'* (*NEB*) or '*to which* Jesus *had directed them*' (*RSV*). But Mark might well have written 'to the mountain where Jesus had appointed *them*' (a more basic use of *tasso*), meaning 'where he first appointed the Twelve as his apostles'; Matthew, missing the point, would then have changed accusative *autous* to dative *autois*, to fit his misapprehension of *etaxato.*[10]

This suggested restoration would improve sense as well as syntax. Since no recorded command to go to Galilee names a particular place, the Eleven, probably with other disciples, must have gathered somewhere already significant during their following of Jesus, and where better than where the Twelve were first appointed? Although *to oros* in Mark often means 'the highlands' (ie. Upland Galilee), here, as in the Transfiguration (Mark 9.2, 9), it must mean a particular hill; very probably the same hill on all three occasions. Here, in the most appropriate place, the Risen Jesus again commissions the Eleven and sends them out to preach.

The New Commission

Major, seeking to recover Mark's original ending, simply took out of Matt.28.9-20 the obviously Matthean episode of Bribing the Guards (28.11-15), and the anachronistic command to baptize in the name of the Trinity in 28.19. The remainder, concluding the episode at the tomb triumphantly (28.9f) and closing with the new commission to the apostles (28.16-20), could have ended Mark's gospel 'with a brevity and dignity like to that with which it opens' (Major, p.102).

Major left it at that; but the whole of Matthew's commission (28.19) is suspect. For **to go and make disciples of all nations** seems as anachronistic as the Trinity, since that was not by any means what the apostles actually did.

The record shows that initially Jesus' followers confined their mission to their fellow Jews

> The command to evangelise all the nations was apparently unknown in the primitive community in Palestine, which, according to Acts [...] looked with suspicion on the Gentile and even on the Samaritan Mission. Even Peter had to be convinced by a special vision from heaven (Green, p.260).

Paul, too, wherever he went, always began at the synagogue, or at **the place of prayer**, where he would meet his co-religionists (Acts 13.5; 16.13; 7.1f; 18.19); and did so after, as well as before, his famous split with the synagogue at Corinth (Acts 18.5-7; 19.8; 28.17). The fact that Gentiles might now be admitted to the church made no difference; it was at the synagogues that 'God fearing' Gentiles were usually found.

Mark had earlier juxtaposed *preaching the gospel to all the nations* (13.10) with being *flogged in the synagogues* (13.9); and to go out and preach the good news *in the synagogues* in all the nations seems, as a fact of history, to have been the apostles' primary understanding of what Jesus now commanded. This meant a major extension of the scope of Jesus' own mission: yet, since his work too had been specifically limited to the Jewish people, this wider field was consistent with his example (Mark 1.39) and precept (Mark 7.27), with the training he had given them (Matt.10.5f), and with the target he had set before them (Matt.10.24).[11] They were indeed to preach worldwide, but still, naturally, to the scattered nation of Israel, on whom the whole world's salvation depended.[12]

It is generally accepted that Matthew has himself inserted the command to baptise in the name of the Three Persons of the Trinity, in line with his tendency to authorise in his text the current practice and doctrine of his church.[13] Since relations with the synagogues were, when Matthew wrote, strained if not already ruptured, it would have been consistent if Matthew also deleted a reference to synagogues, in order to conform Jesus' original instructions to the church's actual practice in Matthew's day, which was indeed to make converts of every nationality.

A Stronger Motive

The ghost theme suggested for Mark 16.8c might possibly have been omitted by the suggested censors without cutting the rest; but a mission statement irreconcilable with the church's later practice would have been truly embarrassing, and scrapping the entire end of Mark's gospel would have been the simplest solution. So, while no ending for Mark could ever have been totally lost by accident, it need not have been lost before the second century; and by then bishops possessed enough authority to censor it. Although the wording of a hypothetical censored ending must necessarily be conjectural, two phrases, consistent with the narrative, the vocabulary and the teaching in Mark, have been suggested, demonstrating the possibility that what Mark might naturally have written to complete his gospel could also have contained reasons for its own suppression, once Matthew's version had become dominant and Mark was little used.

That Matthew's ending contains certain oddities, which its derivation from a Marcan ending could explain, offers a degree of support for this hypothesis; but the important issue is that it should not in future be maintained that Mark's gospel *must* have been meant to end at 16.8. An alternative is clearly possible.

Little by Little

What could have made quiet censorship effective was widespread indifference; Mark was not now a highly esteemed text, Matthew being preferred at every point; so that Mark eventually came to be thought secondary and derivative, and was largely ignored by Christian authors.[14] Matthew, with smoother style, clearer narrative, greater miracles, well-arranged teaching, additional dramatic episodes, a magisterial and immensely powerful Jesus, and clear support for the practices of the developing church (Matt.18.15-19; 28.19), had everything to recommend it. Possibly only its association with Peter prevented Mark's gospel from going the way of the half-dozen gospels now known only from fragments or quotations; or even from disappearing as entirely as Q. Certainly no one was likely to preserve or even to miss Mark's last few verses, if nobody used them; and any such ending to Mark had disappeared long before Clement claimed, in the third century, that Peter had fully approved Mark's gospel (Eusebius, *EH*, 2.15.2).

New copies of Mark would now stop at **they were afraid**, if the ending of that verse was a sore point; but complete versions of Mark would not immediately dematerialise simply because they were out of fashion. There were still disagreements as to which books were to be accepted;[15] and also about their exact form, since Eusebius in the fourth century and Jerome in the fifth still knew texts ending at Mark 16.8, without either Longer or Shorter Ending. There might still have been full uncensored texts of Mark, gathering dust in chests, and the last complete copy may have disintegrated centuries later; but perhaps few 'old-style' texts of Mark would have survived the Great Persecution of 303-313 AD, which targeted the Christian scriptures.

Some Christian ministers admitted, after that persecution, that they had ostensibly obeyed the edict to hand over all bibles and liturgical books; but not, they said, to the extent of surrendering the gospels, only papers, heretical works or medical treatises.[16] Eusebius reports many subterfuges that were connived at by the authorities;[17] and one possibility might have been to hand in a pile of worthless documents with an old-style copy of Mark on the top, arguing that the 'faulty' ending made it no 'true' gospel.

Therefore, supposing that Mark 16.8 concluded with some reference to the youth being taken for a ghost, which remains the only sensible explanation of the women's flight, and that there also followed a mission statement which agreed with the church's earliest, but not its later, practice, there is no problem as to why nor how a longer original ending could have disappeared, ignored when not destroyed. All this is necessarily conjecture; but the theories which sustain that Mark designed his gospel to end at 16.8 are equally speculative, and possibly less tenable. Of the two additional phrases conjectured here, the first is trebly supported, by Mark's usage with *gar*, by the need to explain the women's panic, and by the need to conclude properly at least that episode; the second likewise, by the general need for a proper conclusion to Mark's gospel, by Matthew's acknowledgedly anachronistic phrasing of the last part of the charge, and by the fact that what the apostles are recorded as doing was *not* what Matthew later says they had been told to do.

Notes to Chapter Seventeen

[1] Or words to that effect; what I have suggested has Marcan vocabulary and Marcan brevity.

[2] Earlier fragments of papyri cannot, being fragmentary, tell us where a complete gospel would have ended.

[3] Wright 2003, p.623, suggests censorship of the original manuscript of Mark by some Christian who disagreed with what it said; but such a censor, again, would surely have added a 'sound' ending before general publication.

[4] The Longer Ending, cited c.180 AD as Mark's work (Irenaeus, *Adversus Haereses*. 3.10.6), was probably known to Justin, as early as 150 AD.

[5] This phrasing is typically Marcan. *Dokeō* is also used like this in Luke 24.37 and John 20.15b, but neither uses *phantasma,* and both add physical evidence for the reality of Christ's risen body. Wording apart, Ignatius would have disliked deluded, rather than briefly mistaken, witnesses.

[6] Origen, *Contra Celsum*, 1.68.

[7] J. Armitage Robinson, in *Excluded Books of the New Testament*, Everleigh Nash & Grayson, 1927, Introduction, p.xv. For 'phantom', p.78.

[8] *Adversus Marcionem*, 5.7.5: ***si phantasma fuit Christus …***

[9] Mark only uses *proskuneō* twice, of the Gadarene lunatic and the mocking soldiers; the latter are **kneeling** (*tithentes ta gonata)*, so he means 'paid homage' rather than 'prostrated themselves'. Matthew prefers *proskuneō* to Mark's *gonupeteō* (Mark 1.40: Matt.8.2).

[10] Or possibly Matthew's copy of Mark, closely written in small capital letters, had been miscopied already, rendering **AYTOYS** (*autous*) as **AYTOIS** (*autois*).

[11] These two Matthean sayings contradict the later position of the church as given in Matt.28.19, so are probably genuine.

[12] Although many scholars claim that Jesus never proclaimed the Kingdom of God in an eschatological sense, he was surely, as man, bound by the mind-set of his time; and would have used 'Kingdom of God' in the sense which he knew his hearers would understand. For the restricted focus of his mission, Mark 7.27, perhaps 5.19; Matt.10.5-6.

[13] Eg., Green 1936, p.7.

[14] Lightfoot 1951, pp.2-5; V.Taylor 1953, p.9.

---

[15] Eusebius, *The Ecclesiastical History* 3.3.1-6, on differences of opinion in the 4th century.
[16] Surrender of bogus documents, Augustine, *Contra Cresconium* 3.30 and 3.33.
[17] Eusebius *The Ecclesiastical History* 8.2.1 (scriptures burnt); 8.3.2 (authorities connive at pretences).

CHAPTER 18

The Resurrection Appearances

Starting Points

Although in Mark's Gospel, as we have it now, only the second century Longer Ending (Mark 16.9-20) offers any account of resurrection appearances, yet since we have claimed that the two appearances in Matthew derive from the original ending of Mark, the reliability of Mark as a record must now be tested also in the light of the resurrection of Jesus. All who soberly consider the historical evidence of the existence and development of the Christian church after the crucifixion of Jesus may take as common ground that his disciples were convinced beyond all doubt that they had seen him alive and well after his death on the cross; but how soundly based was their belief?

The resurrection is, of course, a key factor, and hence a sensitive point, in most systems of Christian belief; and those who already accept it as the miraculous dematerialising of the dead physical body of Jesus, which could then rematerialize to be seen and inspected by the disciples on any occasion, will find no problem with the ending now suggested for Mark. But, although the case for the conventional belief has been strongly and clearly restated by N. T.Wright in *The Resurrection of the Son of God* (2003), not all Christians have this certainty of the miraculous, and for them and the rest of the world an alternative explanation will be offered here.

Initially, Wright's statement of the position is unarguable. The Sadducees apart, the general belief of Jesus' time was that the righteous would be restored to a physical life at the Day of the Lord, but:

> there was no clarity as to precisely what (*the resurrected body*) would look like or what sort of continuity or discontinuity there would be with present existence (Wright 2003, p.205).

Therefore, he argues, the Christian belief was such a new and uncharacteristic development that it could not 'have generated spontaneously from within its Jewish context', but must have sprung from the combination of the empty tomb, and the appearances of Jesus, alive and well, taken together.

> It is therefore historically highly probable that Jesus' tomb was indeed empty on the third day after his execution, and that the disciples did indeed encounter him giving every appearance of being well and truly alive (Wright 2003, pp.686f).

So far we may all endorse Wright's view, together with the general grounds from which he has argued it, for the nature of the earliest Christians' beliefs about the bodily resurrection of Jesus cannot well be explained on any other basis. But when he asks, 'What explanation can be given for these two phenomena? Is there an alternative to the explanation given by the early Christians themselves?' I suggest that there could be.

Evidence

After careful rebuttal of some alternatives others have suggested, Wright returns to this theme:

> the challenge is: what alternative account can be offered which will explain the data just as well, which can provide an alternative sufficient explanation of all the evidence and so challenge the right of the bodily resurrection to be regarded as the necessary one?' (Wright 2003, p.718)

This challenge must be met; and the first step is to decide what should be considered as evidence. First must come Paul's succinct list of those who on various occasions saw the risen Jesus (1 Cor.15.5-8); but his resurrection theology is only evidence for how he and others interpreted the facts, not for the facts themselves. Then comes Mark's story of the women at the tomb and, with caution, Matthew's accounts of Jesus appearing to the women, and later to the disciples on a Galilean hilltop; which, as suggested above, probably derived, slightly enhanced, from the original Mark. Finally, Luke offers a parallel report which lends some confirmation of the foregoing. (John need not be considered as having any historical value so far as the facts of resurrection are concerned.)

Accepting, then, Wright's position that both appearances and empty tomb are required to explain the particular, indeed peculiar, way in which the apostles conceived the resurrection of Jesus to have taken place, nonetheless it must have been the appearances, in which they met a patently living and commanding Jesus, which alone convinced them that he was alive; the empty tomb by itself, if Luke is to be believed, did not (Luke 24.21). Once the apostles were convinced that Jesus lived, the empty tomb added a belief that the nature of Jesus' new, risen, life had involved the reanimation of his dead body; but without that first, compelling belief, resurrection was the last thing an empty tomb would suggest. Therefore it is the appearances which are crucially important.

The Nature of the Appearances

Wright (2003, p.690) dismisses 'Veridical Visions' as a 'thoroughly insufficient condition for the early Christian belief', holding that:

> They could not possibly by themselves, have given rise to the belief that Jesus had been raised from the dead.

Hugh Montefiore, on the other hand, sets out a some length his understanding of the 'veridical hallucination', to use his more technical term, but is concerned rather with showing the possibility that the resurrection appearances could have been such visions, than with addressing the point made by Wright. He does, however, attempt a definition: veridical means truthful, he explains:

> and for a hallucination of someone to be truthful there must be genuine contact between two persons, even though both are not physically present at the time when it takes place (Montefiore, p.107).

Here, 'vision' will remain the preferred term ('hallucination' has overtones of 'delusion'), and it would be more objective to say that there appears to be genuine contact between two persons. For we can only know – whether visionary or 'bodily' appearances are claimed – how the experience seemed to the percipient.

Using the term 'paranormal', Montefiore deploys various forms of alleged 'paranormal experience', providing often rather dubious explanations for 'miracles', such as 'bilocation' to explain Jesus walking on the sea; and here, he simply mentions that the body 'seems to have dematerialized', which explains nothing at all. 'Paranormal', I suggest, is no more valid a category than 'miraculous'; but visions and mystic experiences, although not everyday happenings, are a recurrent fact in *normal* human life. The vital point, generally overlooked on both sides of the argument, is that visions of the dead, which are not perhaps common but have frequently been reliably reported, can be assigned to two main classes: mere apparitions, which may alarm the beholder but otherwise do not signify – the common ghost-story, in fact – and 'veridical visions', which seem to involve an active interchange with the dead person, and matter deeply.[1]

Types and Levels of Visionary Experience

A good modern example of the first category is given by Arthur Grimble (*A Pattern of Islands*, Penguin 1981, pp.156-163) who met the apparition of an islander just dead, but was merely puzzled that this man should pass him with no glance nor greeting – until he reached the village where the dead man was laid out for burial. The disciples thought that they saw a ghost when Jesus came walking out from the shore, seemingly upon the water (Mark 6.49); the women at the tomb were probably terrified because they thought the young man they found in the tomb was a ghost; and Luke, although this may be for artistic effect, has this as the first reaction of the disciples when Jesus appeared to them that evening (Luke 24.37). Peter, miraculously freed from prison, was assumed to be a ghost by those who had thought that they would never again see him alive (Acts 12.15b).[2] Such apparitions might be dismissed by the scientific as without objective foundation (Pliny, *Natural History*, 2.52.188f), but were generally held to be the spirits of the dead.

Of such manifestations it is indeed right to say that they could not possibly account for the disciples' belief that Jesus had risen from the dead; but the genuine veridical vision is very different. A modern example is given by J. B. Phillips' account of his own seeings of the lately dead C. S. Lewis; a firsthand account whose reliability is perhaps enhanced by Phillips' own conviction that such a vision would *not* sufficiently explain all the narrated resurrection appearances of Jesus.[3] He explains how he was watching television when Lewis appeared, sitting in a nearby chair, and 'spoke a few words which were particularly relevant to the difficult circumstances through which I was passing.' A week later Lewis appeared again 'and repeated to me the same message, which was very important to me at the time.' Phillips clearly was under some emotional strain or stress, of which he gives no details, which this experience addressed. It was, of course, nothing to do with believing Lewis to be alive – an irrelevance, since both men held conventional Christian beliefs about life after death. The vision simply addressed, effectively, a real problem which Phillips was experiencing.

Such a background of emotion – of strain, grief, bereavement, or loss of direction – is common to many such personal experiences. Gerd Ludemann cites many instances of such visions by people mourning those close to them; for example, the case of a girl who lost her father when she was nine, but who (still grieving, although years later) had an experience when she, in bed, 'heard' the house door open, and steps, and then her father appeared to her, beautiful, 'shining like gold and transparent like mist'. Instantly recognisable, he came to her bed and gave her such a kind look and smile that she felt deeply at peace and happier than she had ever been. Then he went away.[4]

Objectively, such experiences have no physical reality outside the chemistry of the brain; but I hold that such experience – it may be termed 'mystic' – may come to us from God, it may convey a true message, and it may guide us to some new purpose not of our choosing. Such an experience is mediated to us, necessarily, through those parts of the brain which normally translate visual or auditory stimuli into what we see and hear, but which in this case are responding, not to external stimuli from the physical world, but to internal stimuli given by, or through, the subconscious.

The point must be stressed that the veridical vision is, to all practical purposes, an encounter with the person seen. Although the percipient sees only an appearance, the overmastering nature of the experience makes it totally convincing. As William James says, 'well-developed' mystic experiences are 'absolutely authoritative *over the individual* to whom they come' (James 1902, Lect.xvii, conclusion, pt.1; my italics). Two main classes of vision of the dead have been indicated; but the reality is a wide spectrum of experience, in which that of Phillips, while clearly a veridical vision, is not the most intense. He was not someone bereft by Lewis' death, his trouble was of another sort; although the experience was a true 'encounter' which, as Quakers say, 'spoke to his condition'.

The distinction implied by James' use of 'well-developed' acknowledges that there are different levels, as well as different types, of mystic experience, but that when these go deep there is no arguing with them. One might distinguish, in another wide-spread type of mystic experience, between an enhanced sensitivity to the world around us, which may be little more than euphoria, 'the runner's high', or being in love, and that rapt level at which a similar experience turns into, as it were, a sudden window into the heart of the universe, a revelation of eternal truth. The former is lovely while it lasts; the latter, speaking from experience, is something which endures unshaken for the rest of one's life; even though it may have lasted mere seconds, while time stood still. Grimble's experience of seeing a man just dead left him puzzled at the time and astonished later, but had no life-changing significance; Phillips' much deeper experience was 'a present help in trouble'; but the experience of the apostles and the other witnesses would have been deeper still, a transforming of their world and their future: on a par, in this respect, with Jesus' own baptismal experience; and identical, it seems, in process and effect, with what happened to Saul on the Damascus Road.

Appearance to the Women.

Consider, then, two relatively simple and undeveloped accounts of such visions. According to Matt.28.8ff, the women, running from the tomb, meet Jesus, who greets them, and they advance to prostrate themselves and grasp his feet in homage. Jesus then repeats more briefly the charge they had received from the angel.

The precondition of this and all the Easter appearances was the mental turmoil which must have overtaken all Jesus' followers and friends at Jerusalem. From sunset on Good Friday until sunset the following day the disciples must have kept the Sabbath; not rigidly, perhaps, but certainly properly, as Jesus had always done. (If it was also the day of the Passover, the men must, like every male Jew in Jerusalem, have eaten the ritual meal that Friday night, however little they wished to celebrate.) And all the time they were tormented by unanswerable questions. Why did Jesus let himself be captured? Since he had foreseen treachery, why did he take no steps to avoid or prevent? Why did God not save him from the cross? Did his crucifixion mean, as Deuteronomy proclaimed, that he was now accursed? What now became of his mission? Were his disciples to try to persuade their compatriots that Jesus had been a good man, a teacher to follow, after the high priest, the Sanhedrin and Deuteronomy had all condemned him? All who had followed him to Jerusalem were now grieved, perplexed and troubled, a standard precondition for the veridical vision.

If we may take the women's vision as originally from Mark, then they have come, very early in the morning, to anoint the body of Jesus properly, according to custom.[5] (It seems mistaken to suggest that the ritual requirements had been fulfilled simply because, some days earlier, Jesus had chosen to rebut criticism of a woman's extravagant generosity by saying that her anointing of his head was to anticipate his burial.) Going to perform this practical task, the women are first puzzled to see the tomb open, then terrified as, inside in the semi-darkness, they encounter the white-robed figure of an unknown adolescent; and they dash helter-skelter from the cave, while he is trying to allay panic by calling that Jesus has risen and they are to tell his disciples and Peter that he has gone ahead of them to Galilee, where they will see him. Running from the 'haunted' tomb like women possessed, they next have a vision of Jesus themselves. In Matthew, of course, they were only walking quickly, and indeed it seems likely that they would soon have slowed to a walk; they might even have been dazzled and brought to a halt by the light of a rising sun;[6] in any case, they would have come down from the height of their terror. Now, to their amazement, they see Jesus, and fall on their knees with bowed heads, and the vision produces a sequence of emotions: calm, joy, a longing to share this joy with the others and for them to see Jesus too. These emotions become concrete thoughts, clothed in words and phrases left in their minds by that encounter with the youth in white: 'Don't fear – tell the others – they will all see me in Galilee.' This message they carry back and deliver.

Any such vision must, in every sense, speak one's own language.[7] We have cited above (Ch.1, *The Call*) instances from early Quakers, showing how verbal messages or commands at this level of experience must always express themselves by using familiar phrases and concepts – naturally so, since the mechanics of 'voice', as of 'vision', can only draw their raw material from what that person's brain already has, consciously or subconsciously, in store. J. B. Phillips' subconscious may perhaps have picked out some phrase from Lewis' correspondence, or his books; the women's minds needed to reach back no further than the enigmatic utterances of that mysterious figure at the tomb.

Only here is there, in Matthew's gospel, a clear suggestion of physical reality in the risen Jesus, as the women grasp the feet of Jesus and worship him (Matt.28.9.b); and we have argued above that Matthew is adapting a Marcan original, with the grasping of feet probably originating from the typically Marcan phrase, **they fell at his feet**. Mark's version of the tradition probably made no reference to physical contact.

Luke and John, while stressing the physical reality of the appearances – Jesus eats and drinks, shows his wounds and invites disciples to touch him – yet stop short of claiming that anyone – excepting, possibly, John's Mary Magdalene at the tomb, actually did touch him; which suggests that the later evangelists had found no other mention of physical contact in earlier traditions. Nor is there any such suggestion about Paul's encounter with Jesus on the Damascus road; and Paul always speaks simply of 'seeing', whether by himself or others; making no distinction between those resurrection appearances which closely followed the death of Jesus and his own vision a few years later. Therefore it would seem that, notwithstanding the exaggerations which crept into the later tradition, it is straightforward visual appearances of Jesus to his friends which must be accounted for: real appearances of a dead person to real people: 'the disciples did indeed *encounter* him giving every *appearance* of being well and truly alive' (Wright 2003, p.687; my italics).

If this is so, then, even though the insistence of Luke on the risen Jesus breaking the loaf (Luke 24.30), showing his wounds and actually eating with the disciples (Luke 24.39, 43), and the even more elaborate stories of John 20.24-29; 21.1-23, can be taken as later exaggerations of a simpler tradition,[8] they nonetheless attempt to make a true point: that the appearances of Jesus were not the apparitions of a ghost, a shadowy, less-than-alive, spirit from a gloomy underworld, but, as veridical visions can be, moments of intense experience in which the dead truly appear to be present with, and often to speak with, those who see them, communicating a sense of life, of joy, of peace, of comfort or new purpose.

The evangelists wrote in terms of their own time, when eating and drinking were considered proof that what was seen was more than mere appearance.[9] To many people today, testimony to the eating of food as proof of the 'physical reality' of the appearances might seem pointless; for if God is already supposed to have abrogated the normal laws of the universe to the point of causing a body to vanish out of the world, the vanishing of food proves nothing more; and, in such a context, neither disappearance can prove anything about the physical reality of what may be seem to be perceived with the eye, but certainly is interpreted, if not created, by the brain.

Appearance to the Brethren.

Before the encounter in Galilee, the disciples had presumably remained in Jerusalem until the end of the feast. That was their religious obligation; moreover, anyone leaving earlier would have been very conspicuous, whereas at the end of the week they would mingle with the usual throng of departing pilgrims. So this last appearance will have taken place perhaps a fortnight after the first one, and its timing does not conflict with other stories of appearances – to Peter, for example, to James, and to **the Eleven and those that were with them** – which probably took place during that week of festival. However many individual or group appearances happened at that time, it would be unlikely that these would have led the apostles to ignore their responsibility to return to that same hill where Jesus had given them their first commission as his apostles.[10]

It seems probable that the Eleven would have spread the word and summoned all the disciples to this special meeting; since the instruction, as recorded, was not to 'tell the Eleven', but to **'tell his disciples'** (Mark 16.7a; Matt.28.7) or **'tell my brothers'** (Matt.28.10b). One need not wholly trust Luke's total of 120 persons (Acts 1.15) as disciples at this time, still less Paul's figure of a gathering of 500, since numbers of any size in ancient histories are seldom reliable; but this is a likely occasion for all Jesus' disciples, one might guess between 50 and 80, but possibly many more, to have assembled. A large gathering might best account for the hesitation of some as the vision spreads telepathically, but unevenly, amongst the crowd.

This is not the place for a detailed study of the nature of the 'multiple vision'; on which topic Ludemann cites some interesting parallels.[11] Two examples of visions telepathically shared by two or three people – with no apparent cause nor result in either case – are cited by G. N. M. Tyrrell (1947, p.63-6); and what can be telepathically shared by two could equally well spread through any number of persons who share a sufficiently strong emotional bond at the time. Here the precondition is not, as it was for the women, a state of shock and terror, and then joy, shared by all three; in Galilee the disciples, whether the Eleven only or ten times that number, would rather have returned to the master's favourite hilltop, no longer grieving, but in a state of the highest expectation.

Let us repeat that to class the resurrection appearances as veridical visions is not to devalue their importance. Such visions can be, as these were, not merely life-enhancing but life-changing experiences. This is the same experience as the call of the prophet: the hearing of the voice of God, which, through whatever senses or brain-cells it is mediated, changes one's life for ever; and like that call, it has Truth without having physical reality. No such experience can prove in objective terms either the existence of God or the reality of life after death; but those who have had a compelling – for want of a better word – mystic experience, at any level, know what they know, which is real and vital to them in a way that nothing else is. The early church was therefore perfectly correct in its rejection of any idea of ghostly or phantom appearances of the risen Jesus; what had happened to the disciples was real in a way quite different from those.

This collective vision would have impressed on the 'brethren' the power and the enduring love of their Master, while the wording of their new commission would arise quite naturally as a variation on the wording of their first one. The messages suggested in the Marcan ending reconstructed above, omitting anachronistic Matthean embellishments, are relatively simple, and their key-phrases are short and clear:

> ***Power has been given to me*** **in heaven and on earth. Go out and** ***preach*** **[in the synagogues?]** ***throughout all the nations*****, teaching them everything which I taught you. And lo,** ***I am with you always*****, even to the ending of this age.**

– and their nascence is easily understood. The words we have are, of course, those found afterwards to express what at the moment of vision may have been only impulses and convictions, deeply felt but barely formulated. The 'hearing' of actual words cannot be entirely ruled out, but is perhaps more likely in the mystic experience of a single person, alone.

Corroboration from Luke

Too much can be made of the discrepancies between Luke's resurrection appearances and those in Matthew. Luke's account of a final experience, given briefly in Luke 24.50-53 and retold in Acts 1.6-12, reads like a typically Lucan – ie. polished and dramatic, but less accurate – version of the same event as Matt.28.16-20; an example of the type of Tale which first loses its details through the erosion of repetition, and is later refurbished by a story-teller, or here, written up by an author who enjoys telling a good story (Dibelius 1934, pp.97-103). As in Matthew, Luke's disciples go out from Jerusalem,[12] go to a significant, familiar hill, and are there commissioned to bear witness **in Jerusalem and all Judaea and Samaria and to the end of the earth.** The last event in Matthew is also the final vision in Luke; and Luke's version too is compatible with the idea that this was a large gathering of disciples (Acts 1.6) although he too does not say so. Luke may then be taken as corroborating the last and crucial experience in the series. Earlier experiences had transformed a theoretical belief in the afterlife into a bedrock certainty of a continuing relationship with the crucified master; but now their future task was set before them and the supreme assurance given – **And see, I am with you even until the ending of this age.**

Since all mystical experience is, in William James' definition, ineffable, not even eye-witness could then have given precise descriptions of such experiences as we could not recount accurately now. Nor, in this particular case, can anyone claim to view the question objectively; for some theologies demand that the resurrection be a uniquely miraculous event, while other concepts of the nature of God and God's working in the universe require that it should not be; while the nonbeliever is committed in advance to disbelief. Here, however, the concern is not theology, but the historical reliability of Mark's narrative. Given above is merely one understanding of the Easter appearances as not, strictly speaking, miraculous, although outside the run of everyday happenings; unique as every historical event is unique, but not altogether outside the bounds of recorded experience. Therefore, those who cannot accept the traditional concept of resurrection need not reject the witness of Mark, even when his gospel is extended to include simpler versions of Matthew's two appearances.

Pentecost: the Spirit in the Church

The disciples had, from the first appearances, been wholly convinced that Jesus was alive, vindicated and exalted, and after their final vision of Jesus they understood that they were to carry on his work all over the world. They still, however, needed to consider and digest these revelations before they were ready to tell the general public.

William James, stating that well developed mystical states were usually 'absolutely authoritative over the individuals to whom they come', adds bluntly, 'but not over anyone else'. Their proper proof has always been the proof of experience. Jesus had been a prophet 'mighty in deed and word', and in his earthly lifetime had imparted something of the same power to the apostles:

> **and going forth they preached that people should change their ways. And they exorcised many demons, and anointed many sick people with oil and healed them.** (Mark 6.12f)

And this power, they found, was with them still. The Pentecost experience, with its multiple vision of tongues of fire and the hearing of a mighty wind, may be regarded as the proper culmination of the sequence of resurrection visions, the moment when the disciples knew themselves empowered, as well as commanded, to preach widely; and on occasion, to heal as well.

It was, surely, the working of the Spirit in the apostles themselves, of which we have a sketch in the early chapters of Acts (and, I suggest, an exposition in the Last Supper discourses of John 14-16), which persuaded others to listen to and believe their otherwise unproven claim for Jesus' resurrection. What his followers still kept, and lived by, was their continuing relationship with him, the risen Jesus whom they had seen and heard. They put their case, as Acts and Paul's letters confirm, solely on the basis of their encounters with the risen Jesus, but it would have been the love in their lives which convinced other people, then and thereafter.[13]

Many believed them, because of their boldness, undeterred by suffering; because of the occasional manifestation of the power of Jesus through healing, and the daily showing of the spirit of Jesus in **love, joy, peace, patience, kindness and honesty, loyalty, gentleness and self-discipline**, to quote from Paul, who himself could not come to terms with his own vision until he was lovingly welcomed into friendship by Ananias as **'Brother Saul'** (Acts 9.17). No one is more definite than Paul about physical resurrection; yet his greatest expression of trust is that he is sure that **neither death nor life [...] will be able to separate us from the love of God...** (Rom.8.38f); Ananias, by his welcome, had shown Paul that love in action. Such love was the solid evidence which, for many, could outweigh the unprecedented and unverifiable nature of what the apostles had to say.[14]

Neither Jesus, who affirmed his belief in the afterlife in terms of a continuing relationship with God (Mark 12.26f), nor, it will be suggested, his disciples, relied on secure knowledge of what would, or had, become of his body; but through their resurrection visions that continuing relationship became intensely real to the disciples. Such experiences, like other commoner moments of 'extended consciousness', for want of a better term, are always totally convincing to the recipient; and one may well live by their light for the rest of one's days. One notable agnostic said of his own recurrent mystic experience, 'I cannot but regard it as the rightful compass-needle of my whole life'.[15] Characteristically, such moments will convince one of being in communion with a reality beyond the limits or limitations of the apparent world. The resurrection visions convinced the disciples of the greater life in which Jesus was now living, and put them in communion with him, or with the spirit which was in him. Their lives became the best evidence for what they had to say.

Notes to Chapter Eighteen

[1] The ghost as a portent of doom appears to belong to legend and fiction, not fact, and may be ignored.
[2] See also Guthrie 1968, pp.274-306.
[3] Phillips 1967, p.89f. He is quite right that some later stories could not be satisfied by such an explanation.
[4] Ludemann 1994, pp.97ff; but I cannot endorse his general view of the resurrection stories.
[5] The decay of the body, after two (possibly cold) nights and one day, would not have been too far advanced; and the Jewish sabbath meant that bodies quite often could not be anointed for at least 24 hours. **Very early** (*lian prōi*) on Sunday morning, Jesus had only been dead some 36 hours.
[6] A **not** (*ouk*) seems lost from Mark 16.2: for if **the sun was up** it was not **very early in the morning**. (cf Mark 1.35). Some texts of Mark omit or alter **when the sun was up;** Matthew and Luke both use phrases meaning 'at first light', the earliest dawn.
7 A veridical vision is quite different from the Pentecost experience of 'speaking with tongues' in a state of 'possession'.
[8] Borg and Crossan, 2008, p.207, correctly point out that visions may also have 'a tactile dimension'; but I incline here towards the natural growth factor of stories.
[9] The converse is stated by Raphael in Tobit 12.19: **All these days I was seen by you; and I did neither eat nor drink, but you were seeing a vision.**

[10] Assuming, as argued already, an original Marcan *hou etaxato* **autous** *ho Iēsus*, 'the hill where Jesus had commissioned them', to lie behind Matt.28.16 which has *autois*. Matthew has missed the point, and created an awkward sentence.
[11] Ludemann 1994, p.106f. He takes the appearance to **over 500 brethren** to mean Pentecost; but in Acts that is not an appearance of Jesus.
[12] Luke has the risen Jesus lead the disciples out on a two-mile walk, perhaps implausibly. Is **He led them out** (*exegagen*, from *exagō*) **as far as Bethany** (Luke 24.50) a distant echo of the earlier tradition, **I will lead you** (*proaxō*, from *proagō*) into Galilee' (Mark 14.28) ?
[13] Nearer the end of that century it is unambiguously claimed, in a passage primarily about the love of God, that **we know that we are living with Him because He has given us a share of His own spirit** (1 John 4.13).
[14] Eg., the mandarin at Yangcheng, won over by the love, goodness and trustful courage of Gladys Aylward (Burgess, 1959, p.144).
[15] Cited by V. H. Mottram 1952, p.153, from Olaf Stapledon; see also Mottram 1952, pp.149-155, Weatherhead 1959, pp.491f, 517ff, and W. James 1902, particularly *Lectures 16 & 17*.

CHAPTER 19

The Empty Tomb

The Puzzle

As we have seen, Mark 16.1-8 presents the quadruple enigma of an open, empty tomb, an unknown adolescent seated inside, a remarkable message to be given to the disciples, and the women's panic-stricken flight. The addition of a slightly modified version of Matthew's resurrection appearances does nothing to solve those problems; and we must sympathise with the later evangelists who thought best to transform the youth into an angel. Unexplained oddities are, admittedly, quite common in Mark, almost a hallmark of genuine Petrine material; but that does not mean that they must still be left unexplained.

So far, explanation has been offered only for the women's flight. The empty tomb has appeared to some a clinching proof of the physical resurrection of Jesus, and to others an obviously invented story intended to supply such proof. Neither position, it was argued above, is correct: an empty tomb proves nothing, and was never worth inventing.

Background – The Tomb

Although the open, empty tomb is still, even today, sometimes invoked to help 'prove' the physical resurrection of Christ, Paul, our earliest witness, never employs that argument, and would have convinced no one if he had; for the Graeco-Roman world of the first century had simpler explanations.

The light fiction of the period, as Wright too has pointed out, is full of heroines who are entombed, apparently dead, but recover later. In *Chareas and Callirhoe*,[1] for example, the unconscious heroine in the family vault regains her senses just in time to be carried off by grave-robbing pirates. Chareas finds the tomb open and the body gone; only much later does he discover that Callirhoe is still alive. Much the same befalls Anthia in the *Ephesian Tale.* In *Leucippe and Clitophon* the hero believes that his kidnapped Leucippe is the woman whom he sees pirates behead and throw overboard, and he buries the wrong corpse. In *Apollonius, King of Tyre,* both the king's wife, apparently dead after giving birth at sea, and later her baby, who grows up as Tarsia, escape death by a hairsbreadth; and an empty tomb is erected, to conceal their guilt, by the foster-parents who wish, and believe, Tarsia to be dead.

In these Greek thrillers, the deceptive tomb, empty of its proper tenant, is a common theme; and the two most straightforward examples given – burial, tomb broken open, 'corpse' removed but later found alive – have probable dates closely bracketing the period 65 to 115 AD, during which our canonical gospels appear to have been written. So it would be easy to infer that the evangelists constructed their stories of the empty tomb and the resurrected Jesus by imitating this theme from popular fiction: but the point of the often complex mechanics of the novels was that a human, believed dead and buried, had never died at all, the very opposite of the gospel message.

Although such fiction was 'popular' only in the sense that it was despised by intellectuals,[2] it is likely that the learned and philosophical would have been yet more sceptical,[3] and the unlettered masses no less cynical, than the middlebrow readers to whom such novels appealed. To have offered an empty tomb as evidence that a real man, truly dead, had been miraculously restored by God to life, would have been futile; the obvious possibilities, all found in the novels, were that either no corpse had been placed there, or human hands had removed it, or the person had never really died; so our evangelists had no motive at all to invent such a thing. Before Mark ever wrote, the apostles had been preaching the resurrection of Jesus for over thirty years on the much sounder basis that they themselves had seen the risen Lord. Nothing would have been gained by inventing the empty tomb, so probably it was only ever related because it was a puzzling fact.

The Dead Man

On the other hand, not even the most dedicated reader of ancient romances would have supposed that Jesus survived crucifixion. Mistaken death was very common in fiction;[4] Leucippe is actually disembowelled and coffined 'before our very eyes', in a fake death which uses a stage-knife with retractable blade, and similar tricks; and genuine corpses can be wrongly identified.[5] But whatever mistaken or sham deaths the ingenuity of novelists can contrive, these never include death by crucifixion.

Rescue at the last moment from a terrible fate was the very stuff of the ancient thriller, and crucifixion, being a protracted death, allows various, more or less realistic, chances of escape; but these always depend, not on mistake, nor rescue, but on reprieve. Chareas is climbing up to be nailed to his cross when reprieved by the satrap of Caria; or, as he tells it later, he had been put on his cross, and was almost dead, before the satrap realised who he was and had him taken down (*Chaereas and Callirhoe*, 4.3; 8.8). Rhodanes, too, is already up on his cross when jealous King Garmus decides to keep him alive to lead the army (*Babylonian Story*, 21; 22). Habrocomes is tied – that, the author explains, is how they do it in Egypt – to his cross; which is then blown from a cliff to float down the Nile, and after signs and wonders he is finally pardoned and released by the prefect of Egypt (*Ephesian Tale*, 4.2; 4.4).

The novels say, in effect, that not even miracles avail without reprieve from high authority: from the satrap, the prefect or the king. So too, in the historical case recorded by Josephus, it was only through the favour and by the order of Titus, the emperor's son, that three of Josephus' friends – one of whom subsequently lived – were taken down from their crosses (*Life*, 420f).

Thus, although apparent or simulated death was common in the novels, and not unknown in fact,[6] no author imagined this as a way of rescuing his hero from a cross. Theories that Jesus simply lost consciousness or was given drugged wine are still occasionally propounded, but the ancient world was realistic in its assumption that no one ever came out of crucifixion alive, except by the direct intervention of authority. Roman auxiliary troops were highly efficient, and usually posted to places where they would have little sympathy with the native inhabitants.[7] Not even at the level of a local prison was any excuse accepted for losing a prisoner, as is shown by Herod Agrippa's reaction to the escape of Peter (Acts 12.2-19), and the gaoler's dismay after the earth-tremor sprang the jail-doors at Philippi (Acts 16.27). Only a reprieve from Pilate himself could have saved Jesus alive: in reality, Pilate double-checked to make sure the man was dead (Mark 15.44f).

Persons Unknown

No one, then, would have doubted that Jesus was truly dead when laid to rest. Therefore the popular reaction to an open tomb and a missing body would be to suppose that the grave had been broken into by some person or persons unknown, who did then 'steal, take, convey or carry away' that body for their own, probably nefarious, purposes. It would not suggest a dead man returning to life. Tomb robbery was common enough, wherever a thief would brave the legal penalties, or the curses invoked in sepulchral inscriptions:[8] in the case of Jesus, however, whose body had to be hastily wrapped in a sheet of linen and left as the Sabbath approached (Mark 15.52-56), there was nothing worth stealing – not even that lavish provision of spices mentioned only in John – and it was the body itself which disappeared. Common sense therefore suggested that some of the late prophet's followers had removed the body (Matt.28.13-15); just as Mark records of the Baptist that **his disciples, hearing [of his death], came and took his body and placed it in a tomb** (Mark 6.29).

Not The Apostles

The apostles undoubtedly believed that the empty tomb implied the physical resurrection, by divine miracle, of the body of Jesus; there was no precedent for such a thing, but nothing in their Easter experiences had followed precedent. Yet while nobody is stronger than Paul in his assertion of the resurrected Christ, what he offers as evidence is, very soundly, the experiences of the apostles and of himself: encounters, for want of a better word, of a kind which were wholly convincing to those who experienced them, and to which they could, and did, testify as, literally, eye-witnesses (1.Cor.15.3-8). To have drawn attention to the all too easily explicable mystery of an open tomb and a vanished body would have been to weaken the effect and to invite, not belief, but ridicule.

This gives the evidence its proper weighting. To those who experienced them, the appearances of Jesus told them unmistakably and beyond all doubt, that he was alive; and this unprecedented and unexpected early resurrection must, as they saw it, be a signal mark of God's favour. Therefore the empty tomb could be understood as another: **he was not abandoned to Hades, nor did his flesh see corruption** (Acts 2.31). By the end of that Easter day, the apostles would have been neither puzzled nor distressed by the disappearance of the body; but the empty tomb was not, they seem to have decided, evidence to present to a sceptical world.

Editing Mark's Account

If we accept the traditional Petrine source for Mark, then, had Peter still been alive when Mark wrote – as Clement of Alexandria would have us believe, but the earlier witnesses contradict him – he might not have passed that episode for publication; but he and Paul had already 'departed'. However, once the Marcan account had been published, with the prestige of the martyred Peter behind it, the church could only make the best of the story as it stood. Its awkwardness is underlined by the eagerness of the later evangelists to alter it.

Matthew, admitting that, when he wrote, the belief current amongst the great majority of his nation was that **his disciples came by night and stole him away** (Matt.28.13, 15b), tackles this head-on, by incorporating into the Marcan account a story of a guard set over a tomb sealed, and only opened by a majestic angel, before witnesses. Luke makes as little as he can, less than twenty words, of the empty tomb,[9] and promptly moves the reader's attention forward to his heavenly messengers; but before recounting the Emmaus appearance he stresses that neither the empty tomb nor that message had been accepted as evidence by the apostles: **And these words seemed like nonsense in their view, and they did not believe the women** (Luke 24.11).

John, like Matthew, expresses the natural reaction: **They have taken the Lord out of the tomb and we don't know where they have put him** (John 20.2). Although he produces an abandoned set of grave-clothes to set against the idea of ordinary tomb-robbery, John does not present the apostles as especially credulous: his unnamed disciple keeps his belief to himself, and Peter is far from convinced.

John's Mary Magdalene repeats to the angels her unchanged conviction that the body has been taken away (John 20.13); she is persuaded only by Jesus' appearance to her, in an episode typical of the non-recognition scenes of Greek drama.[10] It is by capturing the imagination with this vivid scene that John carries his reader past questioning to belief, as was his stated aim.[11] For good measure he does it again, with Thomas as the incredulous one, unconvinced until he has seen the print of the nails (John 20.24-29). Although these are, I suggest, imagined incidents, the skill of the author allows him to convey better than anyone the instant and overwhelming nature of the moment of revelation – **Rabboni!** or **My Lord and my God!** – and both instances display this truth, that it was the experience of seeing the risen Jesus which convinced – **Because you have *seen* me, you have believed** – and which transformed one's life. The empty tomb did not.

'His Disciples Came by Night'

What has been said so far runs parallel to the path which Wright has marked out: the appearances were experiences which convinced the followers of Jesus that they saw him truly alive and gloriously well. Now, we diverge; for to accept that the tomb was truly empty does not compel acceptance of the apostles' interpretation of that astonishing fact. Those of us who live in a world where a disappearing corpse implies human agency, or who hold a miraculous resurrection to be not so much impossible as inappropriate, require an alternative: neither supernatural, nor 'paranormal' – which is the supernatural thinly disguised – but realistic, and not historically improbable. Matthew 28.15 records that there was an alternative interpretation, widely current in the first century.

The Motive.

The first question to ask, then, is not Frank Morison's famous 'Who moved the stone?' but 'Who wanted the body?' Cicero had already laid down that the first line of inquiry should always be *cui bono*, who benefits? In this case, who intended to benefit?

Not Pilate nor Caiaphas. They had achieved what they saw as needful, the execution of the dangerous new leader, and that was that: 'stone dead hath no fellow'. In any movement led by a prophet – the Baptist, for example, or the Mahdi – the leader is usually irreplaceable, and there was no reason to pursue misguided followers, nor to deprive the dead man of decent burial when a responsible citizen offered to see to it.[12] Shrewd practitioners, who between them kept the peace in Judaea for a decade with very little violence, Caiaphas and Pilate had nothing to gain by removing and hiding the corpse.

Jesus' friends from Galilee had the one obvious motive, which would have been to lay the master to rest in his own country, where they could make him a shrine and where many would still wish to honour his name, whatever folk said in Jerusalem. The worthy councillor who had found Jesus a tomb was doing his best, they might think, but Jesus was first and last a Galilean, and his bones ought to lie in Galilee, and be honoured, with affection, where he, and his friends, belonged.

Now Jesus had a wide spectrum of Galilean friends and followers in and around Jerusalem at that time. There were the Eleven, now despondently worrying about their role as the leaders of a dead prophet's following. There was a considerable group of women who had come up from Galilee (Mark 15.41), some of whom were planning to tend the body properly at the first opportunity. Amongst other Galilean pilgrims there would still be some well-wishers; but there were also the rest of his disciples, of whom a large body had been sent on ahead of him into Peraea and had then followed him up to Jerusalem (Luke 9.51; 10.1; 19.37; Mark 10.32). Without relying unduly on Luke's figure of seventy (or seventy-two), Jesus would have had a fair number of other disciples there for the Passover feast. Two such 'followers', it seems, prepared the room for the Last Supper, and perhaps served it;[13] and probably it was two from the same group who were detailed to fetch and return the donkey (Mark 11.1-3).

We have seen above (Ch.6, *His Disciples*) that the majority of Jesus' followers were probably between sixteen and nineteen or so, the normal age to be a teacher's disciple.[14] Religious art usually depicts the apostles as mature, often middle-aged men but most, even of the Twelve, were probably much younger. It would certainly not be surprising to find, amongst the other 'followers', some impulsive youths who, outraged by the execution of their master, and perhaps recalling how the Baptist's disciples had taken their master's body away to entomb it properly (Mark 6.29), determined to take the body of Jesus home to Galilee.[15] Such lads, new bottles for new wine, would be likely to have accepted whole-heartedly the master's teaching that nothing from outside a man can pollute him (Mark 7.14-23), and so might be willing to handle a dead body at need, and abandon early the Feast of Unleavened Bread; whereas most Jews would have shrunk from even going near a corpse during the feast. (Tombs were actually whitewashed at this season, to help visitors avoid them.)

The Method.

The plan, made as they met and talked on that sad Sabbath, could have been to open up the tomb soon after dark on Saturday night, bringing an improvised bier, perhaps simply one long pole and a stout sheet,[16] and to bear away the body as fast as they could by the short route, through Samaria, to Galilee; perhaps resting in the shade of some ravine in the hills for most of the first day, to avoid notice, and again during the hottest part of the next; pressing forward through each moonlit night and, I estimate, reaching Galilee, a matter of some sixty-five miles, on the morning of the third day (Tuesday). There they could lay the body, by now in urgent need of burial, under a cairn of stones somewhere remote, perhaps in the hills near Nazareth; intending later to collect the bones in an ossuary and have a proper tomb set up, where all Jesus' friends would be able to revere the master's memory.[17]

Four fit youths, accustomed as they were to tramping long distances, could have managed this; six would make it easier. The group would be small, however; for avoiding notice was essential if they were not to be stopped, flogged or even crucified, on charges of tomb-robbery with seditious intent. Pilate and Caiaphas would not be concerned to persecute followers who now went peacefully home; but any who seemed determined to carry forward the subversive activity of the dead messianic pretender, which an immediate attempt to possess themselves of his body might suggest, could expect no mercy. Rome was ruthless with all who persisted in flouting her authority; and since these youths would in any case be technically guilty of robbing a tomb, they would have, if detected, no defence.

The Outcome.

Such a group might not only have removed the body but successfully taken it all the way back; yet, even while they did so, visions of the risen master had begun and, long before the flesh had rotted to leave bones ready for an ossuary, the whereabouts of Jesus' human remains had ceased to be of any concern to his followers.

This last point is fact, not surmise. The tomb at Jerusalem where Jesus had been buried was not kept in mind, and is today a matter of pious guesswork. This has been used to argue that the whole burial story is untrue, since, in a world in which the tombs of just and holy men were venerated, it is inconceivable that the tomb of Jesus, had it ever been known, would not have been remembered and continually revisited; Jeremias held that the argument was stronger than mere custom, because 'the one who had lain in the tomb was more than one of those just men, martyrs and prophets'.[18] Yet, while that underlines the strength of the suggested motive for removing the body to Galilee, where Jesus was loved, Jeremias' argument overlooks the quantum leap in thinking about Jesus which was forced upon the apostles when his apparent resurrection took place not, as they might have expected, at the coming Day of Judgement, but some thirty-six hours after his death.

The combination of seeing Jesus alive, and the tomb empty, convinced the apostles that he had been 'raised' ahead of time – just, they now thought, as he had foretold – **the first-fruits of those who have fallen asleep**, as Paul says. This then compelled his astonished followers to believe that the one whom they had known as a man **powerful in deed and word in the sight of God and of the people** had now been lifted onto a supernatural plane, higher indeed than martyrs and prophets, to be God's heavenly deputy, soon to come again on the clouds of glory (Acts 2.23-36).[19] It could then seem irrelevant to revere the tomb of a person you had seen and knew to be alive; it would be nonsensical to venerate the tomb of the apocalyptic Son of Man; and both might seem pointless, since the body itself was not there. For all who supposed its disappearance to have been part of a miraculous resurrection, veneration at a tomb would seem foolish indeed.

There is therefore nothing in the Jewish 'sacred tomb' custom which tells against the validity of Mark's account; rather, it confirms a sound reason why a small group of Jesus' followers might have removed the body to Galilee, as suggested above, before the unexpected visions changed the priorities. The bearers' original plan could have been to keep very quiet about what they had done for, say, a year or two, by when the bones would be ready, and the authorities would have small chance of identifying the 'robbers'. The little band would probably have planned to inform some member of the Twelve later, so that the bones might be collected and a shrine set up, but even then it would still be sensible for the carrying-party not to brag openly: we may note that the women, breaking no laws, nevertheless get up in the dark to go secretly to tend the body, and that the apostles themselves seem to have said nothing in public about their Easter experiences,[20] until at Pentecost a further experience impelled them to discard such caution. Later still, when there was sporadic persecution of the new sect, it would have been extremely foolish for those who had taken the body from its grave to have marked themselves out for reprisal.

As the Apostles Saw It

It has always been a sound argument, however, that if the disciples of Jesus had removed his body they would not then have upheld, and often died upholding, their claim that he had risen from the grave. Certainly Paul's apparent conviction that Jesus' earthly body had been 'recycled', which we may suppose the apostles to have shared, argues strongly that they knew only that the body had gone, and nothing more; for which reason and no other, as Wright also seems to say, they assumed that the process of resurrection must be one of transforming an actual dead body into a different, heavenly body (cf. Wright 2003, pp.209-398). Had the apostles known where Jesus' body had been put, and that it had decayed like any other, it need not, indeed could not, have altered their conviction that he was alive, for they had seen him and heard him speak; they would simply have interpreted resurrection differently. Now, with the tomb found empty, they never doubted that what they saw was Jesus' body, transformed and resurrected; for, crucially, he had told them over and over that he would be raised again **after three days** (Mark 8.31; 9.31; 10.34), or perhaps **on the third day** (Matt.16.21; 17.23; Luke 9.2; 18.33; 24.7,46).

We have suggested (Ch.8 above) that Jesus had meant that he would rise again with the righteous after the Day of the Lord; for the resurrection of the just *on the third day* after the Coming is found later as a piece of rabbinic lore,[21] and was, once the idea of resurrection became current, an obvious interpretation to make of Hosea 6.2: **After two days He will heal us; on the third day we shall arise and live before Him**. But now, the disciples were forced to believe that they had previously misunderstood the time scheme, since Jesus' forecasts now seemed to confirm that the master, whom they saw alive and well, had already risen from the dead, ahead of the expected time.

Understanding the Appearances.

Without those prophecies, which may have been no more than Jesus affirming his trust in God's justice,[22] they might have been less sure of what they were seeing; without the disappearance of the body they would have had to adopt a different concept of the *manner* of resurrection. On this, as Wright (p.129) has shown, there was a wide spectrum of belief: 'dozens of options, with different ways of describing similar positions, and similar ways of describing different ones'. It was the seeing which mattered because, as described above, to have a veridical vision of that calibre was an unarguable and life-changing experience, to which any consideration of the logistics of resurrection was an afterthought. Paul does not admit any difference between the vision which he himself experienced and those which he lists, in detail, of the earlier apostles; nor does he anywhere state that the apostles had touched, or eaten with, the risen Lord. It is neither Paul nor Mark but the three later evangelists, writing fifty to eighty years after the event, who deliberately stress the physical reality of the risen Jesus by giving him a body which eats and can be touched. Later still, the *Gospel of Peter* offers its somewhat ludicrous picture of two vast heavenly figures entering the tomb, to emerge supporting an even larger figure, who comes out followed by the cross itself; thus spelling out what Luke, Matthew and John all seem to have believed,[23] that the body, whether required to contribute to the physicality of the 'risen body' or not, had been removed by supernatural agency.[24]

By the time that these later evangelists were writing, most of the relevant eyewitnesses were dead. Some died long before Paul (1 Cor.15.6); by 85 AD, an approximate date for the writings of Matthew and Luke, even the youngest disciples would have passed seventy. The fourth Gospel, so strongly associated with the province of Asia, where tradition says the apostle Philip lived until the reign of Domitian, and Irenaeus claims that John of Ephesus remained **until the reign of Trajan**, was written probably no earlier than 100-110 AD. In other words, although datings are approximate, those gospels which stress the physical reality of the risen Jesus were probably not written with any eyewitness at hand to verify or refute their claims. Like many other stories in these gospels, their versions of the resurrection seem to be a developed, slightly exaggerated tradition.

On the other hand, Paul, who wrote with eyewitnesses alive and active, speaks only of 'seeing': *ōphthē*, **he was seen**, is the word he uses, in four consecutive verses (1 Cor.15.5-8). This is the same verb which Raphael uses to make the distinction, after finally manifesting himself as an angel to Tobit and Tobias:

> **All this time I have been *seen* by you [*hōptanomēn humin*]; but I did not eat nor drink, you were looking at *a vision* [*horasis*, once again from the same, irregular, verb, *horaō*]** (Tob.12.19).

It is the same verb used by that youth at the tomb; **'There you shall see him'** (*opsesthe*) (Mark 16.7b). 'He appeared to' is strictly a more exact translation, as Wright indicates, than 'he was seen',[25] but it is a distinction without a difference; for it still does not even imply that anything was experienced other than a vision; and when the term is used of ordinary people, it again merely says that they were seen. At the very least, Paul states his case in terms which neither claim nor suggest more than vision, and affirms that that is what he was taught (1 Cor.15.3).

I have suggested that it need not have mattered if the apostles had known what really became of the body of Jesus; but evidently they did not. The imagined group of headstrong youths might originally have planned to tell them later and reap due credit; but events had moved past them. Had they ever spoken of their action, they might soon have found it hard to interest anyone, for the resting place of the dead master did not compare with visions of the risen Lord, as he might now be titled; more probably, feeling rather foolish at the waste of their heroic effort, they would never have told anyone, for that would have been needlessly to admit what was technically crime and certainly folly. It may be that they were present at the vision on the hill in Galilee, they might even have been the ones who hesitated, but once drawn into that experience, they too would have found it so overpowering that knowledge of where the physical body lay would hardly signify. They would have needed to take a slightly more sophisticated view of the nature of resurrection than did the others; but their silence would be unimportant, for it was the living Lord, not the empty tomb, that was proclaimed. On that point, the silence of Paul and Acts about the tomb is confirmed by Mark 16.1-8, which reads as unvarnished, almost incoherent, reminiscence, and plainly has never been eroded by preaching.

If it is not in human nature to keep such a secret forever, one of the party might perhaps, in the fullness of time, have told somebody; but it is also human nature to refuse to accept an unromantic truth undermining a cherished myth. It is clear from the gospels of Matthew and Luke that, before they wrote, the oral tradition had already acquired a great deal that was legendary; so that a truth which clarified Mark's account would contradict Matthew's guarded tomb opened by the angel, and Luke's risen Jesus who eats and drinks, or at least the beliefs which those stories embodied. If the story were told to some wise and open-minded elder in their church, would they not have been advised to leave well alone? The growing legends had done no harm, but to contradict them now could only cause distress, anger or bewilderment within the church, while encouraging hostile opponents to claim, untruly, that the Christians had faked the evidence all along. It is hard to imagine such unwelcome information, had it ever become known, being published; rather, it would quietly have been put aside as irrelevant.

For, although my hypothesis would mean that the apostles were mistaken in believing that the body of Jesus had been miraculously transformed by God into the 'heavenly' body which they saw, that mattered no more than Columbus' belief that the new land which he had found was India. The apostles were right, we may say, in their conviction that they saw Jesus alive and well; that they may have been mistaken as to exactly how this came about was unimportant. The living Christ was the heart of their *kerygma*: the empty tomb, so far as we can tell, was never mentioned. Only when the later gospels published exaggerated versions of the story did that empty tomb gather importance.

The Youth in the White Robe

If a handful of enterprising young disciples could explain the disappearance of the body, what would account for Mark's white-robed *neaniskos* and his announcement that Jesus is risen? He is not dressed for travel, nor for moving rocks and carrying bodies; it seems unlikely that he had anything to do with that. If the angelic interpretation is now doubly inadmissible, what of the human who remains? While it will never be possible to know exactly who this youth was nor what he was doing, a reasonable explanation is not hard to find.

There is nothing very puzzling about the youth's presence at the tomb: he has clearly slipped out of the house sometime on Saturday night, apparently unable to change out of his Sabbath best without alerting his parents. The real difficulty lies with what he said to the women. In what circumstances could any normal human pronounce so confidently that Jesus had been raised, and say where they would see him? It is that enigmatic message, to which we shall come later, which does most to excuse the later evangelists for their transformation of the young man into a heavenly being.

Most probably, he was a devoted young follower or admirer of Jesus, who wished to ease his grief in a mourning vigil outside the tomb; just as the women were hoping to ease theirs with the proper laying out of the body. His parents might not have favoured their young son's parading his allegiance to the disgraced prophet; but in any case, spending the night by the tomb was just the sort of romantic undertaking about which one can never tell one's parents, because it sounds so embarrassingly silly. After sunset, however, when the sabbath was over, he could go out 'to see a friend'; but changing his clothes first might have prompted awkward questions.

His Message

Possibly, if he reached the tomb before the suggested carrying-party had left with the body, the youth knew what they had done; in which case his words were not perhaps recalled exactly. They are reported as:

> **'Don't be frightened. You are looking for Jesus of Nazareth who was crucified. He has been raised, he is not here. Look, that's the place where they laid him. But go and tell his disciples and Peter that he is going to Galilee ahead of you. There you will see him, as he told you'** (Mark 16.6-7).

It needs only to suppose that he actually said, not *ēgerthē*, 'he has been raised', but *ērthē*, 'he has been taken away'; and that he called after the fleeing women, not *ekei auton opsesthe*, 'there you shall see him' but, perhaps, *ekei auton heurēsete*, 'there you will find him', to change the statement into a hasty and half-heard report of the body's removal. The women next have their own vision of Jesus, if Matthew is correct on that point, and their recall of the youth's message would inevitably be coloured by that.

This possibility of mishearing, however, seems less likely than that the young man had himself 'seen the risen Lord'; that he had already experienced what the women were about to, and that that was how he knew and why he was so sure. Certainly the simplest explanation would be to assume that, when he arrived, he found the tomb empty and the body gone. With shock and bewilderment added to distress, he might have been in a state particularly receptive to the experience which we call a 'veridical vision' (Ludemann 1994, p.96ff).[26] It seems unlikely that anyone could speak as confidently as he reportedly did of seeing the dead alive, except from such personal experience; otherwise, like John's Mary Magdalene, he would more likely have supposed simply that the body had been taken away. Quite possibly, then, he had been the first to see Jesus on that memorable day.

His Identity

Whether correctly reported or not, the terms used in the youth's cryptic message, and especially the rider **as he told you**, would still link him with Mark's other *neaniskos*, the one who accompanied (*synēkolouthei*) Jesus to Gethsemane; and who therefore, as Morison pointed out,[27] heard Jesus say that after he was raised up he would lead them, or go ahead of them, again to Galilee (Mark 14.51, 28).[28] Jesus had probably been referring to the joyful life to come, when he, with all the just, would be raised to new life in God's kingdom on this earth. To that he had already referred at supper, saying that he would not drink wine again **until the day when he drank it new in the kingdom of God** (Mark 14.25); probably he expected the Day of the Lord to follow his own death very quickly. On Sunday morning it would be natural, almost inevitable, that the youth, if he were the same one, should interpret a mind-shaking vision by using those words which he had heard from Jesus himself, as best he recalled them.[29]

Can this be the same youth? Even without his message, that would at least be the minimal assumption. Here are two adolescent lads, both showing by their actions devotion to Jesus; both prepared to slip out of the city at night, and both, it would seem from their dress, finding it necessary to leave home without stopping to find more appropriate clothing. Neither seems to be known to Jesus' close followers, which suggests that they are not from Galilee; and their actions are more consistent with a home in Jerusalem. It is more probable that these two *neaniskoi* were one and the same, than that there were at the feast of Passover that year two different youths answering to that specification.[30]

An Unforgettable Image

A strong indication that Mark is recounting, not composing, this story, is that he seems quite unaware of the true relevance of the white robe. Why is it still recalled by his source, maybe thirty years later? The answer is obvious, from Mark's own words, once we forget the angel and think in terms of real people.

The women, not wishing to be seen, make their way to the cave in the dark hours, lit by a full moon. It is **very early morning** (*lian proi*); as they approach, they see in the moonlight that the stone door has been rolled back (Mark 16.4). In some uneasiness they enter the chamber to seek the body they wish to tend (16.5). Peering in the dimness, they expect to find a corpse, covered in *sindon,* fine linen (15.46f); instead, they see an empty shelf. Then, amongst the shadows on the other side, there *is* a white-clad figure, but sitting up; **and they went into shock** (*exethambēthēsan*, 16.5). Then it spoke! (16.6). **And they scrambled out and fled from the tomb, like women possessed, shaking and frenzied** (16.8).[31]

Naturally enough, the women said nothing to anyone as they fled, but it is foolish to suppose that they would not, after such an experience, have told family and friends just as soon as they were safely back and coming out of shock. Whether the women managed to report exactly what words the youth was calling after them as they ran may be doubted; but *visual* trauma is embedded in one's mind for life. They would certainly have remembered all too clearly that glimpse of the pallor of a beardless face above a long white robe, which had given them such a shock; while the unfortunate resemblance to the shrouded dead created by his dress must have been central to their explanation of that startled flight. So the lad's best clothes became part of the record, Mark uncomprehendingly repeated what he had heard, and the later evangelists concocted the best explanation they could for the youth, his clothes, and his message.

Everything in Mark's enigmatic account of the women's visit to the tomb, therefore, becomes credible when considered as an episode of real people in an unusual situation. Although we can never be sure exactly what happened, and the way is still open for anyone to believe that the best explanation of the body's disappearance is unique miracle, yet a common sense interpretation of Mark's data suggests the removal of the body by devoted followers with good reason for secrecy; the presence at the tomb of the same teenage enthusiast who had accompanied Jesus to Gethsemane; and the natural fright of the women when startled by a ghost-like figure inside a tomb. This led them to flee in terror while the youth was trying to convey, in terms which he had heard from Jesus, his own conviction – based more probably on a vision of his own rather than the mere absence of the body – that the master was truly alive as never before.

Notes to Chapter Nineteen

[1] One of the earliest surviving novels; by Chariton. For date see Reardon 1989, pp.17f.

[2] Philostratus is scathing about Chariton; the emperor Julian about the whole genre; others ignore the novel entirely (Reardon, p.12).

[3] Pliny, *Naturalis Historia*, 2.52.173-177, cites a number of cases of people mistakenly thought dead but discovered to have been still alive. He is also very scornful of any idea of survival after death.

[4] As well as Callirhoe, Leucippe, Tarsia and her mother, there are also Rhodanes and Sinonis in Iamblichus' *Babylonian Story,* taken for dead while unconscious

from eating poisoned honey, or when sprawled in alcoholic stupor at the bottom of an empty grave; empty because the young woman for whom it had been prepared was, at the last moment, found to be still breathing.

[5] Eg. the beheaded slave mistaken for Leucippe (*Leuc.*5.7); Trophime's mutilated body taken for Sinonis (*Babylonian Story* 13, 18).

[6] Even today: a case was reported from Belo Horizonte in Brazil in January 2011. Some of Pliny's examples woke up on the pyre! Jairus' daughter was mistaken for dead by everyone except Jesus; the widow's son at Nain (Lk.7.11-16) may have been another such case. The fourth evangelist has tried to ensure that the same could *not* be suggested about Lazarus (John 11.1-44).

[7] The Tigris Boatmen, *Barcarii Tigrenses*, posted to Hadrian's Wall, are an extreme example. Syrian or Samaritan troops were usual in Judaea.

[8] Even in Galilee: see R. A. Horsley 1996, p.63, for such an inscription in Aramaic.

[9] **They found the stone rolled away from the tomb; but having entered, they found not the body** (*of the Lord Jesus*). (Luke 24.2-3).

[10] Eg., Electra's recognition of Orestes (Soph. *Electra* 1210-80). The novelist Heliodorus describes the reunion of his heroine with her stepfather as a **theatrical recognition scene** (*Aeth.*5.11).

[11] **These have been written down so that you shall believe that Jesus is the Christ, the Son of God** (John 20.31a).

[12] Philo, *In Flaccum*, 82: **I have known cases when, on the eve of a holiday, crucified men have been taken down and their bodies handed over to their relatives, because it was thought proper to have them buried and allow them the customary rites.**

[13] The claim that these were Peter and John (Luke 22.8) will not stand against Mark's statement that **When it was evening, he came *with the Twelve*** (Mark 14.17).

[14] Josephus, aged 16, lived in turn as Pharisee, Sadduccee and Essene; then he spent three years in the wilds as the zealous disciple of an ascetic called Bannus, before returning, aged 19, to the city (Josephus, *Vita* 10-12). Had this been evidence of precocity, he would have made that boast.

[15] The wish to bury the beloved teacher in some place he loved is natural. Antonio Machado (Spanish poet, d.1939), lamenting a beloved teacher, calls on his friends to take his body to the blue hills of Guadarrama, where once the master dreamed of Spain renewed. The theme of Browning's *Grammarian's Funeral* is similar.

[16] A light stretcher, allowing four bearers, would be better. I estimate five minutes at the tomb. The linen wrapping would be kept on the body. The grave-clothes left lying (John 20.5-7) are probably pure invention, and the same detail found in many texts as Luke 24.12, is probably an addition from John (Aland *New Testament* includes, Throckmorton *Gospel Parallels* omits); but could be an embellishment by Luke, borrowed by John.
[17] Such a tomb for Jonah exists, near Nazareth; but probably built after Jesus' time (Reed 2002, pp.205-208).
[18] Jeremias, *Heileigegengraber in Jesu Umwelt (Mt. 23.29; Luke 11.47). Eine Untersuchung zur Volksreligion der Zeit Jesu*, 1958, p.45. Cited in Ludeman 1994, p.208, nn.206, 207)
[19] This speech may not be historical, but is probably a fair reconstruction of the original kerygma.
[20] That is at least implied by Acts 1.12-26, dealing only with internal issues, behind closed doors.
[21] See H. K. McArthur, 'On the Third Day', *New Testament Studies 18, '71-72*, pp.81-86.
[22] Although prophecy is not impossible, more probably Jesus had simply tried to reassure them, from his own belief in resurrection – like a Christian telling friends that 'we shall meet again in heaven'.
[23] But it is a mistake to attach importance to **for I have not yet gone to the Father** (John 20.19), which is the author's excuse for presenting Jesus here in the plain clothes necessary if Mary is to take him for a gardener, not in the shining garments appropriate to his glorified, heavenly status.
[24] Mark, if Peter is his source, would have believed the same; but the story is told without addition.
[25] Since ***ōphthē*** is followed each time by a Dative; but this follows Semitic usage, as in Mark 9.4, where Elijah, with Moses, **appeared *to them*** at the Transfiguration, and there is no suggestion that that was anything but visionary.
[26] Ludemann 1994, pp.96ff.
[27] Morison 1944, p.161. *Synēkolouthei* means he was *with* the party, not trailing behind.
[28] Mark 14.27f: **You will all fall away [...] but, after I have been raised, *proaxo humas eis ten Galilaian***,
ie. **I shall lead you** (or **go ahead of you,** or **walk at your head) to Galilee**. Prophecies are rightly suspect; but it is reasonable that Jesus should that night have held firmly to the hope of future happiness.

[29] On this hypothesis, Jesus might rather have spoken of leading them again *in* Galilee rather than *to* Galilee (Mark 14.28). The empty tomb could have prompted a subconscious change to the wording.

[30] By contrast, the traditional identification of John Mark of Acts as the evangelist who was Peter's interpreter or guide in Rome is based only on an imperfect coincidence of common names, with all the circumstances different: Peter's assistant needed Latin as well as Greek and a comprehensive knowledge of the vast city of Rome, with its million inhabitants. John Mark from Jerusalem does not qualify, and should have had a better knowledge of Palestinian geography than the evangelist can show; which also means that he must not be identified with this unknown youth, either.

[31] Literally, **for trembling and frenzy** (*ekstasis*) **possessed them**. Semantically, *ekstasis* implies being beside oneself, from shock or rapture.

CHAPTER 20

The Recapitulation and Coda

The Jesus of History

J. D. G. Dunn (2005, 31) has well said that 'the only Jesus available to us [...] is *Jesus as he was seen and heard by those who first formulated the traditions we have* – the Jesus of faith'; but this perhaps need not dispose for ever of the Jesus of History, even though the Synoptic Gospels are all by authors who truly believed that Jesus was, in some sense, the son of God, and are only to a small degree independent traditions – whereas for Socrates, by contrast, we have Socrates as seen by Xenophon, as seen and imagined by Plato, and as caricatured by Aristophanes, all eye-witnesses. However, this study has shown that there is no good reason why the Gospel of Mark should not be accepted as deriving from the eyewitness of the apostle Peter; as remembered, set down and arranged by Mark, his guide and interpreter in Rome, after Peter's death; and it is, I suggest, a very short step from the Jesus of Peter's faith to the Jesus of history, since whatever Peter believed derived primarily from his experience of his master's personality, teaching and actions. His beliefs about Jesus may not always be right, they may distort his interpretation of events here and there, but they should not have greatly altered the actual facts on which he based them.

The Witness of Peter

Form Criticism, when revised to a better understanding of the wide spectrum of oral transmission, confirms that the text of Mark is precisely what its traditional authorship would lead one to expect: a mixture of sayings and parables, stories used in preaching, and personal reminiscence. Later criticism has fully exploited the over-zealous judgement of the Form Critics that *all* the gospels should be considered far removed from eyewitness, but has offered nothing new to support that verdict; which, although sound enough in respect of most gospels, now seems mistaken as applied to Mark.

The historical evidence remains strong, once we have disallowed such dubious later enhancements as the claim that the author was John Mark from Jerusalem, or that Mark wrote his gospel while Peter was alive, and with his approval. What Papias had to report, with a disciple of Jesus as his source, was that Mark, with no personal knowledge of Jesus, but having been Peter's guide and interpreter in the great city of Rome, wrote down accurately all that he remembered, but not entirely in the correct order, trying neither to leave out nor to falsify anything. Two early witnesses support this, stating outright what Papias only implies, that this was after Peter was dead.

The internal evidence is equally strong: the unnecessary detail, inexplicit narrative, redundancy and poor syntax so often seen in the Tales all indicate the peasant, speaking in his own rambling but vivid way of his own experience; the rounded down examples indicate the preacher he had, perforce, become; and while the traces of genuine Palestinian background and vocabulary point to Peter, the terse style of the connecting narrative suggests the compiler, and the ignorance of Palestinian topography betrays the Roman interpreter. The unvarnished portrait of the human Jesus, and the often unflattering depiction of the disciples, imply both an honest witness and a faithful reporter. Yet it is clear that both of them can make mistakes. Peter has misinterpreted the fates of the Gadarene swine and the fig tree as deliberate acts of Jesus; and perhaps thought that the whole Sanhedrin was assembling in the high priest's house when he saw various representatives entering. Mark has misunderstood what Peter told him about Jesus walking on the water, and probably about the feeding of the large crowd also; and almost certainly, since the Asian church which had preserved and always celebrated the actual date of the crucifixion is against him, has attached the wrong date to the Last Supper, mistaking it for the Passover.

The Interpreter's Version

This gospel, then, is not a consecutive eyewitness account, but separate episodes, reported at second hand, and set, with parables and sayings, into a brief narrative outline, probably written down by Mark himself from what he had learned from Peter; generally reliable, therefore, but brief. Into this he has fitted stories and teaching as best he might: not, according to Papias, always in the right place, and more appropriate contexts for one or two incidents have been suggested. Included also are a few oddments from, probably, other sources (Mark 8.1-10; 13.14-27); and certainly Mark has also used a short, presumably pre-existing, narrative of the Passion, clearly written by another hand, which he has supplemented with material from Peter. All the material has been subject to the possible inaccuracies of oral transmission; but to no great extent, since most of it passed directly from the eyewitness to the evangelist. Indeed, much may well consist of the authentic words of Peter.

Such information, which might be termed 'Grade B reliable', is on a par with the best written evidence in ancient history; more reliable in some ways than accounts like those of Caesar and Thucydides, whose eyewitness is slanted to personal and political aims, for neither Peter nor Mark suffer from these. Inevitably the gospel shows traces here and there in its account of Jesus' life, and notably in its understanding of the terms 'Son of Man' and 'Son of God', of an interpretation of the person of Jesus which was presumably developed after his death, arising from the apostles' astonishing resurrection experiences. Yet it seems possible, guided by the evidence of Luke and Matthew and the later gospels, to chart a steady movement further and further away from fact: the beginnings of such exaggeration can then be traced back into Mark, where common sense can confirm how much, or rather how little, distortion entered his historical account. If the best picture of Jesus we are offered is the Christ of Peter's faith, this does not prevent our looking behind Peter's presentation.

So, in '*Mission to Galilee'* and *'Challenge to Jerusalem*', key themes and roles of Jesus have been examined, in the light of what Mark's gospel can say about them. Other interpretations of the same matter are possible; but it has been shown that a rounded, credible picture of Jesus and his work can be derived from what Mark has set down. Mark can sometimes, notably in respect of Jesus' teaching, be corroborated and supplemented from Luke and Matthew; but should never be subordinated to their inferior, less realistic, traditions. Only their Q material can be allowed equal standing with Mark.

'Ending in Triumph' examines the various problems posed by Mark's abrupt conclusion, and shows that there are alternatives to rating the author as some kind of literary or theological genius, never recognised until twentieth century scholarship rescued his reputation. We have argued that the proper ending of Mark has been preserved, slightly altered, within Matthew's final chapter; readers will decide whether the case has been made out. If it has, then the restored ending of Mark would provide our simplest, and probably most reliable, account of the resurrection. If this leads to a conviction that Mark, whether or not this study has always interpreted correctly what he says, is a sound witness, not a theological nor literary inventor, then in his gospel there is an immensely valuable resource for the life, and teaching, of Jesus; provided only that the exaggerations and Christologies of later evangelists are not allowed to obscure the Marcan picture and undermine its validity.

A Leading Case

This point may be illustrated by returning to the case of Barabbas and the customary release of a Passover prisoner. That Josephus, who has little good to say of any Roman governor, and none of Pilate, does not mention this custom is unimportant: it may, indeed have been wholly forgotten by his day, for if such a custom was created by the shrewd Pilate-Caiaphas team, it might not have survived their dual dismissal from office. The strong objection to the story is that no Roman governor would ever have released a prisoner guilty, as Barabbas is said to have been, of armed revolt and murder; but those charges are later exaggerations. In Mark, as we saw, Barabbas is only **imprisoned *with* the rioters who had committed murder in the riot**, which suggests that he personally may not have killed, nor led any riot; to concede his release would therefore be credible. But then Matthew calls Barabbas **notorious**, Luke asserts that he had been **imprisoned for a riot started in the city, and for murder**, and John claims that he was an **outlaw brigand** (*lēstēs*), thus making his release historically incredible.

Mark should be allowed to stand alone as historical evidence; then, with a little caution – regarding Barabbas, for instance, it is not clear whether Peter's information was first or second hand, nor how well Peter himself understood the Passover custom – this gospel furnishes a very good source about Jesus; and indeed, except for Paul's tiny contribution, the only one to any degree historically reliable. Matthew and Luke are treasuries for the teaching of Jesus, but very suspect historically wherever they diverge from or embellish Mark's account. John, as Clement of Alexandria points out, was never intended as history: on an imaginative or spiritual level it has much to offer, but as history it is utterly unsound, and in its dominant blanket-identification of Jesus' opponents as 'the Jews', it has been, perhaps unintentionally, disastrous. Mark alone can bring us closer, perhaps very close, to the Jesus who, in first century Palestine, walked and talked, ate and slept, healed and taught so unforgettably, until he was crucified under Pontius Pilate; and of whose life beyond death his disciples became absolutely convinced by the unusual experiences which followed.

Jesus, according to Mark

Yet we have to accept Mark's picture of Jesus as a whole, if at all. While we may reasonably adjust the detail here and there to account for such marvels as defy our common sense, we must not simply shut our eyes to aspects of Jesus which do not sit well with modern ideas. Mark's Jesus is unashamedly an apocalyptic prophet, his whole mission stemming from a correct premonition that disasters were coming soon to his nation, and the mistaken inference that the sequel would be the Day of the Lord, when, without warning, God's heavenly Son of Man (by which, whatever Mark and his church believe, Jesus did *not* mean himself) would come **on the clouds of glory** to take over the whole earth and rule in justice that peaceful future world where everyone would delight to do the will of God.

Jesus became an intuitive healer and exorcist, but the healings reported in Mark lie within the range of such healings as have been reported of other people, in many times and places. (Matthew and Luke have preferred exaggerated versions of such stories, while John apparently created new episodes of a uniquely miraculous nature.) Nevertheless, Jesus' healings greatly enhanced his prestige, making people more inclined to hear what he said.

And this was new teaching: for the *metanoia*, the change of heart which Jesus demanded, went so far as to ask the well-off to give away their wealth, commonly regarded as the sign of God's approval, with its consequent power and status; and to live very modestly, giving their surplus riches to relieve the needs of others. This does not seem to have attracted many wealthy adherents, yet it still remains as part of Jesus' enduring legacy to the world. Similarly, his teaching that we should love our enemies, and do good to those who ill-treat us, remains a constant inspiration. Above all, perhaps, it is his urgency that folk should start to live like this now, as though God's new world had already come, without waiting until better times arrive, which has so often led individuals and groups successfully to attempt the apparently impossible.

He had started with four disciples, probably all of young adult status; later, from the many, probably still younger, men who followed him, he selected eight more, making a symbolic Twelve as a suitable cadre to be specially trained. There seem also to have been three mature women who regularly accompanied them around the country. But soon his mission in Galilee was handicapped by sensation-seeking crowds, who denied him the peace and quiet needed for this training, and he withdrew northwards to less accessible Upland Galilee; from where he sent out, in due time, the Twelve, in pairs, to preach and to heal.

Jesus may have hoped to find himself free of the curious when he returned to Lowland Galilee, but that was not to be. There was immediately an inconsiderate crowd, almost besieging their house in Capernaum, and pursuing him when he went off for a quiet day with the Twelve. So finally he left the country altogether, and travelled with the Twelve in the lands to the north, and then to the east, of Galilee. While training his disciples he also reconsidered his own mission, and by the time they reached the territory near Caesarea Philippi he had come, we may say had been guided, to see that he must now take his mission to Jerusalem itself, although any prophet preaching a change of the world order there, under direct Roman rule, would have very short shrift from the authorities.

As he worked his way slowly southward he repeatedly warned his disciples of his own coming fate, with the consolation that he would rise **after three days**. By this Jesus may be supposed to have meant 'at the resurrection of the righteous', in which he certainly believed, due three days after that Coming of the Son of Man, which he had prophesied would be no long time distant. So indeed the disciples probably understood at the time; but later events persuaded them that they had mistaken his meaning.

We have suggested that Jesus rode a donkey, to the gates of Jerusalem only, for no purpose of his own, but only in obedience to such a prompting by the spirit as sometimes comes to a prophet. Next day, however, by his deliberate action at the temple he not only, it seems clear from Mark, evicted the traders, but took command of the court of the Gentiles, and maintained his rule there for the next three days, in defiance of the temple executive, the 'chief priests'. On Thursday he had his Last Supper with the Twelve and created an easily memorised new rite, to which he gave, along the lines of Passover custom, a profound meaning, for them to remember and use thereafter.

Arrested at Gethsemane, he was brought to Caiaphas for questioning, so that sufficient evidence might be found to persuade the Sanhedrin next day that it was proper to hand him over to the Roman governor – who would certainly execute him. Challenged to say on oath whether he was God's Anointed, a man speaking as God's representative, Jesus found no alternative but to say flatly 'I am', and, almost as corroboration, prophesied the doom of those who arraigned him. He was condemned, for blasphemy, by all those present. At daybreak, the Sanhedrin in executive session concurred, and sent him on to Pilate.

Pilate, while having nothing personal against Jesus, can never have had the slightest intention of letting him go; his task, like that of any colonial governor, was to take effective action against any popular prophet preaching a change of regime, before riot or rebellion could ensue and cause great and needless loss of life. Jesus was, by due process of Roman law, convicted of sedition and sentenced to the standard penalty, flogging and crucifixion, and humiliated with a placard proclaiming him **King of the Jews**.

Taunted by a hostile crowd, but watched by male and female disciples, Jesus suffered for six hours before he died. Mark's description of the unusual events attending Jesus' death, including the centurion's verdict that '**This was a son of god**', are best explained by freak weather, of the nature of a 'dry thunderstorm', with a lightning strike on the temple, which would naturally be regarded as a portent. Pilate, once Jesus' death had been confirmed, released his body, which was entombed by Joseph of Arimathaea.

Some thirty-six hours later, very early on Sunday morning, the women found the tomb open, the body gone, and a youth sitting in the tomb who told them that Jesus had risen and would meet the disciples again in Galilee; but the women, mistaking the white-robed youth for a ghost, fled in panic. Originally, however, Mark's gospel probably went on to recount briefly the women's meeting with Jesus as they fled, and finally the meeting with the disciples on a Galilean hilltop, where Jesus gave them their new commission to carry his message into all lands.

Mark's adolescent youth in white, neither fully adult nor brilliantly dressed, inspiring panic and not reverence, lacks the authority required by an angel; and no writer of that time – nor, probably, of any other – could have left the story unfinished, to end in bathos. It seems quite possible that second century bishops might have quietly agreed to censor Mark's original ending, particularly if it had mentioned ghosts – fear of ghosts being the best explanation of the women's flight – or, worse, culminated with a mission statement no longer compatible with the church's practice. It seems likely that a version of Mark's ending can be recovered from Matthew, relating the appearances of Jesus, to the women, and to the brethren in Galilee; these being the first and last, as known to Peter.

These appearances are basically credible and probably historical; and if a non-miraculous interpretation of that evidence is preferred, this need not detract from Christian faith. We have suggested, as an alternative to the dematerialising of the physical body in a process of physical resurrection, that Jesus' grieving friends saw 'veridical visions' in a profound mystical experience which transformed their lives. This, we maintain, sufficiently explains both the stories of visions and the subsequent actions of the disciples; who were then not so much able as compelled, for the remainder of their lives, to testify truly that they had seen the Lord, alive and well after his death.

The residual puzzle of the empty tomb cannot be dismissed as Christian invention. Since a mysteriously empty tomb would have been, and was, attributed to the removal of the corpse by human agency, it would have been pointless to invent such a story to support the physical reanimation of the body, although that reanimation was undoubtedly the belief of the apostles: therefore the empty tomb should be taken as fact. That it apparently was hardly mentioned, and never proclaimed, until Mark had published the story, is consistent with the apostles having chosen not to preach about it; but we may accept N. T. Wright's case that Paul almost certainly knew of it. With regard to Wright's central thesis, however, there is at least one possible alternative to the transformation of the dead physical body of Jesus into a semi-physical 'resurrection body'.

Fiction and fact combine to emphasise the impossibility of Jesus having survived the cross; but there is no improbability about Pilate's conceding his body for burial, a concession for which precedent is known, nor for the women's intention to lay his body out properly, according to custom, as soon as the Sabbath was over. Nonetheless, it is not necessary to accept that the apostles were correct in their interpretation of the disappearance of that body. Its removal by human hands was physically possible, psychologically even likely.

An alternative to the 'unique miracle' is that some of Jesus' younger followers **came by night and stole him away**, and carried the body to Galilee, reburying it there so that Jesus' bones might later have a memorial tomb in his own country. Jewish custom at that time meant that some would certainly have wished to do this, the political context dictated that it could only be done secretly; and, since the empty tomb never featured in apostolic preaching, there was never a pressing need to tell what had been done. The empty tomb was irrelevant to the *kerygma*, and might never have been heard of again had not Mark, according to Papias, conscientiously set down everything he had heard Peter say, in what is a mixture of exemplary anecdote and casual reminiscence.

Mark's youth at the tomb might best be accounted for as a teenage enthusiast who aimed to spend the night in a vigil at the master's tomb; and was himself very possibly the first see the risen Lord, since that experience would account for his certainty that Jesus had risen. If he were also, as seems likely, the same youth who ran naked from Gethsemane, that would account for the wording of his message to the women.

This hypothesis, then, offers an alternative explanation for the disappearance of the body of Jesus from the tomb; while fully accepting the fact of its disappearance and allowing that the apostles truly believed this to have been miraculous, as evidently they did. The suggestion can neither be proved nor disproved, but constitutes a feasibility study, setting out one simple scenario accounting for the disappearance of the body without supernatural agency. Its purpose is to show both that Mark's Easter morning story ought not to be dismissed as impossible, nor even as improbable, just because the grave was open and the body gone; and, conversely, that to accept Mark's tale does not compel the acceptance of a miraculous physical resurrection of that body. In the end, all beliefs about the resurrection are conditioned by different understandings of God's relations with man and with the universe.

It would be a mistake, however, to suppose that if the disciples saw Jesus alive again in veridical visions, their experience was therefore any less 'real' – or convincing – than the conventional supposition, in which what they saw was a transformation of the physical body of Jesus into something which had the appearance of and could sometimes act as a normal body, but which appeared and disappeared at will. Mystic experience, a prime factor in all religion, has its own validity, and could have given the disciples as firm or firmer a foundation for their faith. Paul's conversion typifies that process in fact, and the Fourth Evangelist brilliantly illustrates it for us in, most probably, fiction. The experience of the witnesses was that, whatever they saw, or seemed to see, conveyed to them the vital truth that death was not the end, that their friend and master was now in a greater life, that they must spread his teaching worldwide, and that he would always be with them; which the joy and confidence of living with his Spirit confirmed to them, again and again.

A Pearl beyond Price

That, or something like it, is the historical record which can be found in Mark. Its relatively realistic portrayal of events, and its close-up picture of Jesus himself, offer the final confirmation that this is a genuine tradition; not faultless, but usually to be relied upon. Jesus is shown as fully human, known to his disciples as a prophet **full of the power of God**, but never, even though they had come to think of him as the Messiah, considered superhuman until after those Resurrection appearances. He can be angry, grieved, bewildered and afraid, but his courage and trust in God carry him through. He is also a man of wit and humour, friendly and approachable, fond of children, a man who enjoys the simple pleasures of food and drink and the beauties of nature, and a welcome guest to people of all classes. He has a strong sense of right and wrong, seeing both principally in the way we treat others, especially those less advantaged. He is never exaggeratedly devout, but seeks guidance in solitary prayer; he has no wish to alter his Jewish religion, but only to bring men to follow its teachings of generosity more fully. He is thoroughly human, but a man who constantly reveals the God who works in him; a man from whom, indeed, we can see what God must be like. He is, above all, a man to follow.

Mark is, therefore, an incomparable source for our understanding of Jesus, provided that this gospel is allowed to stand by itself, undistorted by the more developed Christologies of the later gospels which, whether their theologies be right or wrong, are markedly less accurate as history. How this record is understood and interpreted, however, will always be a matter for the interpreters.

SELECT BIBLIOGRAPHY

Ancient Authors

Clement of Alexandria, *The Rich Man's Salvation*, LCL (Loeb Classical Library), Heineman, 1919.

Eusebius, *The Ecclesiastical History*, LCL (Loeb Classical Library), Harvard U.P., 1998 [1926].

Josephus, *Bellum Judaicum*, tr. H.St.J.Thackeray, LCL (Loeb Classical Library), Harvard U.P. 1929-65.

-----------, *Antiquitates Judaici*, lib.XIV-XX, tr. R. Marcus, A. Wikgren, L. H. Feldman, LCL, Harvard U.P. 1963-65.

-----------, *Vita*, tr. H. St. J. Thackeray, LCL, Harvard U.P. 1926.

Philo, *In Flaccum*, tr. F.H.Colson, LCL, Harvard U.P. 1954.

-----------, *De Legatione ad Gaium*, tr. F.H.Colson, LCL, Harvard U.P. 1962.

Plato, *Phaedo*, tr. H. N. Fowler, LCL, Harvard U.P. 1940.

-----------, *Symposium*, tr. W. R. M. Lamb, LCL, Harvard U.P. 1946.

Pliny, the Elder, *Naturalis Historia*, tr. H. Rackham, LCL, Harvard U.P. 1938.

Suetonius, *Vitae Caesarum*, tr. J. C. Rolfe, LCL, Harvard U.P 1914.

Tacitus, *Historiae*, tr. C. H. Moore, LCL, Harvard U.P.1951.

Modern Authors

Alston, R., *Aspects of Roman History, AD 14-117*. Routledge, 1998

Anderson, H., *The Gospel of Mark*, Marshall, Morgan & Scott, 1976.

Anderson, J .C. and S. D. Moore, eds., *Mark and Method*, Minneapolis: Fortress Press, 1992.

Barrett, C. K., *Jesus and the Gospel Traditio,*. SPCK, 1967.

------------, *New Testament Essays,* SPCK, 1972.

-----------, *The Gospel according to St. John,* 2nd ed. SPCK, 1978.

Bauckham, R., *Jesus and the Eyewitnesses*, Grand Rapids, Michigan: Eerdmans, 2006.

Best, E., *Mark, The Gospel as Story*, Edinburgh: T&T Clark, 1994 [1983].

Borg, M. J., *Meeting Jesus Again for the First Time,* New York: Harper Collins, 1995.

Borg, M. J. and J. D. Crossan, *The Last Week,* SPCK, 2008.

Boulton, D., *Who on Earth was Jesus?*, Ropley, Hants: O-Books, John Hunt Publishing, 2008.

Buckman, R. and K. Sabbagh, *Magic or Medicine,* Macmillan, 1993.

Burgess, A., *The Small Woman,* Pan Books, 1959.

Burridge, R., *What are the Gospels?* CUP, 1992.

Brandon, S. G. F., *The Trial of Jesus of Nazareth,* Batsford, 1968.

Bultmann, R., *Jesus and the Word,* first pub. 1926, tr.L. Smith & E. Lantero 1934. rep. New York: Scribner, 1958.

-----------, *Primitive Christianity in its Contemporary Setting* tr. R. H. Fuller, Thames & Hudson, 1956.

-----------, *The History of the Synoptic Tradition,* 3rd rev. ed. 1958, tr. J.Marsh. Oxford: Blackwell, 1963.

Burge, G. M., *Interpreting the Gospel of John,* Grand Rapids, Michigan: Baker Books, 1992.

Carcopino, J., *Daily Life in Ancient Rome* first pub. 1939, tr. E.O.Lorimer. Penguin Books, 1956.

Catchpole, D., *Resurrection People,* Darton, Longman & Todd, 2000.

Crossan, J. D., *The Cross that Spoke. The Origins of the Passion Narrative,* San Francisco: Harper & Row, 1988.

-----------, *The Historical Jesus: The Life of a Mediterranean Jewish Peasant,* Edinburgh: T&T Clark, 1991.

-----------, *Jesus, A Revolutionary Biography*. San Francisco: HarperSanFrancisco, 1994.

Dibelius, Martin, *From Tradition to Gospel*, rev. 2nd ed., tr. B. L. Woolf. Nicholson & Watson, 1934.

-----------, *A Fresh Approach to the New Testament and Early Christian Literature,* tr. anon. Nicholson & Watson, 1936.

Dodd, C. H., *New Testament Studies,* Manchester: Manchester U.P., 1953.

-----------, *More New Testament Studies,* Manchester: Manchester U.P., 1968.

-----------, 'The Framework of the Gospel Narrative', 1st pub. *Expository Times* 1932, repr. in *In Search of the Historical Jesus*, ed. H. K. McArthur, SPCK, 1970.

Drury, J., *The Parables in the Gospels,* SPCK.1985.

Dunn, J. D. G., *A New Perspective on Jesus*, SPCK, 2005.

-----------, 'The Messianic Secret in Mark' in *The Messianic Secret* ed.C.Tuckett, SPCK 1983: 116-131

Ehrman, B.D., *Jesus, Apocalyptic Prophet of the New Millennium*, OUP 1999.

Farrer, A., *A Study in Mark*, A & C.Black 1951.

Fenton, J., *More about Mark*, SPCK 2001.

Fieney, D.A., *The Social History of Palestine in the Herodian Period: the Land is Mine*, New York: Edwin Mellen Press, 1991.

Finegan, J., *Handbook of Biblical Chronology*, Princeton: Princeton U.P., 1964.

Fortna, R.T., *The Gospel of Signs. A Reconstruction of the Narrative Source underlying the Fourth Gospel*, Cambridge: CUP, 1970.

Fox, George, *The Journal* ed. N. Smith, Penguin Books, 1998.

Freyne, S., *Galilee from Alexander to Hadrian, 323 BCE to 135 CE*, Indiana: Notre Dame, 1980.

-----------, *Galilee, Jesus and the Gospels*, Dublin: Gill & Macmillan, 1988.

-----------, 'Archaeology and the Historical Jesus' in *Archaeology and Biblical Interpretation* ed. J. R. Bartlett, Routledge 1997.

-----------, *Jesus, a Jewish Galilean*, T&T Clark International, 2004.

Fuller, R.H., *The Formation of the Resurrection Narratives* rev. ed., SPCK, 1980.

Funk, Robert. W., Roy. W. Hoover, and the Jesus Seminar, *The Five Gospels*, New York: Scribner, 1996.

Gardner R., *Healing Miracles*, Darton, Longman & Todd, 1988.

Green, F. W., *The Gospel according to Saint Matthew*, Oxford: Clarendon Press, 1936.

Gruen, E. S., *Diaspora. Jews amidst Greeks and Romans*, Cambridge MA, Harvard UP, 2002.

Gundry, R. H., *Mark – A Commentary on His Apology for the Cross*, Grand Rapids, Michigan: Eerdmans, 1993.

Guthrie, W. K. C., *The Greeks and their Gods*, Methuen, 1968 [1950].

Hagg, T., *The Novel in Antiquity*, Oxford: Blackwell, 1983.

Harvey, A. E., *Jesus and the Constraints of History*, Duckworth, 1982.

Hengel, M., *Property and Riches in the Early Church* tr. J.Bowden, SCM Press, 1974.

-----------, *Studies in the Gospel of Mark* tr. J.Bowden, SCM Press, 1997 [1985].

Hooker, M. D., *The Gospel according to St Mark*, A&C Black, 1991.

-----------, *The Message of Mark*, Epworth Press, 2005 [1983].

Horsley, R. A. with J. Harrison, *Bandits, Prophets and Messiahs*, San Fransisco: Harper & Row, 1988.

-----------, *Archaeology, History and Society in Galilee*, Valley Forge, Pa: Trinity Press International, 1996.

James, W., *The Varieties of Religious Experience* first pub.1902, Fontana, 1960.

Jeremias J., *The Eucharistic Words of Jesus* 3rd ed., tr. N. Perrin, SCM Press, 1966.

-----------, *The Parables of Jesus* tr. S. M. Hooke, rev. ed., SCM Press, 1972.

-----------, *Jerusalem in the Time of Jesus*, tr. F. H. & C. H. Cave, SCM Press, 1969.

Jones, A. M. H., *The Herods of Judaea*, first pub. 1938, Oxford: Clarendon Press, 1967.

Kelber,W. H., *The Oral and the Written Gospel*, Philadelphia: Fortress Press, 1997 [1983].

Kidd, B. J., ed., *Documents Illustrative of the History of the Church*, SPCK, 1920.

Kloppenborg, J. S., *The Formation of Q*, Philadelphia: Fortress Press,, 1987.

Kummel, W. G., *Introduction to the New Testament* tr. J. A. Mattill, SCM Press, 1966.

Levick, B., *The Government of the Roman Empire* 2nd ed., Routledge 2000.

Lightfoot, J. B., James, M. R., & Swete, H. B., eds. & trs., *Excluded Books of the New Testament*, Everleigh Nash & Grayson, 1927.

Lightfoot, R. H., *The Gospel Message of St. Mark*, Oxford: Clarendon Press, 1950.

-----------, *St. John's Gospel. A Commentary*, Oxford: Clarendon Press, 1956.

Lindars, B., *Jesus Son of Man*, SPCK, 1983.

Ludemann, G., *The Resurrection of Jesus*, tr. J.Bowden., SCM Press, 1994.

Mack, B. L., *The Lost Gospel. The Book of Q and Christian Origins*, Shaftesbury: Element Books, 1993.

Major, H. D. A., *The Reminiscences of Jesus by an Eyewitness,* John Murray, 1925.

Malina, B. J., *The Social Gospel of Jesus*, Minneapolis: Fortress Press, 2001.

Manson, T.W., 'Realised Eschatology and the Messianic Secret' in *Studies in the Gospels* ed. D. E. Nineham, Blackwell, 1957.

Marsh, F. B., *The Reign of Tiberius*, OUP, 1931.

McArthur, H. K., ed., *In Search of the Historical Jesus*, SPCK, 1970.

Meagher, J. C., *Clumsy Construction in Mark's Gospel*, New York: Edwin Mellen Press, 1979.

Mealand, D. L., *Poverty and Expectation in the Gospels*, SPCK, 1980.

Meyers, E. M. and J. F. Strange,, *Archaeology, the Rabbis and Early Christianity*, SCM Press, 1981.

Montefiore, H., *The Miracles of Jesus*, SPCK, 2005.

Morgan, J.R. and R. Stoneman, eds, *Greek Fiction. The Greek Novel In Context*, Routledge, 1994.

Morison, F., *And Pilate Said*, Rich & Cowan, 1939.

----------- *Who moved the Stone?* 2nd ed., Faber, 1944.

Mottram, V. H., *The Physical Basis of Personality* 2nd ed., Penguin Books, 1952.

Nineham, D. E., *The Gospel of Saint Mark* repr. Penguin Books, 1992 [1963].

Nineham D. E. ed., *Studies in the Gospels*, Oxford: Blackwell, 1955.

Perrin, N., *Jesus and the Language of the Kingdom*, SCM Press, 1976.

-----------, *The Resurrection Narratives*, SCM Press, 1977.

Petersen, N. F., 'When is the end not the end?', *Interpretations* 34, 1980.

Pritchard, J. B. ed., *The Times Atlas of the Bible*, 1987.

Quaker Faith and Practice, pub. by British Yearly Meeting, Friends House, Euston Road, London NW1 2BJ.

Reardon, B. P. ed,, *Collected Ancient Greek Novels*, Berkeley: Univ. of California, 1989.

Reed, J. L., *Archaeology and the Galilean Jesus*, Harrisburg, Pa: Trinity Press International, 2002.

Rhoads D., J. Dewey, and D. Michie, *Mark as Story,* 2nd ed., Minneapolis: Fortress Press, 1999.

Rosten, L., *The Joys of Yiddish*, Penguin Books, 1971

Sanders, E. P., *The Historical Figure of Jesus*, Penguin Books, 1991.

Sayers, D. L., *The Man Born To Be King*, Gollancz, 1943.

Schweitzer, A., *The Quest for the Historical Jesus,* tr.W.Montgomery, 2nd Eng.ed. 1911, repr. A&C Black, 1922.

Schweizer, E., *The Good News according to Mark*, first pub. 1967, tr. D. H. Madvig, SPCK, 1987.

Scramuzza, V. M., *The Emperor Claudius*, Cambridge: CUP, 1940.

Seager, R., *Tiberius*, Berkeley: Univ.of California Press, 1972.

Shelton, J- A., *As the Romans Did*, Oxford: OUP, 1988.

Sherwin-White, A. N., *Roman Society and Roman Law in the New Testament*, Oxford: Clarendon Press, 1969.

Smith, Morton, *The Secret Gospel. The Discovery and Interpretation of the Secret Gospel according to Mark*, Gollancz, 1974.

Stanton, G., *The Gospels and Jesus* 2nd ed., OUP 2002 [1st 1989].

Stibbe, M. W. G., *John as Storyteller: Narrative Criticism and the Fourth Gospel*, Cambridge: CUP, 1992.

Stoneman, R., *The Greek Alexander Romance*, Penguin Books, 1991.

Taplin, O., *Greek Tragedy in Action*, Routledge, 1989

Taylor, D. B., *Mark's Gospel as Literature and History*, SCM Press, 1992.

Taylor, V., *The Formation of the Gospel Tradition*, Macmillan, 1949.

-----------, *The Gospel according to St. Mark,* Macmillan, 1953.

Tolbert, M. A., *Sowing the Gospel*, Minneapolis: Fortress Press, 1996.

Tuckett, C., ed., *The Messianic Secret*, SPCK, 1983.

Turner, C. H., *The Gospel according to St. Mark*, SPCK, 1931.

Tyrrell, G. N. M., *The Personality of Man*, Penguin Books, 1947.

Vermes, G., *Jesus the Jew* 2nd ed., SCM Press, 1983.

-----------, *The Changing Faces of Jesus*, Penguin Books 2000.

Weatherhead, L. D., *Psychology, Religion and Healing*, Hodder & Stoughton, 1951.

Wills, L. M., *The Jewish Novel in the Ancient World*, Ithaca, NY: Cornell U.P., 1995.

-----------, *The Quest of the Historical Gospel*, Routledge, 1997.

Wright, N. T., *The Resurrection of the Son of God*, SPCK, 2003.

Yoder, J. H., *The Politics of Jesus*, Grand Rapids, Michigan: Eerdmans, 1972.